Marketing Communications:

An advertising, promotion and branding perspective

2nd Edition

Babak Taheri & Hamid Shaker

(G) Goodfellow Publishers Ltd

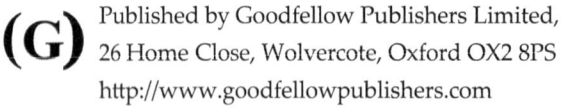 Published by Goodfellow Publishers Limited,
26 Home Close, Wolvercote, Oxford OX2 8PS
http://www.goodfellowpublishers.com

First published 2017

British Library Cataloguing in Publication Data: a catalogue record for this title is available from the British Library.
Library of Congress Catalog Card Number: on file.

ISBN: 978-1-915097-78-1

DOI: 10.23912/9781915097774-5790

 Design and typesetting by P.K. McBride, www.macbride.org.uk

Cover design by Cylinder

"A brand is not so much about rational arguments, but the way that the company resonates with people emotionally"

Steve Jobs (1955-2011)

Contents

Acknowledgments

This book builds upon our journey in the field of marketing communications which has been shaped by years of dedicated learning, practice, teaching, and research. We aim to support undergraduate and postgraduate students in mastering marketing communications as they advance through their education and as they prepare for their professional careers in business and marketing communications. In this new edition, we have updated and expanded the content to reflect the latest trends, technologies, and best practices in the field.

We would also like to express our deep appreciation to Geraldine Bell for her invaluable contributions to the first edition of this book. We wish her a fulfilling and well-deserved retirement. We extend our heartfelt thanks to our colleagues at Goodfellow Publishers for their unwavering support and collaboration.

BT & HSh

Dedication

To my beautiful wife, my daughter Lia, and my parents and brother.
Thank you!
BT

To my wife, Naghmeh, and my parents, Nahid and Ali. Thank you!
HSh

Biographies

Geraldine Bell BA (Hons) MBA ACIM is Assistant Professor, Marketing, with 25 years' industry experience in marketing management and marketing communications roles. With a degree in the History of Art, she started her career as a graduate trainee in a global advertising agency in London working on a variety of FMCG accounts including jeans, tights, toothpaste, whisky and leisure. After a short stint at Revlon International, she handled the advertising and PR for Scottish brands such as Harris Tweed and Shetland knitwear. She then moved to British Airways Holidays, working on the Sovereign and Enterprise brands – a brand portfolio that grew to include Falcon and Twenty's after acquisition by Owners Abroad – all of which is now consolidated in the First-Choice brand and owned by TUI. The mid-nineties, and into the noughties were spent as UK Group Brand Manager at the Scottish Tourist Board/VisitScotland managing Scotland's Autumn Gold campaign, before moving into education. She currently teaches Leisure Marketing, Marketing Communications and International Marketing.

Elaine Collinson (PhD) has over 30 years of experience teaching Marketing at undergraduate, postgraduate, and executive education levels. Her expertise includes Marketing Strategy, Branding, Marketing of Education, Entrepreneurship, Services Marketing, and Small Business Growth. She has extensive experience working with industry to enable growth, delivering training programs, and collaborating with economic development agencies. Her research has informed economic policy, and she mentors for Interface. Elaine has led several research projects and published in various academic journals and books on business development and support.

Ross Curran (PhD) is the Associate Head of the Department of Marketing and Operations at the Dubai Campus, and the Global Programme Director for the MSc in Digital Marketing. Ross leads several undergraduate and postgraduate courses delivered across Heriot-Watt's three campus locations and has published in academic journals, and practitioner media.

Chris Dodd (PhD) is a Consumer Psychologist with a particular interest in the social, psychological and experiential aspects of consumption. He has developed and delivered many programmes and courses within marketing, communications, psychology and management, catering for both academic and practitioner audiences. His research is particularly informed by a focus upon people and their relationships with social and physical environments. His work has been published in numerous international journals and he sits on the Editorial Advisory Board of the journal *Young Consumers*. He is a Chartered Psychologist and Associate Fellow of the British Psychological Society.

Martin Gannon (PhD) is Senior Lecturer in Entrepreneurship at the University of Edinburgh Business School. He has a track record of publishing in internationally leading journals and an active interest in philanthropy, family business, tourism development, and sustainability research.

Sean Lochrie (PhD) is an Associate Professor in Management at Heriot-Watt University, Dubai. His primary research interest focuses on the creation of custodianship behaviours within World Heritage Site management. Recent publications have explored stewardship and local community engagement in World Heritage Site management. He has published research in journals including the *Journal of Marketing Management*, and the *International Journal of Contemporary Hospitality Management*.

Andreea Oniga (PhD) is Assistant Professor in Digital Marketing at Edinburgh Business School, Heriot-Watt University. Andreea completed a PhD and an MLitt in Marketing at the University of St Andrews. Andreea has 10 years of experience teaching in Higher Education, and has taught courses in digital marketing, customer experience, and marketing communications, amongst others. Her current research interests revolve around digital marketing, online communities and digital consumer behaviour. Andreea also has experience working with the industry, as academic supervisor on a Knowledge Transfer Partnership (KTP) in the area of digital marketing strategy.

Rodrigo Perez Vega (PhD) is an Associate Professor in Marketing at Henley Business School. His research interests are in social media, digital marketing and the interaction between consumers and new technologies. Prior to finishing his PhD, Rodrigo had marketing experience in several digital marketing and brand management roles within FMCG and service industries.

Mostafa Purmehdi (PhD) is a social scientist with a doctorate degree in Marketing from HEC Montreal. Mostafa is interested in questions around sustainable marketing strategies, web 3.0 markets and applications of blockchain technology in digital marketing. At New York Tech, he co-chairs the Sharpening Institutional Identity committee, sits on the Vancouver Research Grants Committee, and is the Director of Business Outreach at the Vancouver campus.

Hamid Shaker (PhD) is a Senior Lecturer in Marketing at Nottingham Business School, Nottingham Trent University. His research interests include online consumer behavior and the impacts of transformational technologies on consumer behavior. His work has been presented at and published in major marketing conferences and journals.

Kitty Shaw (PhD) is a teaching fellow at the University of Edinburgh Business School and an experienced marketing practitioner with 22 years' experience in the financial services sector, working in a variety of research, communications and planning roles. Her current research interests include the marketing of pensions; financial education; and engagement with financial services. She teaches Marketing Communications and Financial Services Marketing.

Babak Taheri is a Full Professor in the Department of Hospitality, Hotel Management & Tourism at Texas A&M University. He has an established reputation in the marketing field with a specific expertise in marketing management, consumer research, hospitality, tourism, leisure and cultural consumption. The innovative nature of his research traces to multidisciplinary work and to methodologically robust measurement and assessment of key concepts. In recent years, he has over 150 academic publications, a significant number of which are in internationally rated top-tier journals with high impact factors. He is Associate Editor of two journals: *The Service Industries Journal* and International *Journal of Contemporary Hospitality Management*. Furthermore, he received extensive coverage in media outlets such as *The Conversation, The Irish Times, Travel Daily News*, and *Esports News*.

Kathryn Waite, BA (Hons), Dip CIM, MBA, MSc, PhD, is Associate Professor of Digital Marketing at Edinburgh Business School, Heriot-Watt University. Kathryn is the Global Head of the Marketing and Operations Department. Kathryn's research interests relate to information provision and use within the online environment. Her current work has focuses on how online provision by financial services organisations support family carers of those living with dementia. Kathryn is interested in trust, engagement and empowerment strategies used by organizations within the digital environment.

Preface

Overview

In today's dynamic marketing landscape, the marketer's paramount challenge is to craft and select the optimal promotions mix to achieve business objectives. This process of designing, developing, and implementing promotional campaigns unfolds in an environment of rapid and constant change. Both marketers and consumers navigate an information-driven world, saturated with diverse media and an overwhelming array of brand choices. The technological revolution has fundamentally altered how consumers perceive, process, and react to communication messages. In this media-rich era, brands must break through the noise by being not only engaging and compelling but also empowering and inclusive, ensuring they stand out amidst the plethora of marketing activities. The advent of digital transformations, including artificial intelligence (AI) and extended reality (XR), has further revolutionized marketing communications, offering new ways to personalize and enhance brand experiences. To run a successful marketing communications campaign, your brand must resonate deeply with audiences, fostering genuine connections and fostering a sense of community.

This book aims to equip you with the essential knowledge and skills to navigate the evolving field of marketing communications. While we cannot cover every aspect, we provide comprehensive insights into key areas to support your academic and professional journey. Here is an overview of the structure and content of our book on marketing communications, designed to guide you through the essential concepts and practices in the field.

Book contents and layout

Chapter 1: This chapter attempts to tackle the existing theory of communications as it applies to consumer and marketing communications in particular. In outlining the topic of marketing communications, it details the marketing communication mix and makes an attempt to explain the processes of communications using the models which underpin of understanding of this topic. It also explores the role of AI in the marketing communications. Last but not least, this chapter gives an overview of marketing communications research in the academic and practice contexts.

Chapter 2: This chapter on advertising as a discourse delves into the realm of languages as places, which helps us to further our understanding of the present. Discourses are places which are the means by which, according to Foucault, we *"reproduce ideologies and interpret cultural materials"*, and nowhere is this more so than in advertising. Depth is provided with a meaningful discussion on semiotics, which looks at the relationship between image and texts. The chapter also draws on the illustration of political marketing and PR as an exemplar of marketing communications discourse.

Chapter 3: The focus of this chapter is on consumer decisions when consuming communications. It explores why consumers are driven to make certain decisions, and how they manage their experiences before, during and after consuming marketing communications. It draws on consumer values, motivations and involvement as a means of framing our understanding around what consumers do in terms of behaviour, what they feel by way of emotion and what they think in terms of cognition.

Chapters 4, 5 and **6**: A judicious approach to marketing communications calls for an analysis of the tools available and planning for marketing communications looks at planning in order to achieve the required outcome in terms of marketing communications strategy. Chapter 4 argues that whilst there is no particular distinction between the various parts of strategy, there is a need for a structure in evaluating strategy and the discussion concludes with a suggested framework for marketing communications planning. While Chapter 5 provides an approach to planning for marketing communications, Chapter 6 outlines the key points to consider when not just planning for the short term with brand communications, but when building long term brands. This chapter draws on the science of semiotics outlined in Chapter 2 and makes the link to how brands use signs and symbols to leverage advantage. This chapter also draws on the concept of positioning, first posited in planning for marketing communications, taking the concept deeper to further develop our knowledge, so that marketers can be more efficient in designing brand communication strategies. Chapter 6 gives us a more detailed look at the impact a clear market positioning has on the promotions mix, and on integrating marketing communications. It examines the efficiency gained from market positioning as it is used to maximise the effect of using multiple media platforms which also allows managers to save on resources

Chapter 7: This chapter explores the nature of creativity within an advertising context, making the case for the one 'big idea' which can be translated from the positioning concept into a creative platform of aesthetic values (content and appeals), which will further benefit and deepen integration.

Chapter 8 explains the importance of digital media within the multiple platforms available, saying that digital marketing is a new and exciting phase in the development of marketing communications. This section of our book looks at how to use digital media to best effect when developing marketing communications. It aims to provide you with core knowledge so that you can navigate this stimulating communications landscape.

Chapter 9 explores the transformative role of Artificial Intelligence (AI) and the Metaverse in modern marketing. It explains AI and its different levels—Mechanical, Thinking, and Feeling AI—and sees how they apply to automating processes, generating cognitive insights, and enhancing customer engagement. This chapter also examine the darker sides of AI, such as bias, privacy concerns, and sustainability issues. Finally, you'll delve into the Metaverse, uncovering its potential as a new frontier in branding and marketing.

Chapter 10: This chapter on international advertising presents you with a global view of marketing communications. It covers the challenges that the culture brings to the question of whether marketing communications should be standardised or localised. It explores the degree to which country of origin affects the perceptions consumers have and the decisions they make about certain products and services, and how marketing communications can exploit this and leverage it to best effect.

Chapter 11 holds several case studies for you to develop and deepen your core knowledge, allowing you to gain insight by applying knowledge to practice. This also gives you an idea of how some firms tackle marketing communications in this modern communications environment.

We wish you all the best,

Babak and Hamid. *Eds*

1 Introducing Marketing Communications

Babak Taheri and Hamid Shaker

One of the key features to managing marketing operations and marketing communications in particular is how best to select optimum promotions mix to achieve your objectives. This implies that you know what your objectives are, (which you may not know at this stage) and how the elements of the marketing communication and promotion mix works best to deliver on your objectives (which you may have some knowledge of already from previous feedback or again, you may not know). Within the practice of promotion, a good starting point is to review the nature of the communications process so that you have an understanding of the role it plays in shaping the thinking behind the choices you make (for example media, appeals and timing). Therefore, it is useful to examine the theory of communication as it relates to both how it is reviewed, and how it influences decision making. This introductory chapter attempts to do this.

Our journey begins with an overview of marketing communications, leading us to explore the nature of the communication process. We emphasize the insights that marketers must leverage to design and develop effective marketing communications. In the subsequent step, we delve into Word of Mouth Marketing (WOMM) and also examine the role of Artificial Intelligence (AI) in shaping communication strategies. Recognizing that marketing communications cannot exist in isolation from consumption patterns, we highlight likely consumer responses. Finally, we delve into how practitioners and academics apply marketing communications theory through research. But first, let's establish a baseline: What exactly is marketing communications?

What is marketing communications?

The purpose and intention of marketing, according to Baker, is *"the creation and maintenance of mutually satisfying exchange relationships"* (2016, p.5). The inference here is that both parties enter an exchange on a voluntary basis. The value in the exchange is that both parties will be satisfied – so much so that they will want to repeat the exchange and further the experience should the need arise.

From a management perspective, marketing communications has a prominent role to play in a range of other managerial domains, for instance, in competitive strategy. Marketing communications is relevant when considering the three resource-based marketing strategies – undifferentiated, differentiated and concentrated. Take for example, launching a new product or repositioning an existing product which suits the undifferentiated approach and requires marketing communications effort. So does the differentiated approach whereby products and services are modified to suit subgroups. This segmented tactic requires a different approach to the marketing mix – pricing, distribution and in particular promotion. For a smaller enterprise, a more concentrated strategy may be appropriate because of resource allocation. In this case marketing communications plays a key role in the promotion of its products and services. Simply put, marketing communications is significant in terms of supporting the marketing mix underpinning marketing strategy and therefore has a prominent role in generating value in achieving competitive advantage.

The job of marketing communications, as pointed out by marketing gurus Kotler et al, is to inform, persuade and remind customers (both internal and external) either through direct (for example, TV or cinema advertising) or indirect means (for example, Instagram giveaways) about the products, services and brands the enterprise seeks to exchange. Kotler et al. go on to say that in a way, *"marketing communications represents the voice of the company and its brands, and are the ways in which it can establish a dialogue and build relationships with customers."* (2016, p.630). Marketing communications also has several functions surrounding the market offering, which sends out a signal helping both the firm and customers to better understand and further the exchange as clarified below:

- How and why a market offering is used: what type of person is it for/is using it; where and when it can be used?
- Who is it that has designed, developed and produced the market offering?
- What is the reward for the customer for usage?
- What are the opportunities for me as a business to get involved in partnership with your (?) products and services?

In short, marketing communications plays a key role in contributing to brand equity because it helps to:

- Establish the brand in customers' long-term memory
- Create a brand image
- Drive sales
- Affect shareholder value.

The marketing communications mix

Marketing communications works through a platform known as the marketing communications mix, also known as *promotion mix*, which is made up of methods and activities to engage consumers with the brands. It offers one-to-one communications, one-to-many or many-to-many forms of marketing communications activities. Table 1.1 gives a brief overview of different components of marketing communications mix, their objectives and methods to achieve them.

Table 1.1: The marketing communications mix in general.

Marketing comms mix	Communications objective(s)	Marketing communications methods & activities
Advertising	Paid, non-personal, identified sponsor designed in the main for awareness.	Product & services, direct response advertising, corporate.
Direct Marketing	Communicate directly, solicit a response, prompted information	Direct mail/email, telecon, mobile - information services (contact centres & websites & mobile technology).
Sales Promotion	Short term incentives designed to stimulate trial and purchase, merits of personal experiences.	WOM, trialling, packaging, point of sale, promotions, exhibitions, merchandising.
Public Relations	Project and protect image, reputation, and market offerings (products/services/ideas) – to gain positive editorial, to address crises, to correct information	WOM, sponsorship, publicity, stakeholder communications, corporate identity, lobbying, familiarisation trips/trialling for editorial gain, event management.
Personal Selling	Company sponsored activities developed and produced to create product/service or brand exchange and interaction	Direct sales, over-the-counter, telemarketing, trade fairs, factory tours, event experiences, presentations.

Activity

List as many marketing communications methods and activities as you can. There are some illustrations in Table 1.1 but these are generalisations. For example, what about company museums, chatrooms, and annual reports?

The artistry in marketing communications is planning how best to use all the different methods and activities to optimise effectiveness and to manage resources in a competent manner. In this regard, and to move forward with this book, first, we look at underpinning theory and then we take a more detailed look at the subsequent consumer response models.

Understanding marketing communications effects: how does it work?

To help us better understand how marketing communications works, it is beneficial to start with communications theory because it provides a rationale for how and why certain marketing communication activities happen like they do. The delivery of marketing communications involves complex processes that need to be understood. By grasping the foundations of marketing communications, you are more likely to develop and shape effective dialogue, working towards the key objectives of *'sharing meaning'* as Baines et al (2008, p.433) put it. The purpose of marketing communications is to interact with an audience and facilitate exchange both now and in the future. Understanding communications theory helps us to make sense of marketing communications and enables managers and marketers to exploit the opportunities effectively as the sender or the source.

Forms of marketing communications

Communications can be interpreted through three models – the one-step or linear model, the two-step or influencer model, and third, the multi-step linear and non-linear better known as the interactive model.

One-step or linear model of communications

The basic model of marketing communication is developed by Schramm (1955) depicted in Figure 1.1. The model highlights the process of transmitting the message from a sender to the receiver. The source can be a person, a group, a brand, etc. Since the source and the receiver are not necessarily tuned into each other, Schramm argued that the source translates the message into symbols for transmission during the decoding stage. After the message is transmitted to the receiver, the receiver interprets the message through the decoding process.

Most marketing textbooks (see for example, Baines et al, 2008; Baker 2014, Fill & Turnbull, 2016; Smith & Zook, 2011) will give you a detailed outline of Schramm's 1955 linear model of communication and will pinpoint his approach as being that of *"the process of establishing a commonness or oneness of thought between a sender and receiver"* (cited in Baker, 2014, p. 400) implying that communication has a unified aspect to it. The more basic model consists of only three elements:

Sender → Message→Receiver

This implies that both the source and the destination of the communication is tuned into each other but, as humans, this isn't the case. Schramm argued that this was too basic in that it did not allow for the transference of thoughts whereby ideas are translated into symbols for transmission – in other words the conveyance of ideas and the translation into decipherable and meaningful sense. He called this encoding and decoding and added to the basic model thus:

Sender (source)→ Encoder→Message (signal) → Decoder→Receiver (destination)

Whereas in telecommunications, the encoder is the transmitting device, in face-to-face both the source and encoder are the same person. Likewise, the decoder and the destination are the same with the message substituting the signal (which becomes the language used).

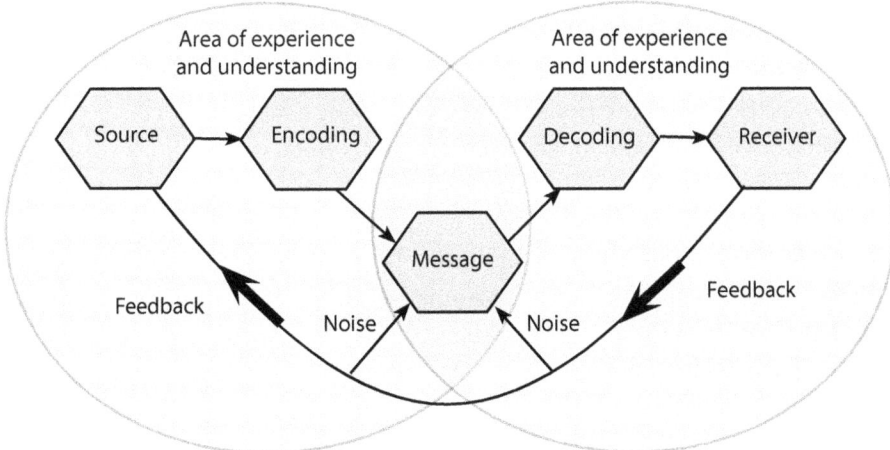

Figure 1.1: The one-step linear model of communication
Source: Adapted from Baker, 2016: 400; Dahlen et al, 2010: 38; and Fill & Turnbull, 2016: 41.

Note the feedback loop in the above model. This tells us that through feedback, the source can determine how its signals are being interpreted. In personal communications feedback is prompt and based on the words we use in the message and the how we use them – signalling the intonation in our voice and/or gesticulation (nod, shrug and wave) whereas it is through mass media that impersonal communication is indicated through circulation figures in the case of newspapers and magazines and, for example, in audience size in the case of radio and TV. The opening episode of the UK programme, *I'm a Celebrity... Get me out of Here!* (#iamaceleb) has a domestic audience of 11.9 million (Goldbart, 2023) and this figure will be used in its contractual negotiations with the BBC over transmitting the show in the next few years to come. As the model depicts, the more that both sides are attuned to each other, the more likely there is to be an overlap. And the bigger the overlap, the more likely there will be shared meaning (the more effective the message is likely to be). The final point in the model is the noise which surrounds the exchange of meaning or as Baker calls it, the *'fields of experience'* (2014, p.401) between the source and destination which is subject to not only the extent to which we are tuned in, but also environmental disturbance. This disruption is prevalent between encoding the message, message delivery (channel) and decoding the message. What's important to note is that there is no such thing as a perfect transmission – there is always noise and some form of potential disruption to contend with whether it be *"selective attention, distortion and retention"* operating within the realms of experience and understanding (Kotler et al, 2016, p 634). As Dahlen et al concurs, this area represents both the sender and receivers frame of reference (2010, p 38)

Despite advances in marketing communications (see below), and along with the cries that mass media is dead, there is still a valid role for this more traditional form of mass communication. This is because advertisers can reach large audiences very quickly and at reasonable cost and through a medium which provides a dynamic, filmic environment where the creative appeal is often more compelling than any other medium. In 2016, the producers of a UK's popular TV show, *The Great British Bake Off*, decided to move to Channel 4 which is reportedly paying in excess of £25 million a year to transmit the show. (Sweney, 2015) And why are these popular entertainment programmes so highly prized by commercial broadcasters? Because they can command huge advertising airtime costs. The format will also include the patronage of products and services related to baking such as small and large electrical items along with kitchenware. This proves that despite audience fragmentation, there is still a big role for mass communications, especially in television where the programming provides an environment where airtime can be commercialised through advertising to a mass audience.

The one-step linear model is the most basic of models in helping us to understand communications and is a two-way process in that communication travels from the source to destination with feedback. The next model develops the basic one into a two-step model to include personal influencers, of which there are two key types which filter communications.

Two step or influencer model of communications

The influencer model of communications assumes that there are two key filters in mass communication – opinion leaders (OL) and opinion formers (OF). Katz and Lazarsfeld's (1955) hypothesis argues that whilst the sender directs communication to a target as in the linear model, there are also personal influencers who act as intermediaries in the form of opinion leaders and formers which filter messages altering the shared meaning between sender and target destination. (Smith & Zook, 2016, p. 151). In short **opinion formers** are formal experts whose opinion has influence through their authority, and **opinion leaders** may be amateurs but who are connoisseurs who have profile and a status that gives them a view, which makes them in demand and results in them being given airtime. So on the one hand there are specialists (OF) such as governors, judges, MPs, journalists, analysts, critics and even some academics, and on the other hand there are other notables (OL) such as celebrities, bloggers, early adopters as triallists, reviewers, seniors, and other confidantes. Both formers and leaders are sanctioning the communications by endorsing it with either a positive or negative spin – the key point being that communications through these two filters are more persuasive and thus credible. For example, the *London Evening Standard* fashion critic may dislike Victoria Beckham's (VB) new fashion collection and write about it and say so, and meanwhile, Cameron Diaz in Hollywood wears VB's dress from the new collection which has been lent to her by VB's fashion PR team hoping that she'll choose it to wear to the Academy Awards ceremony on the night hence being seen to support the new VB collection! In this case, the fashion critic is the OF whilst Cameron Diaz is the OL, and both of their opinions and views carry weight. Fashion firms regularly send shoes and handbags to both journalist and critics, and celebrities in the hope that they will either write or wear the article to give it editorial profile. This influencer model of communications can be visualised in Figure 1.2.

The two-step model, which as mentioned above is more commonly known as the influencer model of communications, tells us that the power of communication is not just with mass media which tells us about information, but is also subject to personal influences which tells us about information in a more persuasive way, exerting influence over us as the target audience. (Fill & Turnbull, 2016, p. 48). The merit of this form of communication can be illustrated by the popularity of using Instagram influencers by beauty and fashion brands. Social media influencers are considered as informal experts by their followers, so consumers trust their recommendations. Another example is the coffee brand Nespresso, whose George Clooney TV commercials are well known globally. When a rival brand called the Espresso Clubhas used a George Clooney look-a-like in their advertising, the original creators and producers sued the imposter firm for misleading its target audience. This is an indicator of the power of persuasion that George Clooney has as the face of Nespresso as an opinion leader in communications. (Associated Press. (2016)

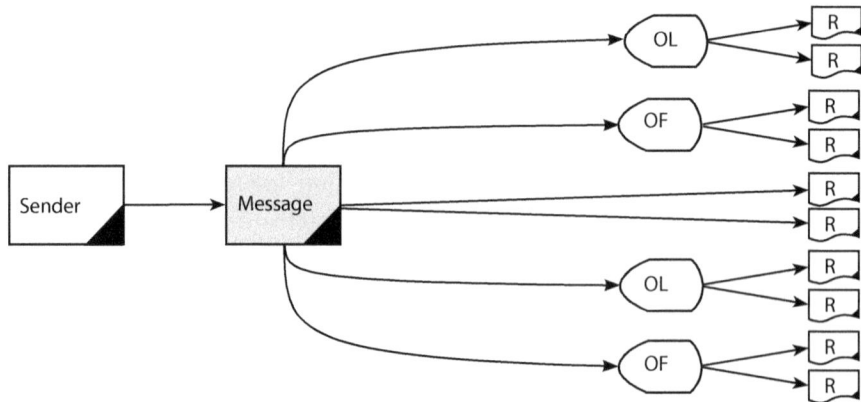

Figure 1.2: Two-step influencer model of communications.
Source: adapted from Smith and Zook (2016:152)

Multi-step or interactional model of communications

The next thought in the progression of our understanding about communications comes from the fact that interaction takes place amongst and between all parties in the communication process. This is referred to as the multi-step model and/or the interactional model of communications.

This model centres around a network of interactions suggesting that influence and persuasion is not just OF's and OL's as in the influencer approach to communications. Whilst persuasion and inducement are exerted through these types of personal influences, the volume of interactions suggest that there are many more types of influences eliciting different responses. Fill and Turnbull suggest that the influence is not only coming from people but is also relative to machines, commenting that communications are increasingly *"characterised by attributing meaning to messages that are **shared, updated and a response** to other messages"*. (2016, p.49). These exchanges of dialogue or 'chats' and reviews are conversations that are interactional in nature as depicted in Figure 1.3.

The internet brought with it a much more useful way of facilitating customer communities where all customers and stakeholders can talk and chat away to each other. This has given rise and more weight to relationship marketing which is now the dominant approach to marketing along with "recombined" and integrated marketing communications (Baker, 2014, p.402).

1

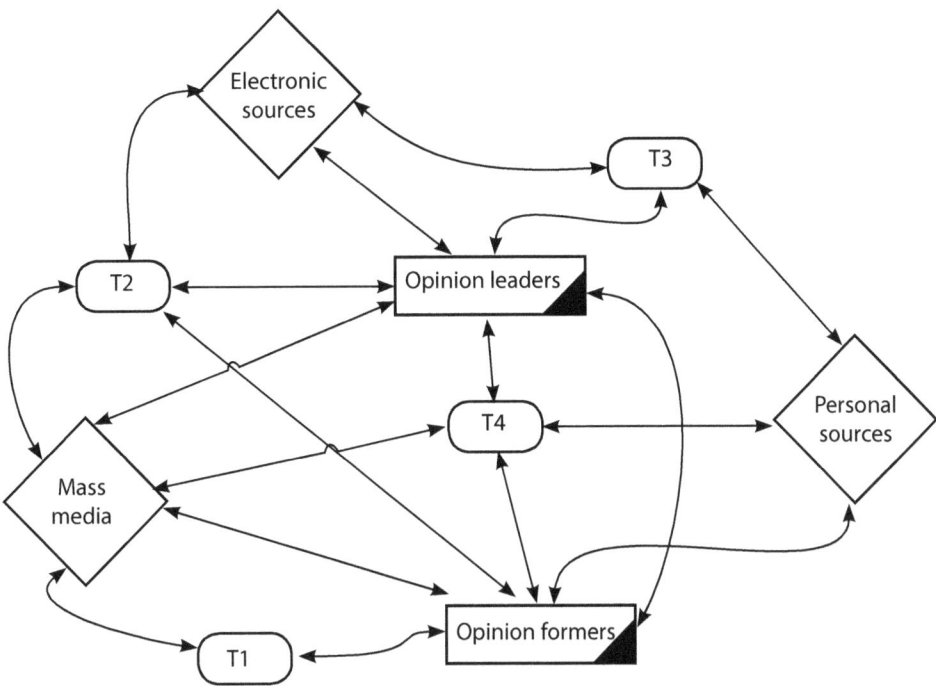

Figure 1.3: The multi-step or interactional model of communication.
Source: adapted from Fill & Turnbull (2016); Smith & Zook (2016) and Kotler et al (2016).

Firms now look to being a key participant in the conversations taking place – so much so that they like to steer the conversations so that the flow of chat is built around the brand and therefore deepens relations. They do this through newsgroups and discussion rooms sponsored by the brand set up to discuss the brand, its applications, problems, issues, ideas, improvements and also include a broader array of topics that can be linked either directly or in some cases indirectly to the brand (Smith & Zook, 2016).

Case: Evian's babies make us 'Live Young'!

There can be nothing more emotional than being at one with our inner-child and #evianbabyandme does just that. "Rollerbabies" was Danone's first taste with its Evian 'Live Young' brand where it reached almost legendary status within the digital-marketing landscape in 2009. Rollerbabies featured computer generated imagery (CGI) babies doing some rather extreme stunts. The clip went viral and made history by being recorded in the Guinness World Records as being the most viewed online ad with up to 25 million views over a two-month period.

Danone's water brand, Evian, has continued with the CGI-aided baby concept where the infants continue to perform hair-raising stunts – as in "Baby Inside" in

2011. Then, in 2013, came Evian's "Baby & Me" which recorded 50 million YouTube views and 100 million total views over several weeks and was seen on 4oD and Videology supported with a Facebook page as well as a raffle draw along with other traditional broadcasts such as TV (during Britain's Got Talent) and Cinema (during The Great Gatsby run) across 15 countries including USA, UK, Germany, France, China and Russia. The advert, or viral clip, featured adults looking into baby-versions of themselves where the CGI-baby copied their grooves and moved in tandem with them. https://www.youtube.com/watch?v=pfxB5ut-KTs

The campaign was strengthened with more innovative online promotion with the introduction of a mobile app which allowed users to upload their photos of themselves and get 'baby-fy-ed' revealing their inner-child and share the results across Facebook, Instagram and Twitter through #evianbabyandme. Most viral campaigns are 'done' and gone but Evian's babies continue to hold good because they never seem to grow old!

Adapted by G. Bell from various sources including Ankeny (2014) and Ridley (2013).

As the example illustrates, there are different means of channelling messages which can lead to a a web of many and different conversations circling around the brand and not just at one time, but at many different times. The key characteristic here with the revolving conversations is that the chat is accelerated by customers themselves becoming advocates. This extends the interaction model to include customers as thought leaders and they too are facilitating conversations – either being more positive, leaning more towards the brand values, or to detract from them, creating a challenge for brands. Of note is that all marketers need to understand more than just the **feedback loop** in the two-step communications model. The modern communications environment now includes, with the multi-step interactional approach, **customer responses** and it is up to the company to turn this into a positive form of communication.

Word of mouth marketing

A prominent topic within marketing communications, enabled by the advancement of new technologies such as social media and mobile internet is word-of-mouth marketing (WOMM). Understandably, this topic has gained significance since the advent of the internet and the resultant usage by both marketers and customers alike leading to conversations being accelerated by customers themselves, hence the notion of amplification where customers can accelerate the chat – the degree of acceleration depending on the level of relationship with the brand with the most intensive **amplification** coming from the tribal fanatic.

WOMM is where firms deliberately shape consumer to consumer communications with purpose and intent. On its own, word-of-mouth is seen to be an organic activity because there is no *"prompting, influence or measurement"* by marketers and is thus considered to be a naturally occurring phenomenon (Kozinets et al, 2010, p.72). However, with intent, comes an active attempt by marketers to affect and change WOM through deliberate marketing communications strategies. This links directly to the previous discussion on the two-step influencer model of communications whereby unwilling consumers are socially engineered into buying through OFs and OLs as a persuasive means of marketing practice. Following on from this is Kozinet et al.'s *"network coproduction model"* which draws on the multi-step model discussed previously (see Figure 1.4) but which has one key element of importance within the topic of WOMM and that is 'seeding'.

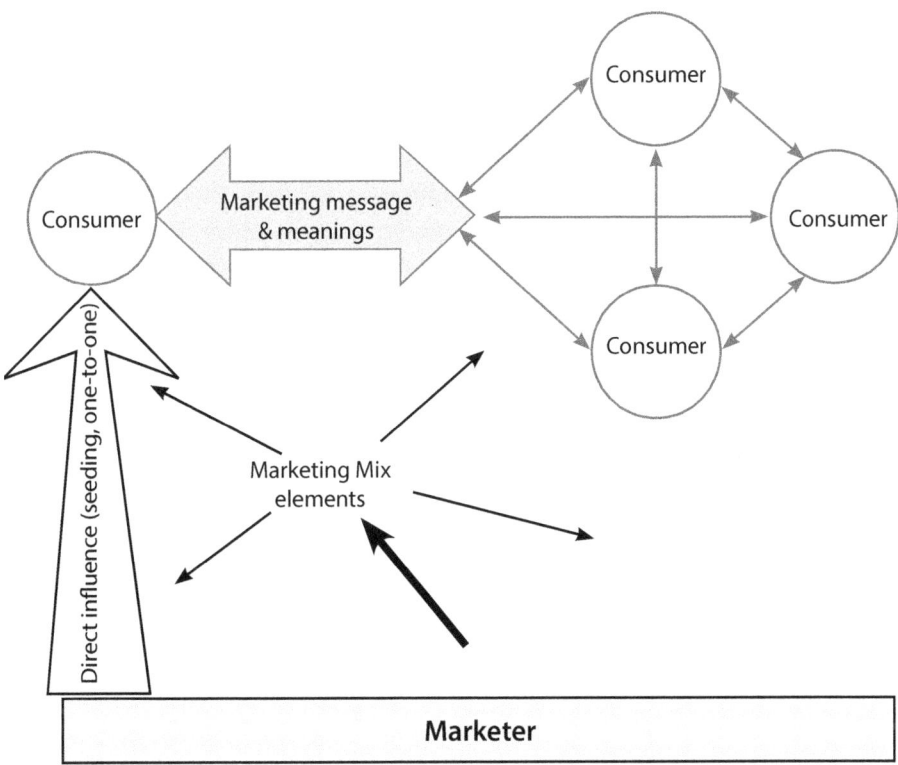

Figure 1.4: How WOMM communications are co-produced in consumer networks - the role of 'seeding'. *Source:* adapted from Kozinet et al., 2010:72.

A seeding strategy is where marketers initiate the communications through the various means available in the marketing mix, and in the marketing, communications mix, in particular as depicted in Figure 1.4. In essence, WOMM is concerned with amplifying a message and content so that it penetrates the communications network – either naturally or judiciously (Fill & Turnbull, 2016; p.60). There's no doubt that social media platforms have led to an exponential increase in the volume of conversations and chat as the multi-step or network communication model explains. But whilst most consumer communications occur spontaneously many conversations are deliberate and are a direct result of a marketer's seeding strategy.

How we brought Trek America to the UK

I Trek Here was an innovative campaign designed to encourage social influencers and TrekAmerica customers to build excitement around their leisure product – adventure tours to the USA.

It was a tailor-made, content-led social campaign aimed at TrekAmerica's core target audience, where the leisure firm employed 10 high-profile, influential bloggers, sent them on a TrekAmerica trip and created social buzz around them experiencing their first trek in Southwest USA.

Source: The Drum Social Buzz Awards.

http://www.socialbuzzawards.com/social-buzz-awards-2015/best-travelleisuresports-social-media-strategy/how-we-brought-trekamerica-to-the-uk

Marketing practice suggests targeted one-to-one seeding within marketing communications programmes as illustrated by Trek America. This depicts the network approach to communications and reminds us that consumers are co-producers in creating value and meaning on the one hand, whilst marketers use innovative tactics and metrics to shape the communications put out by the opinion leaders on the other. What stands is the implication that marketing messages are traded amongst and between members within and around the network.

Lady Gaga and the one-percenters

Jackie Huba is a founding member of the Word-of-Mouth Marketing Association in the USA. Founded in 2004, it advocates *"ethical WOM practices through education, professional development and knowledge sharing with top industry marketers"* www.WOMMA.org. It came into being at about the time of the rise of social media platforms. Today, Jackie is considered a leading expert in customer loyalty and WOMM. You can see her in action giving a keynote speech to the Marriot Hotels at https://www.youtube.com/watch?v=UMWw6V_Ztvl. What's interesting is her stance on customer acquisition vs retention. She cites Lady Gaga as a best practice exemplar. She says that the customer universe is made up of new, existing and advocate-type customers. Of note, is the fact that most companies fail to see the value in WOM relative to advocates. Advocates are those customers who are more loyal than just loyal – they are super engaged in your brand. They want to help you succeed and they will do anything for you. Take Lady Gaga. She has 57 million 'likes' on Facebook and yet her focus is on advocates who make up a small proportion of her followers on social media. Jackie's research says that most brands have a population of advocates of about 1%. These 'one-per-centers' have enormous value because they are the ones that are going to spread the word on your behalf. Because they have an almost evangelical zeal about them, they are likely to shout loud and clear about products, benefits and value propositions. Lady Gaga, Jackie says, has identified one-per-centers as the means of growing her business and giving her longevity in the music business. The focus, for Gaga, is to turn followers into fanatics as this will grow the Gaga brand. (Huba, 2013)

And finally, one further point put forward by Kozinets et al (2010, p. 74) is the fact that whilst co-produced narratives are shaped by character narrative (personal stories/expressions), communication forum (bogs, social networking sites), communal norms (age, lifestyle, interests, ethnicity, social class) and the nature of the marketing promotion (type of product/service, compelling nature of message/visual e.g., humour, hard sell or soft sell, aim/objectives), marketers need to be aware that marketing messages and meanings are also altered systematically when embedding them into the narrative. They are altered in a way that is 'attuned' to the consumer's own likes/dislikes when operating either as an individual or in a communally appropriate context. This then is familiar in that in more traditional communications, such as PR, the control and shape of the message is with the journalist as intermediary. In the online world, the consumer now has control and is the intermediary, and the consumer's approach and context matters.

Amplification accordingly (Fill & Turnbull, 2016) comprises both the behavioural and cognitive elements of the marketing-to-consumer, and the consumer-to-consumer concept. This involves searching, reading and writing of reviews about a brand as well as actions such as trialling (as in the TrekAmerica example where they take a familiarisation trip and follow this up with writing about it as a positive experience), other experiences and purchase, and subsequently sharing it with several networks. Trending content (popular topics) is amplified as a direct result of embedded tweets, sponsored stories and social advertisements. This has changed the way we view consumer behaviour as a topic several texts specialising in this specific field of enquiry aim to enlighten us to the changes and highlight the considerations within this area of marketing. Meanwhile, it is still incumbent on us to have a baseline awareness of how consumers are likely to make a response to marketing effort and the next section explains this.

Communication in the age of Artificial Intelligence (AI)

Artificial intelligence (AI) is revolutionizing marketing communications. Increasingly, consumers rely on variety of AI-powered smart tools, such as Amazon's Alexa, for various needs such as searching for information or putting orders for their groceries. These devices, which mimic human intelligence through autonomous processes, are changing how brands engage with consumers.

Dawar (2018) suggests that consumers soon will delegate portions of their decision-making processes to trusted smart assistants. This shift will transform the communication dynamic between brands and consumers to include interactions between AI assistants and both consumers and brands. For instance, rather than manually searching for Colgate toothpaste on Amazon, consumers might simply ask Alexa to add toothpaste to their shopping list. While such digital transformation and technological advancements might suggest a diminished role for branding, Dawar (2018) emphasizes that AI systems depend heavily on the information provided by brands, along with data from sources like social media comments and consumer feedback. Therefore, in the age of AI, brands must not only engage in traditional marketing practices to influence opinion leaders and consumers but also develop strategies to communicate effectively with AI-powered tools.

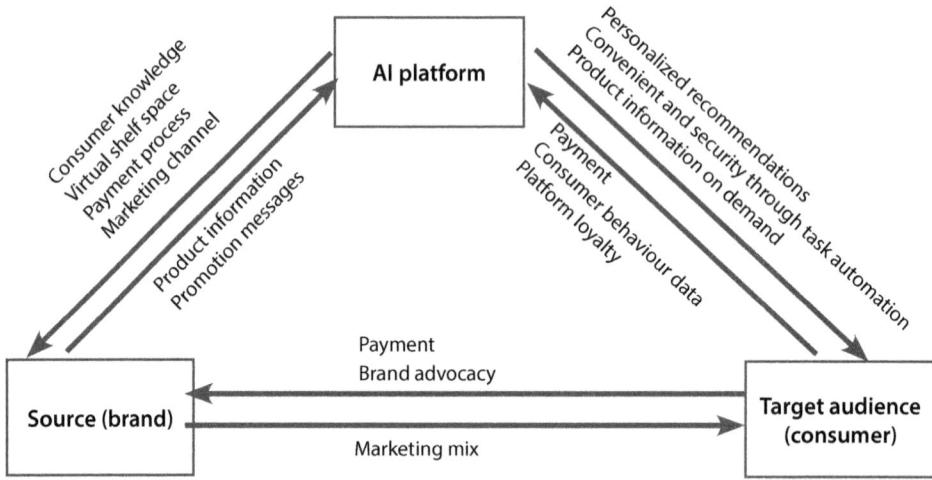

Figure 1.5: The role of AI platforms in marketing and branding. *Source*: adapted from Dawar (2019)

In conclusion, integrating AI into marketing communication requires a dual approach: maintaining strong, clear brand messaging for consumers and ensuring that AI systems have accurate, comprehensive information to facilitate informed decision-making. Brands that can adeptly navigate this new landscape will be better positioned to succeed in an increasingly AI-driven market environment. Figure 1.5 depicts the role of AI platform in the marketing communications and

1

branding. Chapter 9 provides further details on the applications of AI in marketing communications and branding.

Consumer response models

The models discussed so far focus on the message transmission process between the sender and the receiver, i.e., consumers. However, to understand how consumers respond, we need to examine the mental processes through which consumers make decisions before committing to a brand. For decades, most marketers and practitioners have subscribed to the view that consumers go through several sequential stages before feeling positive about a product or deciding to buy it; this process is often referred to as the 'consumer journey'. (cf. Taheri et al., 2021).

For example, when a consumer wants to purchase a new dishwasher, they start by searching for brands that come to mind. These are the brands that they are aware of due to advertisements, suggestions from friends, or recent exposure to relevant stimuli. Consumers then shortlist some of these brands, research them, evaluate some alternatives based on their research, and eventually make a purchase. After purchasing the brand, they continue their decision. This evaluation forms the basis of their post-purchase behaviour, such as recommending the brand to others, becoming loyal and repurchasing from the brand, or writing a negative review on social media. Chapter 3 provides more in-depth explanation of consumer behaviour and product purchasing steps.

Based on this journey, we can model consumers' responses to marketing communications. For example, Figure 1.6 shows the adoption model (Rogers, 1962), which assumes that consumers are initially unaware of brands, and after initial exposure to marketing stimuli, they gather more information, and if their evaluation results in a positive attitude towards the product, it can lead to purchase and loyalty.

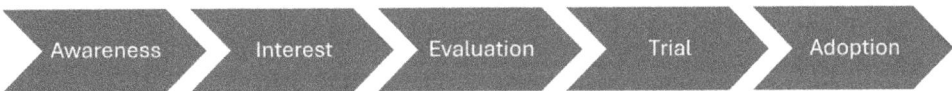

Figure 1.6: Adoption model (Rogers, 1962)

The adoption model belongs to a category of models known as hierarchy of response models. Other examples include infamous AIDA (Strong, 1925) and more recent Hofacker's online information processing model (2001). Table 1.2 provides an overview of response hierarchy models. These models help identify the sequence of mental stages consumers go through from the time they are unaware of a brand until they become loyal to it. As explained by Smith and Zook (2019), these models help the goals of marketing communication: whether to prioritize increasing brand awareness through billboard ads (i.e. cognitive response), creating positive attitude through social media campaign (i.e. affective response), or encouraging purchase through promotion codes (i.e. behavioural response).

Table 1.2: Summary of customers' likely response to communications: response hierarchy models.

Stages	AIDA	Purchase (Baker, 2016:201)	Hierarchy of effects	Innovation adoption	Communications (Kotler et al., 2016: 635)
Cognitive thought	Attention	Problem recognition	Awareness	Awareness	Exposure
			Knowledge		Reception
					Cognitive response
Affective (emotion)	Interest	Evaluation and research	Liking	Interest	Attitude
	Desire		Preference	Evaluation	
			Conviction	Trial	Intention
Behaviour (conative/ motive	Action	Purchase	Purchase	Adoption	Behaviour

Source: Adapted from Baker, 2016: 201; Kotler et al., 2016: 635, and Fill & Turnbull, 2016: 120.

While these models are useful for identifying the mental stages that consumers typically go through, they have several limitations. First, these models presume that consumers respond in a rational manner. There are times, however, when consumers respond in an irrational way – for example when they are making a purchase on impulse! Second, advancements in digital technology have altered the classic purchase funnel. Consumers now interact with various touchpoints, both online and offline, that can be personalized based on each individual journey. For instance, when a consumer is buying a product on Amazon, they are exposed to personalized product recommendations during checkout, based on data Amazon gathers from various touchpoints. Technologies such as AI, Internet of Things (IoT), and mobile internet provide brands with unprecedented opportunities to personalize the consumer journey using on vast amount of collected from different touchpoints. This shift is why marketing communications have increasingly moved towards a more 'integrated' approach.

Integrated marketing communications approach

In this introductory chapter, the focus has been on understanding the classic or more traditional approach to marketing communications, and introducing the changing nature of marketing communications as it moves to a more integrated marketing communications (IMC) approach – a summary of the key characteristics of which is outlined below in Table 1.3.

Table 1.3: Summary of changes in characteristics between traditional and contemporary marketing communications

Traditional communications	Contemporary approach
Acquisition strategy	Retention strategy
Mass, volume communications	Targeted and more focussed communications
Monologue	Dialogue
Information is sent	Information is requested
Information provision	Information retrieval
Sender takes initiative	Receiver takes initiative
Offensive	Defensive
Repeated information	Relevant information
Hard sell	Soft sell
Brand salience	Brand confidence
Transaction	Relationship
Advertising management	Relationship management
Aim to change attitude	Aim to achieve satisfaction
Modern: linear, volume	Postmodern: cyclical, fragmented

Source: Adapted from De Pelsmacker et al, 2013: 9.

IMC is when there is a plan which evaluates the strategic roles of the different elements of the marketing communications mix (the toolbox as outlined in Table 1.1) so that the combination of the mix provides clarity, consistency and thus enabling the marketer to maximise the effect of communications (Baker, 2014). Understanding each of the different parts of the marketing communications mix (advertising, DM, PR, PS & SP) aids comprehension of, for example, the implications and impact each part has so that these component parts (either singularly with each other or collectively) can be *"recombined and integrated"* to best effect so that our understanding of how they work together either with each other or collectively in practice is important (Baker, 2014, p. 402). But managing IMC is a challenge in practice and assistance comes from the basic 4Cs framework.

The 4Cs framework (Picton & Broderick, 2005, p. 28) is useful as a basis for the evaluation of IMC. It stands for coherence, consistency, continuity and complementary and explains the intended outcome of IMC as follows:

- **Coherence** – logically connected as opposed to disparate parts
- **Consistency** – multiple messages support and reinforce the overall strategy as well as each other, as opposed to being disjointed and unclear
- **Continuity** – not just connected but consistently so, rather than erratically so
- **Complementary** – synergistic by way of working together and harmonising together, as opposed to being isolated and cut off from the purpose and intent of marketing communications

The rationale behind looking at marketing communications in a more integrated way is acknowledgement of the customer approach to communications. Customers and other stakeholders may or may not be that aware of the subtleties between for example, Nivea for Men's sponsorship of English football and a Boots on-pack promotion in-store. Customers just see the means of transmission of messages through various on and offline channels trying to persuade us to either attend to the message and content, to do something about it or to entice us to talk and chat about it online. IMC adds value in that it offers a deeper and a speedier means of comprehension of the communications. And integration is not obligatory – it is planned carefully in order to optimise the objective of achieving the 4Cs as outlined above.

Moreover, the planning of an integrated approach to marketing communications takes into account the ability to control the method of marketing communications (for example the level of control in advertising is limited should the context change, making it not that easy to adapt quickly and efficiently); the ability to manage the resource and costs (for example cost per contact or the cost of the amount of wastage); the degree to which the audience is likely to perceive the credibility of the communications (for example a narrative through an editorial intermediary in the *Financial Times* either online or offline is highly likely to be more believable and trustworthy than an advertisement) and also the role of the communications itself, for instance, what is the job it is trying to do (for example, the DRIP elements of aiming to differentiate, reinforce, inform and persuade).

Table 1.4 provides an overview of the criteria for consideration in relation to the means of communications available.

Table 1.4: Key selection criteria relative to the characteristics of the marketing communications mix

	Advertising	Sales Promotion	Public Relations	Personal Selling	Direct Marketing
Control:					
By manager and by audience, ability to target, to be flexible	Med Med	High High	Low	Medium Medium	High High
Costs:					
By investment, return, & cost per contact & wastage	High High waste	Med Med waste	Low High waste	High Low waste	Med Low waste
Credibility:					
Sincere, believable, reliable & trustworthy	Low	Med	High	Med	High
Communications:					
Level of dispersion, interaction & ability to forward	High Low Low	Low Med Med	Low Med Low	High Low High	High Medium High

Source: adapted from Fill 2013, p. 27.

Marketing communications research

Research in marketing communication is indispensable for both academics and practitioners. For academics, it provides a foundation for developing theories and models that explain consumer behavior and the effectiveness of different communication strategies. Practitioners rely on research to make informed decisions about campaign development, execution, and evaluation. This dual focus ensures that marketing communication strategies are both theoretically sound and practically effective. Agencies act as intermediaries, needing research knowledge to generate actionable insights and craft skills to implement these insights effectively. Despite debates on the methods and relevance of various research approaches, the consensus remains that research is crucial for eliminating ineffective communications and enhancing successful campaigns. While a thorough review of marketing communications research is out of the scope of this chapter, it is important that we be familiar with the main types of research. To delve deeper into research methods in marketing and management, please read major research method textbooks such as Easterby-Smith et al. (2021).

Uses of research in marketing communications

Hackley (2010), categorizes research in marketing communications into three stages of initial, creative and copy-testing research. Before a campaign begins, **initial research** utilizes secondary data from market reports, industry publications, and competitor analyses. This foundational stage helps understand the brand, market dynamics, and consumer behavior. This information is critical forming a strategic direction for the campaign.

During the campaign development, **creative research** uses primary qualitative data, such as focus groups, in-depth interviews, and naturalistic experiments. This stage aims to uncover consumer thoughts, feelings, and behaviors to generate insights that guide the creative process. By understanding the target audience more deeply, brands can craft messages that resonate and engage effectively.

After the campaign is launched, **copy-testing** methods predict consumer reactions to the marketing communication mix. **Tracking studies** are then used to measure the campaign's effectiveness, often involving surveys and other quantitative techniques to gather data on consumer responses. These studies provide evidence of the campaign's success, helping agencies demonstrate their value to clients and refine future strategies.

In marketing communications, **Key Performance Indicators** (KPIs) are essential metrics that help marketers evaluate and measure the success of their efforts. Table 1.5 lists the main KPIs for marketing communications along with their definitions and examples of their use in digital marketing. To collect and interpret these KPIs, tools like Google Analytics and similar platforms are invaluable. They provide detailed reports and visualizations, helping marketers track performance in real time. Additionally, advancements in Artificial Intelligence (AI) have enhanced the ability to gain deeper insights from data. AI-powered tools can analyse large datasets, identify patterns, predict trends, and even suggest optimizations to improve campaign effectiveness.

Table 1.5: Common KPIs in digital marketing

KPI	Definition	Example in Advertising
Impressions	The total number of times an ad is displayed, regardless of whether it is clicked or not.	An online banner ad is shown 10,000 times across various websites.
Reach	The number of unique individuals who see an ad.	A social media post reaches 5,000 unique users.
Click-Through Rate (CTR)	The percentage of people who click on an ad after seeing it.	An email campaign is sent to 1,000 people, 100 of whom click on the ad, resulting in a 10% CTR.

1

Conversion Rate	The percentage of users who take a desired action (e.g., make a purchase) after clicking an ad.	An e-commerce site sees that 50 out of 500 visitors who clicked on an ad make a purchase, yielding a 10% conversion rate.
Cost Per Click (CPC)	The average cost paid for each click on an ad.	A company spends $200 on a Google Ads campaign and receives 400 clicks, resulting in a CPC of $0.50.
Cost Per Thousand (CPM)	The cost of 1,000 ad impressions.	A video ad campaign costs $500 and achieves 100,000 impressions, resulting in a CPM of $5.
Return on Ad Spend (ROAS)	The revenue generated for every dollar spent on advertising.	An advertiser spends $1,000 on ads and generates $5,000 in revenue, resulting in a ROAS of 5:1.
Bounce Rate	The percentage of visitors who leave a site after viewing only one page.	A landing page from an ad has a bounce rate of 60%, meaning 60% of visitors leave without further interaction.
Customer Acquisition Cost (CAC)	The total cost of acquiring a customer through an ad campaign.	If a company spends $1,000 on an ad campaign and acquires 50 new customers, the CAC is $20 per customer.
Lifetime Value (LTV)	The predicted net profit attributed to the entire future relationship with a customer.	If the average customer has monthly average value of $50, and the rate at which consumers cancel their subscription is 5%, the LTV is (50/0.05=)$1,000.
Engagement Rate	The ratio of interactions (likes, comments, shares) to the total number of impressions.	A Facebook post gets 500 likes, 100 comments, and 50 shares from 10,000 impressions, resulting in a 6.5% engagement rate.
Social Share of Voice (SSoV)	The percentage of mentions of a brand versus its competitors on social media.	During a product launch, a brand achieves 40% SSoV on social media, indicating strong visibility compared to competitors.

Methods of research

Generally speaking, there are two major categories of research methods in marketing and marketing communications: quantitative and qualitative. **Quantitative research** involves structured data collection techniques that produce numerical data. For example, for copy-testing, experimental research designs gauge audience reactions through controlled experiments. To collect data simple tools such as questionnaire or more advanced tools like psycho-galvanometers and eye-tracking devices that measure physiological responses to marketing communications stimuli such as an advertisement are used. Survey research, another quantitative method, gathers data on consumer attitudes and behaviors through structured questionnaires. Quantitative methods are essential for establishing causal relationships between marketing communications efforts and consumer behavior.

Qualitative research focuses on understanding consumer emotions, attitudes, and behaviors through methods such as ethnographies and in-depth interviews. These techniques, rooted in anthropology and cultural sociology, allow researchers to delve into the complex, subjective experiences of consumers. By capturing the intricacies of consumer perceptions, qualitative research offers deeper insights that can inform creative strategy and execution.

The advent of big data and advanced analytics has revolutionized marketing communications research. Big data encompasses vast amounts of information generated from digital interactions, social media, and other online activities. Advanced analytics techniques, including machine learning and AI, enable researchers to identify patterns and trends that were previously undetectable. Content analysis uses algorithms to analyse textual, visual, and audio content from various media sources, providing insights into consumer sentiment and engagement. AI-driven tools can predict consumer behavior, personalize marketing messages, and optimize campaign performance in real-time. These technologies enhance the precision and effectiveness of advertising research, allowing for more targeted and impactful marketing communication strategies.

Summary

As we progress through this book, the introduction has provided a comprehensive overview of communication theories, helping us understand how marketers and consumers interact in various contexts, including one-to-one, one-to-many, and many-to-many scenarios. We have also delved into contemporary topics such as word-of-mouth marketing and AI-powered platforms and explored the sequential nature of consumer responses. Using this background, we have explained the importance of Integrated Marketing Communications (IMC) in today's marketing world and examined the key criteria for selecting different forms of consumer communications. Additionally, we have emphasized the vital role of research in marketing communications for both academics and practitioners. This foundation prepares us for a deeper exploration of the essential concepts in marketing communications.

Further reading

Batra, R., & Keller, K. L. (2016). Integrating Marketing Communications: New Findings, New Lessons, and New Ideas. *Journal of Marketing, 80*(6), 122–145.

This paper provides a good review of new media and the consumer decision journey in the age of divided consumer attention. More importantly, authors outline a comprehensive framework to understand how consumer process marketing communication and how to improve integrated marketing communications.

Cambier, F., & Poncin, I. (2020). Inferring brand integrity from marketing communications: The effects of brand transparency signals in a consumer empowerment context. *Journal of Business Research, 109*, 260–270.

In marketing communications, a significant challenge arises from consumers' increasing scepticism toward marketing claims. This research paper highlights the importance of transparency in increasing consumers' trust. While the authors focus on consumer-ideated new products, their findings can be generalized in other marketing communications.

Corkindale, D., Neale, M., & Bellman, S. (2023). Product Placement and Integrated Marketing Communications Effects on an Informational TV Program. *Journal of Advertising, 52*(1), 75–93.

Product placements and IMC such as program sponsorship billboard or commercials during the program are inseparable parts of TV programs. This paper examines the interaction of these two on the entertainment experience of consumers.

Costello, J. P., & Reczek, R. W. (2020). Providers Versus Platforms: Marketing Communications in the Sharing Economy. *Journal of Marketing, 84*(6), 22–38.

Peer-to-peer (P2P) platforms such as AirBnB or Uber are popular these days. This research paper examines how consumers interpret the marketing communications if they focus on the firm (i.e. platform) or the provider (i.e. peer). This paper is good example of using experimental design research in Marketing Communications.

Rosengren, S. and Dahlen, M. (2015) Exploring Advertising Equity: How a Brand's Past Advertising May Affect Consumer Willingness to Approach Its Future Ads. *Journal of Advertising*, 44 (1).

This paper introduces conceptualizes 'advertising equity' relative to measurement in marketing communications. It focusses on past advertising being an influencing factor in building up a catalogue of perceptions about a brand. This gives brands a global value which is further merit in measuring brand equity. It also discusses advertising budgeting and forecasting, pretesting and evaluating advertising plus negotiating media as well as co-branding partnerships.

Review questions

1. The role of marketing communications is to

   a) Inform
   b) Persuade
   c) Remind
   d) All of the above

2. The marketing communication mix consists of the following:

   a) Advertising, direct marketing, sales promotion, personal selling and public relations
   b) Advertising, direct marketing, sales promotion, personal selling, WOM, and PR
   c) Advertising , direct marketing, sales promotion & e-vouchers, personal selling, and PR
   d) Advertising, direct marketing, sales promotion, personal selling and online chats, and PR

3. Marketing communications in the main takes the form of three models of communication which are:

   a) the one to two, two to three steps and the multi-step models of communications
   b) the one-step, two-step and multitude of step models of communications
   c) the one to two, two to three and the multi-award winning models of communications
   d) the one-step, two-step and multi-step models of communications

4. _____ and _____ can alter the shared meaning between target and destination in the influencer model of communication.

   a) Opinion formers, consumers
   b) Opinion formers, opinion leaders
   c) Influencers, opinion leaders
   d) Marketers, consumers

5. Social media platforms have brought about ways of facilitating

   a) Revolving contradictions
   b) Revolving conversations
   c) Revolving conflaborations
   d) Revolving contra-indications

6. The role of a seeding strategy is to affect change by

   a) Initiating marketing communications activity
   b) Deliberating marketing communications activity
   c) Engineering marketing communications activity

d) All of the above

7. The innovation-adoption model of consumer response suggests the following stages

   a) Awareness, interest, evaluation, trial and adaption
   b) Awareness, interest, evaluation, trial and adulation
   c) Awareness, interest, evaluation, trial and adoption
   d) Awareness, interest, evaluation, trial and addiction

8. Which two characteristics best sum up the differences between the more traditional and the more contemporary view of communications.

   a) Monologue/dialogue
   b) Offensive/defensive
   c) Mass/selective
   d) All of the above

9. The elements of the 4Cs framework which provides a bases for evaluating IMC are:

   a) Coherence, consistency, contemporary and complementary
   b) Coherence, consistency, continuity and complementary
   c) Coherence, consistency, contingency and complementary
   d) Coherence, consistency, contradictory and complementary

10. Which stage of research in marketing communications typically involves analyzing secondary data from market reports and competitor analyses?

    a) Copy-testing research
    b) Creative research
    c) Initial research
    d) Post-campaign analysis

Answers

The answers to these questions can be found at the back of this book, or at the Marketing Communications page at Goodfellow Publishers:

https://www.goodfellowpublishers.com

References

Ankeny, J. (2014) 'How these 10 marketing campaigns became viral hits', *Entrepreneur*. https://www.entrepreneur.com/article/233207.

Associated Press. (2016) 'Nespresso sues rival for using George Clooney lookalike', *Daily Telegraph*, 22 January. http://www.telegraph.co.uk/finance/newsbysector/retailandconsumer/12113467/Nespresso-sues-coffee-rival-for-using-Geroge-Clooney-lookalike.html.

Baines, P., Fill, C. & Page, K. (2008) *Marketing*. Oxford: Oxford University Press.

Baker, M. (2016) *Marketing Strategy and Management*. 5th edn. London: Palgrave Macmillan.

Dahlen, M., Lange, F. & Smith, T. (2010) *Marketing Communications: A brand narrative approach*. West Sussex: John Wiley and Sons.

Dawar, N. (2018, May 1). Marketing in the Age of Alexa. *Harvard Business Review*. https://hbr.org/2018/05/marketing-in-the-age-of-alexa

De Palsmacker, P., Geuens, M. & Van Den Begh, J. (2013) *Marketing Communications: A European perspective*. 5th edn. London: Pearson.

Easterby-Smith, M., Jaspersen, L. J., Thorpe, R., & Valizade, D. (2021). *Management and Business Research*. Sage.

Fill, C. (2013) *Marketing Communications: Brands, experiences and participation*. 6th edn. London: Pearson.

Fill, C. & Turnbull, S. (2016) *Marketing Communications: Discovery, creation and conversations*. 7th edn. London: Pearson.

Goldbart, M. (2023). UK TV Ratings Bonanza: The Most-Watched Shows Of 2022. *Deadline*. https://deadline.com/2023/01/queen-elizabeth-funeral-eurovision-im-a -celebrity-uk-tv-ratings-1235197599/

Hackley, C. (2010). *Advertising and Promotion: An integrated marketing communications approach*. 2nd edn. Sage.

Huba, J. (2013) Monster loyalty: How Lady Gaga turns followers into fanatics. New York: Penguin Group.

Katz, E. & Lazarsfeld, P. (2006) *Personal Influence: the part played by people in the flow of communications*. Transaction Publishers, USA. Originally published by The Free Trade Press in 1955.

Kotler, P., Keller, K. L., Brady, M., Goodman, M. & Hansen, T. (2016) *Marketing Management*. 3rd edn. London: Pearson.

Kozinets, R. V., de Valck, K., Wojnicki, A. C. & Wilner, S. J. S. (2010) 'Networked narratives: Understanding word-of-mouth marketing in online communities', *Journal of Marketing*, 75, 71-89.

Picton, D. & Broderick, A. (2005) *Integrated Marketing Communications*. 2nd edn. Harlow: FT Prentice Hall.

Ridley, L. (2013) 'Evian launches global baby and me campaign', Campaign. http://www.campaignlive.co.uk/article/ evian-launches-global-baby-campaign/1179271.

Rogers, E. M. (1962). *Diffusion of Innovations*. New York, NY: Free Press.

Schramm, W. (1954) *How Communication Works (Vol. 586). The process and effects of mass communication*. University of Illinois Press.

Smith, P. R. & Zook, Z. E. (2016) *Marketing Communications: Offline and online integration, engagement and analytics*. 6th edn. London: Kogan Page.

Strong, E.K. (1925) *The Psychology of Selling and Advertising*, McGraw-Hill.

Sweney, M. (2015) 'The Great British Bake Off final gets biggest TV audience of the year', *The Guardian*, 8 October. https://www.theguardian.com/media/2015/oct/08/the-great-british-bake-off-final-nadiya-jamir-hussain-gbbo.

Taheri, B., Prayag, G. & Muskat, B. (2021) 'Introduction to the special issue: Consumer experience management and customer journeys in tourism, hospitality and events', *Tourism Management Perspectives*, 40, 100877.

2 Marketing Discourse and Semiotics

Babak Taheri and Martin Gannon

In everyday life we are regularly exposed to, and interact with, many different forms of advertising. For example, through television and radio commercials, billboards, direct (or junk) mail, and carefully staged large-scale public relations exercises, advertisers draw upon different narratives and discourses to communicate the benefits of their brands, products, and services to us as potential consumers. Within the context of marketing, discourses serve as the places where the advertiser and the consumer communicate, interact and engage in choreographed events within the position of a particular semantic context (Oswald, 2012). Such advertisements are often comprised of several interactive elements which may draw upon images, photographs, music, societal observations, paralanguage, language, scenarios and situations, and the existing preconceptions of consumers in order to spread an advertising message in an effective and entertaining way (Cook, 2001).

There are often extremely strong relationships between the images used and the language employed in advertisements. This study of signs is called *semiotics*. Here, signs, text, and symbols serve as crucial elements of the consumer experience and are vital tools employed throughout advertising and marketing. Language, gestures, art, heritage, television advertisements, films, and even sales pitches and conversations, all contain signs that are used to convey specific meanings or are used to share a precise communicative purpose in marketing a product or service (Cook, 2001). For example, phrases such as 'your flexible friend' (Access credit card), 'naughty but nice' (fresh cream cakes) or 'it's the real thing' (Coca-Cola) have passed into British vernacular from advertising copy. However, contemporary marketing communication is not only concerned with catchphrases and levity, nor is it solely focused on furthering the commercial interests of organisations. Politicians and their advisers also utilise discourse and marketing communication tools to appeal to their followers and voters. As such, this chapter aims to make sense of marketing discourse and semiotics within the context of advertising and promotion, and marketing management in general. It also explores political marketing discourse as a particularly revealing illustration of everyday marketing interactions.

Case Study: Patagonia's Environmental Activism Messaging

Patagonia, the outdoor apparel company, is renowned not just for its high-quality products but also for its robust stance on environmental activism. Its environmental activism is woven into the fabric of its brand identity. This commitment is reflected in their marketing discourse, which goes beyond mere product promotion to advocate for broader environmental issues.

A quintessential example is Patagonia's recent initiative where the company announced a new corporate structure, giving away 98% of its stocks to a non-profit. This initiative is a testament to Patagonia's commitment to fighting the environmental crisis.

In addition to striking visuals, Patagonia employs advocacy language that directly appeals to consumers' sense of responsibility. Their website and social media channels are filled with calls to action, such as signing petitions, participating in environmental clean-ups, and supporting sustainable practices. This language positions Patagonia not just as a company, but as a movement dedicated to environmental stewardship.

One of the most striking examples of this commitment is their *"Don't Buy This Jacket"* campaign (Patagonia, 2018). This campaign boldly combines advocacy language, an urgent tone, and factual statistics to communicate Patagonia's dedication to sustainability. The campaign employs strong advocacy language, encouraging consumers to rethink their purchasing habits. Phrases like *"Think twice before you buy"* and *"Reduce, repair, reuse, recycle"* are central to their messaging, urging consumers to consider the environmental impact of their choices.

The urgent tone of Patagonia's messaging is designed to galvanize action. By highlighting the dire consequences of inaction, such as irreversible damage to ecosystems and loss of biodiversity, Patagonia's discourse creates a sense of immediate need. The tone of Patagonia's communication is urgent and persuasive. By using statements such as *"Environmental bankruptcy"* and *"We are running short on fresh water…,"* the campaign underscores the immediacy of environmental issues, compelling consumers to take action.

This is further reinforced by the use of factual statistics that lend authority to their claims. By grounding their messages in scientific data, Patagonia ensures that their advocacy is both credible and compelling. For instance, Patagonia aims to make approximately 96% of its products by weight PFAS-free by Spring 2024 (Patagonia, n.d.). By grounding their messages in scientific data, Patagonia ensures that their advocacy is both credible and compelling.

The impact of Patagonia's environmental activism messaging is profound. It has successfully positioned the brand as a leader in corporate social responsibility, attracting a loyal customer base that shares its values. This alignment with environmental causes not only enhances Patagonia's brand image but also drives consumer engagement and action. Their commitment to transparency and activism resonates deeply with eco-conscious consumers, fostering a strong sense of community and shared purpose.

Source: Gelles (2022); Patagonia (2022) and Patagonia (n.d.)

Defining discourse

The use and importance of discourse and 'texts-as-statements' are well established within the field of marketing communications and advertising. Indeed, Said (1978: 167) notes the underlying power and ubiquity of text in discourse-building by stating that: *"texts, in fact, are in the world ... as texts they place themselves – one of their functions as texts is to place themselves – and indeed are themselves, by soliciting the world's attention"*. Discourse is the primary way of reproducing and communicating ideas, and discourse provides a platform that allows individuals to interpret a range of cultural materials in an accessible and relatable fashion (Foucault, 2002). The way in which discourse is employed embodies the cultural importance of language and is linked to power relations and reality within any given social context (Fairclough, 1995). This is because actors perceive, and subsequently gain an understanding of, social phenomena by consulting and processing information in the form of texts, symbols, images and photographs (Berdychevsky et al., 2016; Gee, 2005). Some argue that 'language-in-use' exists everywhere and that typically *"people construct situations through language by carrying out seven interrelated building tasks. These are: significance, activities, identities, relationships, politics, connections, sign systems and knowledge"* (Berdychevsky et al., 2016: 111). Table 2.1 demonstrates the interoperation of these seven stages, which Gee (2005) argues can be understood from both a micro- and macro-structure perspective within the marketing and advertising context.

Exercise

Think about an experiential marketing situation, such as going to your favourite nightclub, and consider it in relation to the questions posed by the 'seven building tasks of discourse' model.

Table 2.1: The 'seven building tasks of discourse' (Berdychevsky et al., 2016; Gee, 2005)

Building task	Example question
Significance	What situated meanings are evoked by or linked to some of the words or objects used?
Activities	What activities, actions, or undertakings are linked with the particular term(s) used?
Identities	What type of identity is being invoked by, or is consistent with, a particular term(s)?
Relationships	Which relationships are taken for granted or ignored?
Politics	What social, societal, or political connotations are relevant or irrelevant with regards to the term(s) employed?
Connections	What relationships or linkages are established between the particular term(s) used and existing texts or discourses?
Sign systems & knowledge	What sign systems are relevant or irrelevant with regards to the term(s) employed?

Emerging from social constructionist psychology (Potter & Wetherell, 1987), the utility of discourse has also been noted by scholars such as Elliott (1996), Thompson and Haytko (1997), Thompson (2004) and Fitchett and Caruana (2015) in marketing and consumer research. For example, Thompson and Haytko (1997:15) describe the way in which discourse is used in fashion marketing: "*Fashion discourses provide consumers with a plurality of interpretive positions that, because of their diverse associations, can enable them to juxtapose opposing values and beliefs. Consumers use these countervailing meanings of fashion discourse to address a series of tensions and paradoxes existing between their sense of individual agency (autonomy issues) and their sensitivity to sources of social prescription in their everyday lives (conformity issues)*". However, Thompson (2004:175) criticises advertisement-centric analysis of text and suggests: "*critical consumer researchers should study how power relationships operate and shift through institutional discourses and practices*". Fitchett and Caruana (2015) also argue that the use of discourse in marketing and consumer research has been saturated and paradoxically conceptualised. They suggest possible ways of adopting a discourse perspective in a more robust and consistent fashion within market-based relations, as outlined in Table 2.2.

Consumers typically engage with advertising discourse for different purposes. This engagement can occur in both every day, general consumption situations and when communicating (either directly or indirectly) purposefully with brands (de Waal Malefyt & McCabe, 2016; Hackley, 2012). For example, de Waal Malefyt and McCabe (2016) discuss the use of discourse analysis when exploring advertising relating to women's vulnerability (i.e., menstruation) and its role in the consumer identity formation process, and suggests that advertising is influenced by gendered ideologies into producing different messages. Additionally, the source of cultural materials for evolving creative advertising is problematic, as advertising agencies showing the whole at one view in material located in culture (de Waal Malefyt & McCabe, 2016). Questionably, the ready and craft consumption is more than just customisation, since *"for consumption activity to warrant being described as a craft, then the consumer must be directly involved in both the design and the production of that which is to be consumed"* (Campbell, 2005: 31).

2

Table 2.2: Applying discourse and market-based relations (Adapted from Fitchett & Caruana, 2015: 6)

Market-based relations	Example Questions
Consumer-product	How is the consumer's product knowledge constituted? How is consumer sovereignty constructed, maintained and subverted?
Consumer-market	How is consumption influenced by the institutional context of the market?
Consumer-consumer	How do consumer interactions construct product knowledge? How do some consumers influence others?
Consumer-producer	How do consumption practices co-opt the producers of products and services?
Marketer-consumer	How do consumers and marketers use power to influence each other?
Marketer-corporation	How are functional activities and/or marketing agents constrained by wider corporate discourse?
Consumer-citizen	How do market-based behaviours influence/transform consumer citizenship?
Consumer-society	How does marketing discourse penetrate other public domains such as health and education?
Consumer-environment	How do marketing texts shape consumer relations with the natural environment?

Activity

Identify an example and analyse it using the market-based relations example questions outlined in Table 2.2.

Another example of this stems from the use of discourse in Web 2.0 advertising, where rapidly improving digital technologies have shifted the balance of power between consumer and producer in recent years. Here, discourse challenges the established producer-consumer dichotomy and its dialogical relationship within the advertising environment. The opportunity brought about by technological change subverts Marx's distinction between 'use value' and 'exchange value' by removing the typical, well-defined barriers between production and consumption. Instead, many are now embracing this by turning consumption into a form of temporary employment (often termed 'prosumption') (Cova & Cova, 2012; Humphreys & Grayson, 2008). Beer and Burrows (2010: 4) argue: "the opportunities Web 2.0 has created for forms of consumption that require active participation are crucial in understanding contemporary consumption". Thus, cultural practices, as well as customer engagement, play important roles in shaping narratives and the interpretation of meaning in contemporaneous consumption, advertising and marketing (Jafari & Taheri, 2014; Taheri & Jafari, 2012). Fellesson (2011) expands upon this notion of consumer empowerment by arguing that, from a discourse perspective, customers can now influence organisational culture and practice in three distinct ways (see Table 2.3).

Table 2.3: Capturing the situated customer (Adapted from Fellesson, 2011: 235)

Element	Example questions
Organisational rhetoric	As an organisation, how do we describe and characterise our customers?
Operational procedures	As an organisation, what influence does the customer have on how we operate?
The physical customer environment	In what way is the customer reflected in the design and function of the physical service environment?

Activity

Apply the 'capturing the situated customer' framework to three well-known organisations of your choice.

Political marketing discourse: An example

As a discipline, political marketing was developed in response to the increasing professionalization of political actors and the political marketplace. Political consumption experiences take many forms, such as the act of voting, canvassing for politicians, or taking part in organised protests, and are stimulated by general feelings of democratic freedom (Dermody & Wring, 2001). An individual's political compass and their level of attachment to a political party are influenced by the political orientation of their family circle, their social class, and who they socialise with throughout their formative years. Nevertheless, political loyalty typically lessens over time as voters disengage with, and become more critical of, their political party (Lees-Marshment, 2001), and consumers subsequently use their sovereignty to pledge their support to those who campaign on issues that they consider important for the betterment of society (Moufahim & Lim, 2009; O'Cass, 1996).

Lees-Marshment (2001) defines political marketing as when political organisations adopt marketing concepts and strategies from the commercial world in order to help them achieve their political goals. Political marketing has existed under the guise of *propaganda* since for thousands of years. However, propaganda is concerned with convincing the electorate that a particular ideology is correct. It does not consider the mutual fulfilment of needs between politician and voter, nor is it focused on stimulating the electorate's understanding of the key issues required to encourage political dialogue and empowerment (O'Shaughnessy, 1996). Niffenegger (1989) provides a more contemporary political marketing framework underpinned by the simple marketing concept of the 'four Ps. This adapted framework includes the particular political 'product' on offer to the voter, the 'promotion' of information to the electorate through manifestos and party political broadcasts, the 'price' of the political product for the people (i.e., the potential economic, societal, and civil improvements they are likely to benefit from), and the 'place(s)' where information is communicated to the electorate.

Politicians make broad use of marketing tools (e.g., market research, media campaigns and segmentation) in attempting to achieve their political goals, and political parties spend more time and money on selecting political consultants based on their marketing expertise than their political leanings. This is why we often hear phrases such as exchange, stakeholders, market research and similar marketing jargon across the media during political campaigns (Dean & Croft, 2001). Thus, contemporary political marketing is *"the study of the processes of exchanges between political entities and their environment and among themselves, with particular reference to the positioning of these entities and their communications…As an activity, it is concerned with strategies for positioning and communications, and the methods through which these strategies may be realized, including the search for information into attitudes, awareness and response of target audiences"* (Lock & Harris, 1996: 22).

Marketing helps us to understand discourses and practices and can help to shape society and social relations (Hackley, 2012). Marketing discourse refers to how people view the world, their environment and the consumption of 'space'. Morgan (1992: 154) suggests that it is *"part of the process whereby a particular form of society is constructed, one in which human beings are treated as things, where identity is reduced to ownership of commodities, and all social relations are conceived in market terms"*. It acts as a discourse which allows us to understand actors in relation to social processes, and thus fits well with the purpose of political marketing (Morgan, 1992). Here, discourse considers the dialectical relationship between the structure of sign systems and existing social codes. The next section explores the importance of semiotics in relation to this and associated concepts.

Activity

Identify examples of political marketing discourse. Are they effective in spreading the intended message?

Semiotics

The word 'semiology' has been used interchangeably with 'semiotics' to refer to the science of signs, where "*[the semiotic perspective] interprets reality in terms of cultural codes that structure phenomena into signs and meanings*" Oswald (2012: 8). Contemporary understanding of semiotics is based on the work of the American theorist Charles S. Peirce and the French philologist Ferdinand de Saussure. Peirce focuses on exploring the structure of meanings in the human experience. He defines semiotics as "*…action, or influence, which is, or involves, a cooperation of three subjects, such as a sign, its object, and its interpretant, this tri-relative influence not being in any way resolvable into actions between pairs*" (Peirce, 1934: 411).

Case Study: Apple's Privacy Campaign

Apple's privacy campaign is an example of modern marketing semiotics. Through a careful selection of symbols and imagery, Apple tries to effectively communicates its dedication to user privacy. Apple's advertising campaign for privacy employs these semiotic elements to build a narrative of trust and security.

Central to Apple's privacy adverts are lock icons, which universally signify security and protection. By incorporating these icons into their clean, minimalistic advertisements, Apple leverages a simple, yet powerful design, ensuring that the message is direct and uncluttered and making it easy for consumers to grasp the core promise of data protection.

In TV commercials, the use of dark colour schemes, predominantly black and deep blues, plays a significant role in Apple's visual strategy. These colours are often associated with sophistication, reliability, and authority. They evoke a sense of seriousness and gravity, underscoring the importance Apple places on privacy.

In a video advert, Apple showcases a young woman named Ellie who discovers a hidden world where data brokers trade her personal information. This metaphorical representation brings to light the invisible yet pervasive issue of data harvesting. The ad illustrates how various types of her data, such as emails, drugstore purchases, and browsing history, are sold without her consent. Through the use of Apple's privacy features, Ellie regains control over her data

By using these elements consistently across various media platforms—be it TV commercials, print ads, or digital campaigns—Apple creates a cohesive and compelling narrative. The repetition of these symbols across different contexts helps ingrain the message of privacy in the minds of consumers.

Source: Grothaus (2022)

de Saussure views semiotics from a linguistic perspective and focuses predominantly on how words and language function as a system of signs. He describes the linkages between a signifier (which is a word) and the signified (which is an 'object expressed'). He highlights these two terms by emphasising that a 'signifier' is the physical manifestation of a sign and that 'signified' refers to the mental meaning linked with this physical object. He also defined three main binary concepts that provide insight into how signs are constructed, processed, and understood (Ellis et al., 2011):

1 **Synchronic vs. diachronic**: Many concepts recognise meaning as a result of their location within a series of signs (synchronic), rather than locating changes in meaning over time (diachronic).

2 **Syntagmatic vs. paradigmatic**: Paradigmatic concepts concentrate on the individual element of a sentence (e.g., the choice of verb or adjective) and evaluate the selection made by the writer. The syntagmatic view concentrates on the sequence of words in any sentence and the way in which these words are interrelated.

3 **Metaphor and metonymy**: Metaphors are typically used to explore the paradigmatic position of texts, whereas metonymy is used to explore syntagmatic relationships.

Metaphors and metonyms typically encompass a range of meanings. Ellis et al. (2011) provide an example of an FT advertisement using a paradigmatic metaphor with the image of dark, heavy and oppressive rain and the subheading: *"Where would your money take shelter in turbulent times?"* This arouses notions of *"economic turbulence caused by the financial crisis"* to the reader (Ellis et al., 2011). A visual representation of de Saussure's theory is presented in Figure 2.1.

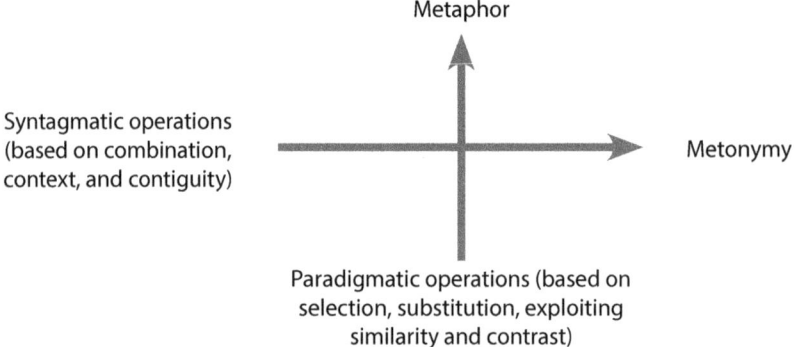

Figure 2.1: Metaphor and metonymy along the paradigmatic and syntagmatic axes (Ellis et al., 2011: 202)

Activity

Identify examples of recent television advertisements. Use Figure 2.1 and de Saussaure's three binary concepts to categorise your examples.

Denotative and connotative meanings

Barthes (1990) investigated the way in which *meaning* is derived from images in advertising. He suggested that all images have different meanings, and categorised these as existing on two distinct levels:

1   The **denotative** level is the basic and constant meaning that a sign or image bears. It allows us to identify the product or service a brand stands for or represents.

2   The **connotative** level refers to the more powerful, emotional level a brand signifies. On this level, a product or service can bes linked to culturally shaped symbolism and values. The higher the number of connotations a brand can generate, the greater its 'connotative index (CI) (Danesi, 2004).

Linguistic messages use denotative and connotative elements to carry out the two main functions of *anchorage* and *relay*. Relay has a narrative ability to carry a story forward, whereas anchorage fixes meaning in order to avoid multiple or undesirable meanings. The prevailing moral ideology of a society stems from those meanings that are fixed through *anchorage* (Barthes, 1990). He also explains that 'non-coded iconic' messages present objects that appear totally natural in an unconditionally analogical manner, whereas a series of signs are apparent in coded messages. It is important to note that semiotics offers an elegant, nuanced and powerful account of the plural and active nature of the process of meaning making.

Activity

Identify examples of denotative and connotative images and signs in recent television advertisements.

Semiotics and the simple marketing communication process

MacCannell (1989, p. 3) defines semiotics as "*a technical perspective for close analysis of the forms and processes of communication. It is a meta-language for describing the hidden ideology of existing theories and methods. Semiotics is not owned by any field or discipline*". In simpler terms, semiotics is the study of signs and their inherent and implied meanings – what they stand for or represent. Consider, for example, the letter 'X'. At a fundamental level its physical appearance, a letter of the alphabet constructed by two intersecting lines, can be considered a *signifier*. This signifier refers to the 24th letter of the English alphabet (the 'object expressed' – signified). Signs are read and their meaning is interpreted based on cultural codes, which we must learn in order to make sense of and process the signs around us (Hackley, 2012). This is how signification occurs. Meaning does not exist in an absolute sense, but in relation to other meanings. For example, the Macintosh (brand) is, to many, synonymous with the terms: 'user-friendly', 'highly functional' and 'well-designed', whereas the 'Apple' name and logo is used to evoke the biblical theme of 'forbidden knowledge' and 'temptation'.

A sign should be communicated through some form of discourse. This mediation is a vital component of the communication process and can be influenced by a range of factors, such as the context where the transmission of the message occurs and the way in which it is delivered. An idea, such as an advertising message, should be passed through a recognisable medium to someone who understands that message, as well as sorting through any noises or disturbance that might impact upon the interpretation of its intended meaning (Oswald, 2012). According to rhetorical theory, the sender's intention is to influence their audience based on creative delivery. The sender constructs the message using shared cultural knowledge of various conventions and connotative indexes (CIs). Thus, it is important for them to utilise visuals which are likely to influence consumers and which represent concepts, actions, metaphors, visual vocabulary or symbolic systems that they are familiar with (Scott, 1994). Based on this principle, Fill ((2009:41 and 2011) describes Schramm's 1955 '*linear model of communication*' (outlined in Figure 2.2).

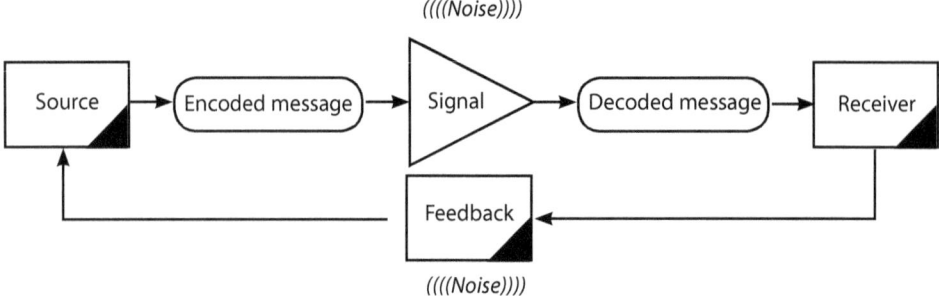

Figure 2.2: The communication process (Fill, 2011)

In this model:

- *Source* represents the individual or organisation sending the message.

- *Encoding* refers to changing the message into a symbolic style that can be easily conveyed. The message that is communicated should come from a source that has authority and the trust of the customer. Using suitable staff members and training them appropriately with regards to how to devise this message is time-consuming and expensive, but it can create trust (Fill, 2011; Hackley, 2012; Percy & Rosenbaum-Elliott, 2012).

- *Signal* refers to the actual transmission of the message.

- *Decoding* describes the process whereby the receiver (or consumer) attempts to understand the message being conveyed. Differences in education, prior knowledge, attitudes and interests will influence the decoding process.

- The *Receiver* refers to the individual or organisation receiving the message.

- *Feedback* is the receiver's communication back to the source on receipt of the message. Feedback is very important as it helps to determine whether communication was successful or not and it can highlight problems with the consumer's interpretation of the message.

- Finally, *Noise* is distortion throughout the communication process, making it difficult for the receiver to interpret the message as intended by the source. Communication is typically considered successful if 'noise' is minimized or eradicated entirely, as there is a higher likelihood that the message will be understood by the receiver as intended by the source (Fill, 2011; Hackley, 2012; Oswald, 2012; Percy & Rosenbaum-Elliott, 2012).

Further, Williamson (1978) argues that for advertisements to be effective they *must* mean something. This typically involves connecting objects and people and making the two interchangeable. Williamson uses semiotic terminology to describe the transmission of meaning to products through *signs*. Goldman and Papson (1996) identify advertising as a key method of producing and reproducing material which can lead to ideological changes and commodity associations. They term this phenomena *'commodity hegemony'*. Advertisements contribute to commodity hegemony as they encourage a range of different people to consider products and services in the same way. Here, the 'mortise and frame' represents the main approach to advert and image interpretation. The mortise structures the creation of meaning within the advertisement via routing the connection between the image (as signified) and the products (as signifier). Regardless of the content of individual advertisements, this represents *"an ideology and practice of commodity fetishism at a deep level of communicative competence"* (Goldman, 1992: 65). Therefore, greater attention and significance is devoted to the rigidity of meaning within advertisements.

2

Activity

Drawing upon Fill's communication process (Figure 2.2), discuss and interpret a recent television advertisement of your choice.

The truth behind signs and polysemy

In order to understand and decode individual advertisements, we must consider the broader promotional system spanning production, marketing, and design (Wernick, 1991). Here, in order to appeal to consumers, the purpose of advertising is to further *"the commodity they project, as the object of desire is simultaneously presented as a cultural symbol charged with social significance; and the ego they seek to engage as the subject of desire is induced to adopt the socio-cultural identity attributed to those who already use the product"* (Wernick, 1991:31).

However, it can be difficult for consumers to understand the truth behind signs. The postmodernist French philosopher Baudrillard (1989) argues that it is not only signs that advertisers use to camouflage the 'truth', and he highlights that simulative signs do not always refer to something 'real'. Here he explores the distinction between 'true' and 'false': *"It is no longer a question of imitation, nor of reduplication, nor even of parody. It is rather a question of substituting signs of the real for the real itself; that is, an operation to deter every real process by its operational double, a metastable, programmatic, perfect descriptive machine, which provides all the signs of the real and short-circuits its entire vicissitudes. Never again will the real have to be produced"* (Baudrillard, 1989: 167).

With this in mind, an advertiser can take advantage of opportunities relating to what is 'true' and 'false', and may create a new spelling in order to engineer a pun in the hope that it appeals to consumers. For example, the maker of Corona Lemonade guaranteed consumers that 'every bubble has passed its fizzical'.

Advertisers also utilise words that are 'polysemous' (a linguistic term employed to explore the semantic process whereby a single word has multiple related meanings). For example, 'foot' can refer to the anatomical structure found at the bottom of the leg, a unit of measurement, or to the base of a mountain. The use of such polysemous terms can result in lexical ambiguity, and advertisers and copywriters often use these multiple meanings strategically. Such lexical ambiguity can also emerge from use of 'homonyms', words with different meanings that are either pronounced the same, (homophones e.g., through and threw), or which are spelled the same (homographs e.g., lead, the metal, and lead, a dog's leash). Some homonyms have the same pronunciation and spelling, but unrelated meanings, for example, bear (the animal) and bear (the verb meaning to tolerate). Here through imaginative use of homonyms and polysemy, social context and interpretive space can play an important role in advertising, whereby the creative use of language and signs help to encourage consumers to engage with advertisements.

Activity

Identify examples of advertisements that utilise lexical ambiguity. Categorise these into those that use homonyms, and those that rely on polysemous terms to get their message across to consumers.

Semiotics and branding

A brand is a *sign* in the semiotic sense. Brands are laden with meaning, represent a range of things and can engender a multitude of feelings to different parties. The semiotic study of brands focuses the capacity that signs have in communicating and generating meaning. It attempts to reveal the codes through which humans draw meaning from signs in particular cultural contexts. Cultural context frames the interpretation of signs; different people utilise different interpretive strategies in deriving meaning from the same signs. Branding allows consumers not only to identify certain products and services, and to distinguish them from those made by others, but also to relate to them in cultural and emotional (connotative) terms. Therefore, such understanding of brands derives from symbolic consumption, which highlights the role of products and services in communicating the social and emotional benefits of consumption that can subsequently fulfil consumer needs such as love, satisfaction and the bolstering of self-image or self-identity (Oswald, 2012). For example, this can help in brand-naming strategies in a multitude of ways.

Some well-known, global examples are outlined below:

1 The use of the manufacturer or founder's name (e.g., Gucci, Armani, Disney)

2 The use of an acronym e.g., (IKEA (Ingvar Kamprad Elmtaryd Agunnaryd), FCUK (French Connection UK), ESPN (Entertainment and Sports Programming Network)

3 Alluding to established (often religious or cultural) organisations (e.g. All Saints, True Religion, Quaker Oats)

4 Referring to a fictitious personality (e.g., Mr Clean, Red and Yellow (M&Ms), Churchill the Dog)

5 The use of descriptive words or phrases. Some of these link the brand to the manufacturer (e.g., Carnation Evaporated Milk, LEGO (a derivation of the Danish phrase 'Leg godt' which can be translated as 'play well', Vanish Stain Remover)

6 The use of place names to identify where a product, service or company is located or was founded (e.g., Hitachi, Bank of America, and Santander)

7 Cars named after animals (e.g., Mustang, Jaguar, and Cougar). This evokes a perception of the automobile as a replacement for animals as transporters of people, or imbues the automobile with some of the animal's desirable attributes.

Consumers generate meaning from brands, and brands can position themselves based on their ability to respond to and satisfy consumers' personal, social, and cultural needs. As such, many brands draw upon multidimensional sign systems in order to fulfil all elements of the consumer interpretation process, and to appeal to as wide a range of potential consumers as possible. Oswald (2012) suggests that there are four dimensions through which we can explore this perspective. These dimensions are: material, conventional, contextual, and performance (Table 2.4).

Table 2.4: The semiotic dimensions of brands (Oswald, 2012)

Material	The intelligible dimension of marketing signs or subunits of meaning (e.g., words, images, spaces, brand names, jingles, trademarks, taglines, logos, packaging, etc.) **Example:** McDonald's 'Golden Arches' logo
Conventional	Different conventions or codes shared by consumers in a market. These include brand codes (linking material signifiers, such as a logo, to a set of connections in the consumer's mind), category codes (consumer expectations about products, retail categories and purchase decisions), cultural codes (consumer's interpretation of marketing communications), and counterfeit codes. **Example:** Products that claim to be healthy (e.g., Pepperidge Farm crackers)
Contextual	The meanings that consumers attach to signs can be changed from one market to the next. They can be observed through the filter of the sociocultural codes that shape meaning in the consumer's world (e.g., gender identity, social identity, religious identity). Here, the denotative and connotative interpretation of marketing signs plays an important role. **Example:** Nike's tagline: 'Just Do It!'
Performance	How the advertiser and consumer use semiotic codes to communicate. This is categorised into subject address (voice) and reference (linking a material signifier to an abstract concept). **Example:** the irony of statements such as 'what a great deal!' is only apparent if the agent recognises that the sale price was too high to begin with.

Summary

This chapter has provided an introduction to the core concepts of discourse and semiotics within the context of marketing communications and advertising. It highlights and explains the important discourse models underpinning contemporary marketing communications, including the seven building tasks of discourse, discourse and market-based relations, and capturing the situated customer. It also explains the crucial role that marketing discourse plays in today's political environment. Additionally, the chapter highlights the importance role of different types of visual messages within the communication process from sender (or advertiser) to receiver (or consumer).

Further reading

Anagnostopoulos, C., Parganas, P., Chadwick, S., & Fenton, A. (2018). Branding in pictures: Using Instagram as a brand management tool in professional team sport organisations. *European Sport Management Quarterly*, 18(4), 413–438.

This research paper examines how professional sport teams use Instagram to communicate their brand attribute and interact with their worldwide audiences. The authors examine the impact of product-related attributes (start player(s), Team Success, etc) and non-product attributes (Club's history, tradition, values or culture, fans, stadium) in Instagram posts on fan engagements.

Azer, J., Anker, T., Taheri, B., & Tinsley, R. (2023). Consumer-Driven racial stigmatization: The moderating role of race in online consumer-to-consumer reviews. *Journal of Business Research*, 157, 113567.

Recognizing the impact of consumer-driven stigmatization is increasingly important as consumers gain more influence in business and marketing. Regulatory frameworks are designed to protect consumers from unfair market practices on the part of firms and businesses. This research paper extends our understanding of racial stigmatization and bias from marketing communications to consumer-to-consumer exchanges.

Cook, G. (2001). *The Discourse of Advertising*, London: Roultledge.

This is a comprehensive and invaluable reference guide to the language advertising.

Lourenção, M., de Moura Engracia Giraldi, J., & de Oliveira, J. H. C. (2020). Destination advertisement semiotic signs: Analysing tourists' visual attention and perceived ad effectiveness. *Annals of Tourism Research*, 84, 103001.

The authors of this research paper employs eye-tracking in their multi-method experiment to examine the influence destination country-brand logo and slogan in the adverts on the tourists' visual attention and ad effectiveness.

Madadi, R., Torres, I. M., & Zúñiga, M. Á. (2024). The semiotics of emojis in advertising: An integrated quantitative and qualitative examination of emotional versus functional ad dynamics. *Psychology & Marketing*, 41(6), 1223–1241.

Employing emojis in the advertisements is not unusual. This research paper examines the impact of this strategy on consumers appraisal of the ads depending on the type of the ad (emotional versus functional).

Review questions

1. What are building tasks of discourse?
   a. Significance, activities, identities
   b. Relationships and sign systems or knowledge
   c. Politics and connections
   d. All of the above.

2. Discourse is the principal way to reproduce ideologies and interpreting cultural materials.
   a. True
   b. False

3. Political marketing is:
   a. A discipline, the study of the processes of exchanges between political entities and their environment and among themselves, with particular reference to the positioning of these entities and their communication
   b. As an activity, it is concerned with strategies for positioning and com-munications, and the methods through which these strategies may be realized, including the search for information into attitudes, awareness and response of target audiences.
   c. a and b

4. What statement below best describes semiotics?
   a. Dialectical in nature and describes the implication of cognitive processes in the consumer – or reader or spectator – in the structure of meanings they encounter in culture.
   b. The word 'semiology' has been used interchangeably with 'semiotics' to refer to the science of signs…
   c. It interprets reality in terms of cultural codes that structure phenomena into signs and meanings
   d. All of the above.

5. The denotative level is the basic (constant) meaning that a sign bears. It allows us to identify the product or service a brand stands.
   a. True
   b. False

6. The connotative level is a more powerful emotional level of a brand. On this level, a brand is linked to the culturally shaped symbolism and values
   a. True
   b. False

7. Polysemy is about many possible meanings for a particular word and phrase.

    a. True
    b. False

8. Homophones are words with different meanings that are spelt the same (e.g., lead, the metal, and lead, a dog's leash).

    a. True
    b. False

9. What are semiotic dimensions of brands?

    a. Material, conventional and theoretical
    b. Material, conventional and contextual
    c. Material, conventional, contextual and performance
    d. Material, conventional, theoretical and practical

10. Which of the below market-based relations answers "how is consumer sovereignty constructed, maintained and subverted"?

    a. Consumer-product
    b. Consumer-market
    c. Consumer-consumer
    d. All of the above.

Answers

The answers to these questions can be found at the back of this book, or at the Marketing Communications page at Goodfellow Publishers:

https://www.goodfellowpublishers.com

References

Barthes, R. (1990). *The Pleasure of the Text*. Oxford: Basil Blackwell.

Baudrillard, J. (1989). *The Consumer Society: Myths & Structures*. London: Sage Publications.

Beer, D., & Burrows, R. (2010). Consumption, prosumption and participatory web cultures: an introduction. *Journal of Consumer Culture,* **10**(1), 3-12.

Berdychevsky, L., Gibson, H. J. & Bell, H. L. (2016). "Girlfriend getaway" as a contested term: Discourse analysis. *Tourism Management,* **55**, 106-122.

Campbell, C. (2005). The craft consumer: Culture, craft and consumption in a postmodern society. *Journal of Consumer Culture,* **5**(1), 23–42.

Cook, G. (2001). *The Discourse of Advertising*, London: Roultledge.

Cova, B. & Cova, V. (2012). On the road to prosumption: marketing discourse and the development of consumer competencies. *Consumption Markets & Culture,* **15**(2), 149-168.

Danesi, M. (2004). *Messages, Signs, and Meanings: A basic textbook in semiotics and communication* (3rd ed.). Toronto: Canadian Scholars Press.

de Waal Malefyt, T. & McCabe, M. (2016). Women's bodies, menstruation and marketing "protection:" Interpreting a paradox of gendered discourses in consumer practices and advertising campaigns. *Consumption Markets & Culture.* **19**(6), 555-575.

Dean, D. & Croft, R. (2001). Friends and relations: long-tenn approaches to political campaigning. *European Journal of Marketing,* **35**(11/12), 1197-1216.

Dermody, J. & Wring, D. (2001). Message: New developments in political communication and marketing. *Journal of Public Affairs,* **I**(3), 198-201.

Elliott, R. (1996). Discourse analysis: exploring action, function and conflict in social texts. *Marketing Intelligence and Planning,* **14**(6).

Ellis, N., Fitchett, J., Higgins, M., Jack, G., Lim, M., Saren, M. & Tadajewski, M. (2011). *Marketing: A Critical Textbook.* London: Sage.

Fairclough, N. L. (1995). *Critical Discourse Analysis: The critical study of language.* Harlow, UK: Longman.

Fellesson, M. (2011). Enacting customers–Marketing discourse and organizational practice. *Scandinavian Journal of Management,* **27**, 231-242.

Fill, C. (2009) *Marketing Communications: Interactivity, Communities and Content.* 5th ed. FT Prentice Hall.

Fill, C. (2011). *Essentials of Marketing Communications* Pearson.

Fitchett, J., & Caruana, R. (2015). Exploring the role of discourse in marketing and consumer research. *Journal of Consumer Behaviour,* **14**, 1-12.

Foucault, M. (2002). *The Order of Things: an archaeology of the human sciences.* Abingdon: Routledge.

Gee, J. P. (2005). *An Introduction to Discourse Analysis: Theory and method,* New York, NY: Routledge.

Gelles, D. (2022) 'Patagonia's New Owner: Earth', *The New York Times,* 14 September. https://www.nytimes.com/2022/09/14/climate/patagonia-climate-philanthropy-chouinard.html (Accessed: 08 June 2024).

Goldman, R. (1992). *Reading Ads Socially*: London, Routledge.

Goldman, R., & Papson, S. (1996). *Sign Wars: The Cluttered Landscape of Advertising.* New York: Guilford.

Grothaus, M. (2022) 'Apple's new privacy ad is a masterclass in marketing', *Fast Company,* 18 May.https://www.fastcompany.com/90753303/apple-privacy-ad-may-2022 (Accessed: 10 June 2024).

Hackley, C. (2012). *Advertising and Promotion: An Integrated Marketing Communications Approach* (2nd ed.). London.

Humphreys, A. & Grayson, K. (2008). The intersecting roles of consumer and producer: a critical perspective on co-production, co-creation and prosumption. *Sociology Compass*, **2**(3), 963–980.

Jafari, A. & Taheri, B. (2014). Nostalgia, reflexivity, and the narratives of self: reflections on Devine's 'removing the rough edges?'. *Consumption Markets and Culture*, **17**(2), 215-230.

Lees-Marshment, J. (2001). The marriage of politics and marketing. *Political Studies*, **49**(4), 692-713.

Lock, A. & Harris, P. (1996). Political Marketing: Vive la difference. *European Journal of Marketing*, **30**(10/11), 14-24.

MacCannell, D. (1989). *The Tourist: A New Theory of the Leisure Class*. London: Macmillan.

Morgan, G. (1992). Marketing discourse and practice: towards a critical analysis. In M. Alvesson & H. Willmott (Eds.), *Critical Management Studies* (pp. 136-158): London: Sage.

Moufahim, M. & Lim, M. (2009). Towards a critical political marketing agenda? *Journal of Maeting Management*, **25**(7-8), 763-776.

Niffenegger, P. B. (1989). Strategies for success from the political marketers. *Journal of Consumer Marketing*, **6**(1).

O'Cass, A. (1996). Political marketing and the marketing concept. *European Journal of Marketing*, **30**(10/11).

O'Shaughnessy, N. (1996). Social propaganda and social marketing: a critical difference? *European Journal of Marketing*, **30**(10/11), 62-75.

Oswald, L. R. (2012). *Marketing Semiotics: Signs, strategies, and brand value*, Oxford: Oxford University Press.

Patagonia. (2011). Don't Buy This Jacket, Black Friday and The New York Times. https://eu.patagonia.com/gb/en/stories/dont-buy-this-jacket-black-friday-and-the-new-york-times/story-18615.html.

Patagonia. (n.d.) Made without PFCs / PFAS. https://www.patagonia.com/our-footprint/pfas.html

Peirce, C. S. (1934). *Collected Papers of Charles Sanders Peirce*. Cambridge: Harvard University

Percy, L., & Rosenbaum-Elliott, R. (2012). *Strategic Advertising Management* (4th ed.). London: Oxford University Press.

Potter, J. & Wetherell, M. (1987). *Discourse and Social Psychology*, London: Sage.

Said, E. W. (1978). *Orientalism*. London: Penguin.

Saussure, F. (1966). *Course on General Linguistics*. New York: McGraw Hill.

Schroeder, J. (2002). Visual Consumption London: Routledge.

Scott, L. M. (1994). Images in advertising: the need for a theory of visual rhetoric. *Journal of Consumer Research,* **21**(2), 252-273.

Taheri, B. & Jafari, A. (2012). Museums as playful venues in the leisure society. In R. Sharpley & P. Stone (Eds.), *The Contemporary Tourist Experience: Concepts and Consequences* (pp. 201-215). New York: Routledge.

Thompson, C. J. (2004). Marketplace mythology and discourses of power. *Journal of Consumer Research,* **31**(1), 162-180.

Thompson, C. J. & Haytko, D. L. (1997). Speaking of fashion: Consumers' uses of fashion discourses and the appropriation of countervailing cultural meanings. *Journal of Consumer Research,* **24**(1), 15-42.

Wernick, A. (1991). *Promotional Culture: Advertising, Ideology And Symbolic Expression*: London: Sage.

Williamson, J. (1978). *Decoding Advertisements*. London: Marion Boyars.

3 Consumer Decisions in Marketing Communications

Christopher Dodd and Andreea Oniga

Introduction

Quite simply, consumers are the primary reason for the existence of marketing communications. Without consumers, there is no commercial imperative for marketers to create even the simplest of messages. The remarkable developments experienced over the last century are testament not only to our creativity and mastery of technology but, more importantly, to the identification of myriad consumer types. Nowhere is this better illustrated than within marketing communications. These consumers are represented through complex and often overlapping needs and wants, and exist within a world of seemingly endless choice. Marketers are driven to define these audiences and to construct tailored communications that typically seek to move beyond simple informational value. Increasingly, the goal is the creation of emotionally and socially engaging marketing communications that serve to persuade consumers not only to purchase or visit but, further, to connect and to become part of a much bigger offering – a relationship. (Costello and Reczek, 2020).

Increasingly, this abstract sense of connectedness between consumers, marketers and brands is being translated into more tangible, financially relevant terms, namely through its inclusion as a component of brand and advertising equity (Rosengren and Dahlen, 2015). It is not surprising, therefore, that marketers are keen to develop brand relationships, with marketing communications offering an expedient, if not always perfect place within which to manage them. The cost to marketers of this approach is the need to understand consumers in ways not previously required. It is no longer enough to identify target groups and fire-off marketing communications in their general direction. Now, consumers exist as an integral part of the communications production process. They are not simply the audience, they are co-creators – designers, developers and users. Quite simply, they are 'one of us' and so it has never been so necessary for marketers to understand 'why' and 'how' consumers behave as they do.

By focussing upon consumer decisions, this chapter seeks to support and further our understanding, explaining why consumers are driven to make decisions and how they manage their experiences. First, we consider who consumers are, exploring definitions relevant to marketing communications that seek to explain their nature, location and value to marketing communications. Second, we present a modelled conceptualisation of this understanding, focusing upon the consumer's decision-making process. Here, we will explore representations of the consumer's journey through their decisions; identify the benefits and costs to consumers and marketers within this process and consider how the contexts of consumption moderate these experiences. Third, we consider some of the overarching theories that seek to explain consumer behaviour. By exploring consumer values, motivations and involvement, we frame this understanding around what consumers do (behaviour), what consumers feel (emotion) and what consumers think (cognition).

Understanding consumers in marketing communications

In Chapter 1, we noted a prevailing conceptualisation of marketing communications, through Kotler et al.'s (2016: 630) definition:

> *"Marketing communications are the means by which firms attempt to inform, persuade and remind consumers directly or indirectly about the brands they market. In a sense, marketing communications represent the 'voice' of the company and its brands, and are the ways in which it can establish a dialogue and build relationship with consumers."*

The first part of this definition offers a fairly traditional interpretation of the role and function of marketing communications. This unidirectional (marketer to audience) approach is symptomatic of earlier attempts to conceptualise consumers and their behaviour, which emphasised the well-established, classical economic formula of production versus consumption. Within such approaches, the marketing environment is seen as a place where products and services are produced and subsequently offered to consumers as part of a wider system of (typically commercial) exchange. Marketing communications naturally fill the void between these ideas, providing information (via numerous forms) that enables these parties to move closer together and achieve satisfying exchanges.

This view has served marketing well for many years, allowing the creation of a readily understandable system of (transactional) exchange for both the marketer and the consumer (see Bagozzi, 1978). The marketing environment has changed, however, with an associated re-conceptualisation of the consumer, the marketer and marketing communications. Whilst some may argue that the traditional view always represented a misconception of this marketing exchange relationship (e.g. Galbraith, 1958; Baudrillard, 1988), the tangible changes in the fabric of the marketing environment (not least through advances in technology) push forward the notion of a radically altered set of parameters/priorities. The second part of Kotler et al.'s definition gives a nod to this changing dynamic, acknowledging that marketers may see value in nurturing collaborative relationships with consumers, around the desired values of their brands (see Dwyer, et al., 1987; Gronroos, 2004). Of course, by labelling consumers as 'consumers', this definition significantly limits the scope of understanding available to marketers to commercial and transactional value.

Perhaps most challenging in the re-conceptualisation of consumers is the notion that consumers exist not only to consume but also to produce. Similarly, to consider marketers as merely producers of communications is to underplay their own consumption of that process and experience. For example, consider how consumers are involved more than ever before in the design process of products and marketing communications, with some markets' existence dependent upon the activity of participant consumers – so called *'prosumers'* (see Cova & Cova, 2012; Martin & Schouten, 2014).

It is likely that you will have contributed to and/or read online reviews, such as those on Tripadvisor. Your review sits alongside other existing reviews and/or elicits more responses regarding the experience. The provider of that experience may also contribute to that discussion, managing interpretations and expectations for the reviewers and readers. The validity of these reviews is bound up with an array of visible evidence to establish the credibility of authors (e.g. contribution ratings and rankings). Ultimately, the marketer may modify their offering and consumers may modify their understanding of the experience. Clearly, in that case, both consumers and marketers have qualitatively changed their position. The consumers (reviewers) have contributed to this offering production and the marketer has actively consumed this development process (at least at an individual level).

Of course, allowing consumers to contribute to marketing does not guarantee that consumers' and marketers' interests are synonymous. It does, however, demonstrate a shared process of marketing that challenges existing adversarial conceptualisations of this relationship. For some, this represents a move from *marketerspace* (where markets control the space) to *consumerspace* (where consumers direct offerings) (Solomon, 2003) although, more realistically, this remains a shared, co-created space!

Thus, consumers occupy various forms. They may be singular or collective; separate or interactive. They are potential consumers; clients and users. They may be advocates or opponents. They may be the target audience and they may also have audiences of their own. They may be passive recipients of marketing communications or they may actively construct marketing communications. They are both consumers and they are marketers. Online or offline, they are ubiquitous. Faced with such varied and complex identities, it may seem an insurmountable task to create meaningful communications. Consumers are, however, bound by one ever present type of behaviour – the need to make choices. We will now turn our attention to explaining the process of decision-making and marketing communication's relationship with this process.

Consumers and choice

Being able to model consumers' decision-making behaviour offers considerable advantage to marketers. At a general level, communications may be assembled to target general approaches to understanding. Consider how bigger brands will focus upon consolidation of brand values within their campaigns. Chanel will routinely offer glimpses of exotic and exclusive worlds wrapped within a sublimely retro feel. Guinness would routinely release big budget, symbolism rich advertisements built around the two-toned colour of its products and brand. Here, the belief is that consumers are aware of the brand and the requirement is to maintain this brand presence as a pre-curser to decisions.

More specifically, decision making may be seen as a staged process, within which the different stages represent different actions on the part of the consumer. This allows marketers the opportunity to tailor communications to the specific behaviours evidenced within each stage (see Figure 3.1).

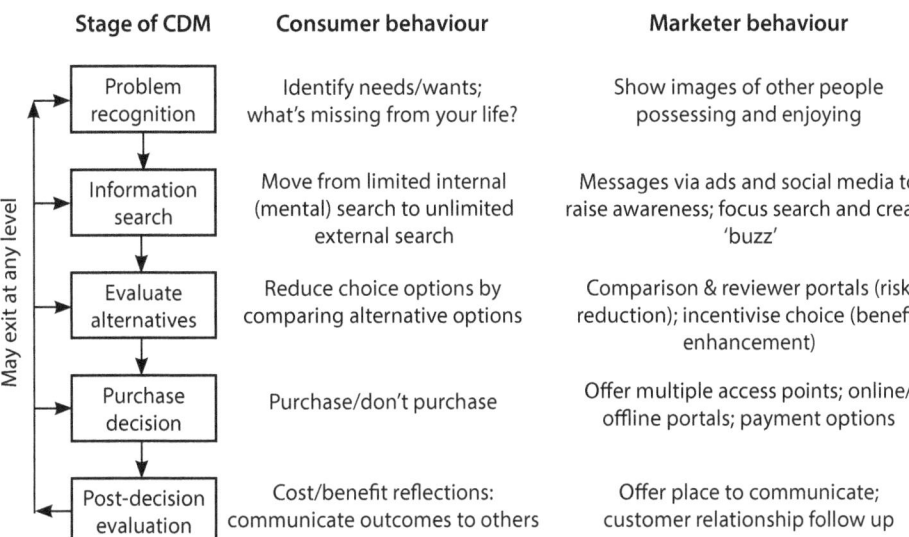

Figure 3.1: Consumer decision making model (CDM) and marketing communications tactics

The value of the CDM model is evident from its use to focus marketing communications activities. The main problem with such an approach however is its reliance on a rational approach to decision making. Clearly, some behaviours are not rational and do not proceed sequentially through stages. Irrational decision-making may be seen within compulsive and addictive behaviours, where consumers act on impulse and/or are less able to control the urge to consume. Marketing communication has been identified as a driver of this irrational consumption, offering unrealistic promises to vulnerable audiences and fuelling a desire to consume (Packard, 1957 and see Desmond, 2003). For effective marketing, there is a need to establish not only how consumers make decisions but, also, why they make decisions.

Drivers of consumer choice

Choice is a fundamental, permanent feature of our lives. We begin our days with a choice (to wake up properly) and fight our way through a seemingly constant process of decision-making until we close our eyes and sleep. (Some would argue that we are still making choices in our sleep!). Some choices are easier than others and some choices seem unachievable. Some choices are forced upon us; others we actively search for. Ultimately, our experience of choice shapes who we are and reveals this identity to others. This presents a fantastic opportunity for marketers to understand you and to influence your decision-making.

For marketers looking to satisfy consumers, identifying needs and wants and explaining why those drives exist offers the opportunity to create more satisfying exchanges. Most people will seek out positive experiences and avoid negative ones. Of course, what people consider to be positive may well differ but most people will be able to offer an explanation for their choices (even if they are not always completely certain why!). Nonetheless, this tendency to pursue outcomes helps us to understand consumers' engagement with marketing communications from a motivational perspective.

Consumer motives

By understanding motivation, we are able to understand why consumers behave the way they do. Much research on motivation takes a psychological perspective and this underpinned most marketing communications insights from the 1950s onwards (see Dichter, 1947). In essence, motivation exists because we recognise the existence of a need or want. This awareness is accompanied by a state of tension that we are driven to satisfy or remove. This is a common perspective in psychology, as cognitive (rational) and affective (emotional) processes are inextricably connected to physiological reactions (behaviours). The strength of your reaction to this tension dictates your drive to resolve it. Consider how you shop for food when you are hungry. Perhaps you make quicker choices, buy more food and eat the food sooner after purchase. The drive to resolve your negative state of tension is much stronger than if you are not so hungry.

Even psychologists are mindful, however, that these psychological processes do not exist in isolation. We are, at least in part, shaped by our experiences and our environments. When explaining hunger, sociologists and anthropologists may point to our fixation with set eating times (e.g. breakfast, lunch and dinner) and suggest that we are conditioned to feel hungry at certain times. Consider how we may sometimes 'forget' to be hungry if we are sufficiently distracted (for example, through work, fun and so on). Anyone who has adopted a nutritional diet will be aware of how many of these seek to subvert our normal embedded expectations of food and satiation of appetite (for example, the 5:2 diet effectively changes your consumption habit on 2 days out of every 7) (www.thefastdiet.co.uk). Clearly, our adoption of certain lifestyles and associated behaviours becomes a significant moderator of our behaviours.

Whilst earlier motivational theories (such as drive theory) emphasise a less controllable biological drive, other theories recognise the cognitive basis of behaviour. For instance, cognitive dissonance theory (Festinger, 1954) suggests that people are motivated to seek balance and harmony in their lives and any choice context will trigger a raised level of tension. Similarly, expectancy theory (Vroom, 1964) suggests that people use their learned experience to set the criteria required to achieve outcomes through, for instance, the setting of goals. Goals may be positive or negative (they have what we call 'valence') and many of us will be aware of setting positive goals that we strive to attain – consider how we may want a new job and will buy new clothes as part of our attempts to achieve this. Not all goals are positive, of course, and you will no doubt have experience of being motivated to avoid negative outcomes – consider how our use of personal hygiene products is driven by a belief that these will help us to avoid rejection and humiliation. The existence of differential valence inevitably causes conflict for consumers and offers marketers the opportunity to resolve this conflict. By grouping conflicts according to a consumer's desire to avoid or approach goals, marketers are able to offer solutions as part of the set of benefits derived from brands and products.

3

This is typically operationalised by three 'motivational conflict' dualisms: approach-approach; approach-avoid and avoid-avoid.

- Whilst **approach-approach** scenarios would seem to offer a win-win for consumers, the reality is that this represents a choice and choices create tension (remember cognitive dissonance!). Marketers may help to make this choice easier by bundling benefits together to create persuasive benefit bundles (e.g. who wouldn't want something that was tasty, filling and nutritious?) but the choice remains.

- **Approach-avoid** scenarios are perhaps more familiar to most of us. Here we want to achieve a goal but recognise that it is perhaps not in our best interests – consider how you feel when you add a large chocolate bar to your lunch or 'go large' at McDonalds. Marketers seek to offset these worries by taking a variety of approaches. Some may embrace over-consumption and incentivise the purchase. Saving money usually makes us feel better, as does believing that we are receiving multiple benefits within one purchase. Others may try to persuade you that you 'deserve' or 'have earned the right' to indulge yourself (https://www.youtube.com/watch?v=LRTq5BImIWg, courtesy of Ford).

- Finally, **avoid-avoid** scenarios see the consumer with a choice few of us want, a choice between two undesirable alternatives. Consider how we often resent having to pay for repairs to products and don't want to accept the cost of replacements. For the marketer, the aim is typically to de-stress this decision. New products may be supported by favourable finance deals; payment plans may offer warranty and service options; all at manageable regular amounts. Of course, reminding consumers of the reliability and trustworthiness of a brand is a regular tactic within marketing communications to offset such concerns.

Consumer values

Your behaviour will, in no short measure, be shaped by your values. Yet this clear link to influencing consumers is not the panacea marketers may hope for. The problem is that values tend to be broad-based beliefs about life in general and your place within it. They may guide people towards certain behaviours but they may not always be so relevant to specific contexts. Further, whilst individuals may exhibit similar behaviours (e.g. food and clothing choices), the belief systems that underpin these behaviours may be different (e.g. religion, health, environmentalism). This makes them seemingly less controllable and less targeted for the specific briefs of brand managers and marketing communications practitioners.

Yet values offer real insights into the beliefs and desires of consumers. Further, our belief systems drive us to relate to others with similar beliefs. This tends to facilitate social network formation that fosters a positively determined consensus (we like to seek out people who agree with us and exclude those who do not) (see Turner et al., 1987). At its broadest level, our core values frame our essential relationship with our world. You may value your freedom, sense of belonging, connectedness and so on. You may also value less abstract ideas, such as cleanliness, privacy, manners or animal welfare.

For marketers, the usefulness of values may lie in identifying relative differences across groups. For instance, where value systems are contained within cultural groupings, we often see striking differences that set those cultures apart. This may be at a general, stereotypical (and often unsubstantiated) level (such as the belief that Germans are organised, Australians are rude and Spanish are passionate). It may also be at a specific, product attribute level (such as the belief that breakfast cereal should contain a particular set of vitamins, cosmetics should be formulated for specific skin types, and the towels in a 4 star hotel should be softer and fluffier than a 3 star hotel).

Schwartz (1992) preferred to create a motivation-based understanding of values. The **Schwartz value survey** accommodates 56 different values and positions them within ten 'motivational domains'. The domains are further contained within two core dimensions. The first dimension concerns our desire to look outwards to others, so at one extreme there is 'openness to change' and at the other 'conservatism'. The second dimension concerns our desire to develop our sense of who we are, identified by Schwartz as 'self-transcendence' or 'self-enhancement'.

For Holbrook (1999), the variations may be more usefully tied to the consumption experience, with consumers actively evaluating the benefits available to them from engaging with the object/offering. Holbrook (and his co-authors) note eight distinct types of consumer value:

1 **Efficiency** – potential for convenience (e.g. how easy is it to obtain/use).

2 **Excellence** – evaluations of quality (e.g. is it well constructed).

3 **Status** – potential for social movement (e.g. will it signal my status; can I manage impressions).

4 **(Self)-esteem** – potential to enhance self-esteem (e.g. does it make me feel better about myself).

5 **Play** – potential for enjoyment (e.g. is it fun to consume).

6 **Aesthetics** – potential to enhance beauty of self and others (e.g. is it beautiful).

7 **Ethics** – potential to support moral/ethical positions (e.g. will it help/harm others).

8 **Spirituality** – potential to transform (e.g. will it enhance experience beyond the norm).

Activity

Assume you have just returned from one of the following: i) a spiritual retreat in Thailand; ii) a spa break in Malaysia; and/or iii) a romantic break in the Maldives. Apply Holbrook's values to your holiday break and make a note of your comments. Can you identify any values which are more dominant than others. What are your reflections on the points you have made?

Rokeach (1973) rather sought to link *terminal* values (a person's desired end-state) with *instrumental* values (the action-based values needed to achieve the end-state). Hence, he suggested for instance that instrumental values such as courage, ambition, politeness or honesty may form the basis to achieve terminal values, such as happiness, friendship, or equality, amongst many others. This link between behaviour and values is further developed through the means-end chain model (Gutman, 1981; 1982), which assumes that people link product attributes to potential end-states. The value of this approach to marketers is fairly transparent. If attributes can be linked to end-states, creating and communicating value may become more transparent.

Example

"Find out what a Boot Camp Fitness Holiday in Spain can do for you" said the headline in the advertisement. The ad went on to ask me whether I was "interested in getting fit, losing weight, and feeling good" about myself. Yes, the voice in my head screamed out to me. "If so", the advert went on to read, "what better environment is there to make the changes to your life than in beautiful Almeria (Spain)". It finished by urging me to "make that change now and find out" what they can do for me!

Source: adapted from www.bootcampspain.net

Of course, life is not that simple. The reality is that whilst attributes may be linked to values, they will exist with varying degrees of importance and abstraction. Establishing exactly which attributes should be prioritised and to what degree of magnitude is enough of a problem to leave means-end analysis to those with enough time and resources to pursue useful answers.

One attempt to operationalise this model, however, has allowed advertisers to generate useful bases for the construction of messages. The Means-End Conceptualisation of the Components of Advertising Strategy (MECCAs) enables a mapping of product/service attributes relative to terminal values (see Reynolds and Craddock, 1988 for an advertising example). By asking consumers to identify and rank attributes of products/services, 'ladders' of expectations are developed for specific products/services. This mapping allows a conceptualisation of the strategy required to communicate effectively with the consumer. For instance, knowing which benefits consumers prioritise allows advertisers to select from those attributes the most appropriate (and so persuasive) features to use as elements within the message. If you believe a car enhances your status if it is fast and loud, then it is a short hop for the advertiser to create advertisements that prioritise speed and noise within the message.

Hence, values help us to understand how consumers prioritise elements of their world, and motivations demonstrate consumers' strength of desire to achieve their goals. Whilst these ideas are clearly useful in understanding consumer behaviour, they struggle to account for the inherent difference between consumers. For instance, whilst you may desperately want the latest version of your favourite tech, your friend may prefer a different brand, may be perfectly content with their older model or even prefer to have no tech at all! Involvement is a concept that allows marketers to explore these differences in preference by building understanding of motives around specific choice contexts.

Consumer involvement

Involvement has been defined as a person's perceived relevance of the object based on their inherent needs, values and interests (Zaichowsky, 1985). When considering *consumer* involvement particularly, 'object' typically relates to one of several contexts: product, purchase decision, advertisements and/or consumption more generally (see O'Cass, 2000). Consumer involvement prioritises, therefore, the consumer's motivation to engage with and manage offering-related information. Consumers do not enter into decisions, however, bereft of psychological baggage. Consumer involvement conceptualises these decisions as part of a process, with antecedents moderating engagement with the context and outcomes offering evidence of decision effectiveness.

There are typically four types of consumer involvement including:

- **Cognitive** (i.e. heightened thinking and processing information about a goal object e.g., a complex purchase; a brand that's new to you),
- **Affective** (i.e. heightened feelings and emotional energy e.g., a consumer responds positively to an ad for tissues featuring a fluffy white kitten),
- **Enduring** (i.e. interest in an offering or an activity over a long period of time; e.g., a parent would consider children's toys important and self-relevant),
- **Situational** (i.e. temporary interest in the goal object; e.g., a childless person would see children's toys as relevant when they need to buy a gift for a child).

Prior research recognises the involvement concept as complicated with various operational and theoretical problems (Laaksonen, 1994). According to Taheri et al. (2017), arguably the discussion on the conceptualisation of involvement concentrates on three categories: the origin of involvement (occurring as a result of practical or role-related needs), the nature of involvement (continuous or dichotomous variable), and the object of involvement (product, person, particular message stimuli or situations). Moreover, there is an overlap between involvement and other similar concepts, such as engagement. Taheri et al. (2014: 322) highlight that *"engagement goes beyond involvement to embrace a proactive consumer relationship with specific objects of engagement"*. They also argue that engagement is broader than involvement and it is a two-way interaction between consumers and brands.

Antecedents of involvement include several broad, overlapping factors:

- **Person** factors, such as needs, values and inherent interest in the object;
- **Situation** factors, such as whether it is a special occasion and/or require for a particular purpose;

- ■ **Object** factors, such as the nature of the communication and/or how the object is differentiated from other objects.

Outcomes could represent anything, from brand preference to how much information the consumer searches for; from how much time is spent considering alternatives to the likelihood of the consumer generating a counter position to an advertisement's message.

We have already seen how values may drive motives to engage with decisions. Consumer involvement suggests that these values are part of a wider set of beliefs that are taken into every decision and moderated by other factors such as the environment within which the choice is being made and evaluations of potential outcomes from the decision. This underpins perhaps the main value of the involvement concept, the notion of levels of involvement.

We will all recognise that some decisions are more difficult than others. For the majority of consumers' decisions, we would expect to see high levels of involvement for high price offerings (such as houses) and low involvement for everyday purchases (such as milk). The value of involvement, however, is that it allows marketers to move beyond these simplistic understandings. Some consumers will find it more difficult to choose a new dress than they will a new car. This may, for instance, be due to their high disposable wealth or because clothes interest them more than cars. Similarly, consumers will buy into brands to the exclusion of other brands. This fierce brand loyalty is a holy grail for marketers, with loyal consumers usually willing to spend more and buy more frequently than for other brands. Of course, some 'brand loyals' may never spend anything on the brand, with their high involvement not translating to purchase (consider the football fan who never goes to a match, never buys merchandise but watches all the games on free-to-air television). They may, however, communicate their affiliation and preference to others and so perpetuate brand values.

If we consider that consumer involvement represents a continuum of a person's engagement with marketing offerings, we see that there may be differences in the way that information is processed depending upon their level of engagement. We may reasonably expect that those less engaged with an offering will engage in more simplistic processing, whilst those at the opposite extreme engage in more elaborate processing. A particular feature of much of our low involvement shopping is inertia. Inertia represents an absence of engagement, thought and deliberation in choices. We buy something because we always buy it. Of course, this does not mean that at some point previously, we have not pursued far more elaborate processing of information. Figure 3.2 represents involvement as an interest continuum.

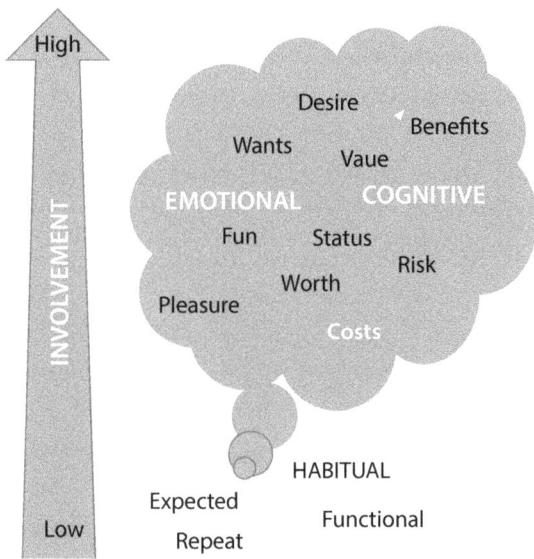

Figure 3.2: Levels of involvement and decision-making

At the higher end of involvement, we notice different types of processing built around cognition (thoughts) and affect (emotion). This differentiation enables advertisers to use different communication tactics. We will often hear marketing communications practitioners talking about selling the 'sausage or the sizzle'. In this analogy, the sausage represents a cognitive approach, where messages will focus on content, ingredients, rationalised inputs and outputs. The sizzle is the affective approach, representing abstract emotional ideas such as fun, fantasy, anticipation, desire, and so on. Would you want to read about the significant features available on a new car or would you like to see it move and hear it roar? Of course, cognitive theorists would argue that emotion does not live in the heart but, rather, in the mind and so everything is cognitive – that is, everything is information that we understand in different ways.

Supporting consumer choice

Whilst marketing communications fundamentally inform consumer decisions, it is clear that they perform many other supporting functions. They assist in evaluations, offering alternatives and suggesting values that may or may not be hidden to consumers. They allow interaction with other people and other environments which, in turn, may allow confirmation of decisions and validate behaviour. They help to position individuals relative to others within their worlds, validating status and identity. Hence, consumers are enabled and empowered by marketing communications in a real and practical way.

Additionally, marketing communications are typically engaging, interesting and enjoyable. By offering consumers the opportunity to have fun; to experience worlds outside of their day-to-day existence and to indulge in fantasies, marketing communications allow separation from consumers' real lives (see Holbrook and Hirschmann, 1982). At both of these levels, marketing communications practitioners employ a variety of tactics to increase consumers' involvement and engagement to support decision-making.

You may recognise some techniques used by advertisers to increase audience involvement with messages. Product placement, for example, is now quite sophisticated. Branded products are not just 'plonked' into content anymore but are intricately woven into the entertainment narrative making a stronger and much more emotional connection with the consumer. Conceptualised by the advertising industry as 'branded entertainment' this concept sees the convergence of advertising and entertainment. (Hudson & Hudson, 2006: 489). Novelty is, of course, still a favourite (see Chapter 7 for further details of novelty within the context of creative advertising). New messages; new ways of constructing the message; unexpected content and delivery will always increase involvement. This perhaps explains the contemporary predilection with unusual approaches to marketing communications. We have seen an incredible rise in the use of interactive media and user-generated content. How many times do you respond to messages asking you to interact with a brand?

Flash mobs take the advertising message to new contexts and audiences. Who wouldn't stop to watch a choir welcome travellers home from their flights (https://www.youtube.com/watch?v=NB3NPNM4xgo, courtesy of T-Mobile); or unlock their inner James Bond for a few minutes (https://www.youtube.com/watch?v=5T6BCHCk6QY, courtesy of Coca-Cola). Of course, creating entertainment out of the messages is not new. Many early television programmes embedded the brand and message so completely into programming that the programmes were effectively an extended advertisement. What has changed is the accessibility of programming. Audiences are now able to control when and where they view their programmes. The rise of social media has enabled variable, consumer-led access to this content. Yet within the channels of YouTube, Twitch and Kick (amongst others) we see a return to the branded entertainment tactics of the 1950s, with the latest generation of YouTubers regularly embedding advertisements within their offerings. So, should we see digital consumers as different to other consumers or consider them in similar terms?

Contexts of consumer decisions – digital consumers

Previous research has referred to 'digital consumers' (i.e. consumers who use digital technologies and access the internet) as mysterious as an undiscovered tribe, existing as a separate entity to 'normal' consumers (Ryan, 2014). However, with widespread technology adoption (over 70% of the world population owned a smartphone by the end of 2023) (Laricchia, 2024) and mixed use of digital and physical channels in purchasing (Flavián et al., 2016), the distinction between digital and 'normal' consumers is becoming increasingly blurred. Importantly, digital consumers are still consumers – still people. The main difference is the environment within which they make decisions. As we have noted previously, consumers are faced with choices, and construct these within an environment of complex information. The digital consumer has the greater potential of broader access to stimuli that may affect this process. For some, this is a simplification process, allowing algorithms to make decisions for them. For others, it is an elaboration, flooding their decision-making with excess information.

Consumer journeys through digital space

The digital environment is characterised by continuous and rapid change, driven by technological developments. For instance, generative AI technologies now allow marketers to create more relevant and personalised content (Kshetri et al., 2023). VR and AR technologies allow the creation of interactive or immersive ads provided through various static or mobile devices (Wedel et al., 2020). External events may also drive change in the digital environment. Widespread restrictions on social space during the Covid pandemic accelerated the growth in use of digital space, both by consumers, and by companies seeking to reach consumers (LaBerge et al., 2020). Post-pandemic, 45% of companies use social media to sell products and 93% to generate brand awareness (The CMO Survey, 2023). Thus, social media has an increasingly important role in a digitalised, post-pandemic world. Not least, social media offers opportunities for multi-way interaction between companies and consumers (Dijkmans et al., 2015). When buying a pair of shoes online, for instance, one may be exposed to various online channels, some of which consumers will have sought (e.g., visiting a company's website, or an external review website) and others which will have been 'served' to them (e.g., a retargeted display advert). The consumer can interact with the brand directly, by commenting on a social media post, and the brand may respond. By publicly expressing their satisfaction or dissatisfaction with a company, their opinions may in turn influence the decision-making behaviour of other consumers. Understanding how consumers navigate this digital space within their choices offers marketers opportunities to shape those decisions and we have, therefore, seen the adoption of digital consumer journeys as a means of facilitating this insight.

The consumer journey concept has evolved from early consumer decision-making process models and is defined as *"the process a consumer goes through, across all stages and touch points, that makes up the consumer experience"* (Lemon & Verhoef, 2016: 71). Touchpoints represent individual contacts with a brand (Baxendale et al., 2015), such as viewing an advert or reading about another consumer's experience. By focussing on interactions at different touchpoints, marketers seek to understand how these interactions affect consumers' behaviour and the experience, at all stages of the journey. Lemon and Verhoef (2016) identify three stages of the journey: the pre-purchase stage (which includes behaviours of need recognition, information search, alternative evaluation), the purchase stage, and the post-purchase stage (See Figure 3.3). This conceptualisation shows close similarity to the decision model explored earlier in this chapter. The main difference is the additional focus on touchpoints. In the digital environment, there may be a large number of touchpoints at each stage. These touchpoints can be under the control of the brand (e.g., digital advertising or other marketing communications) or out with its control (e.g., external review websites) (Lemon and Verhoef, 2016). An understanding of all the touchpoints consumers will encounter in their journey and how they may work together is therefore useful in developing marketing communications which integrate coherently with other touchpoints. Importantly, the journey is dynamic in nature; it is influenced by past experiences and may in turn influence future experiences and behaviours (Lemon & Verhoef, 2016).

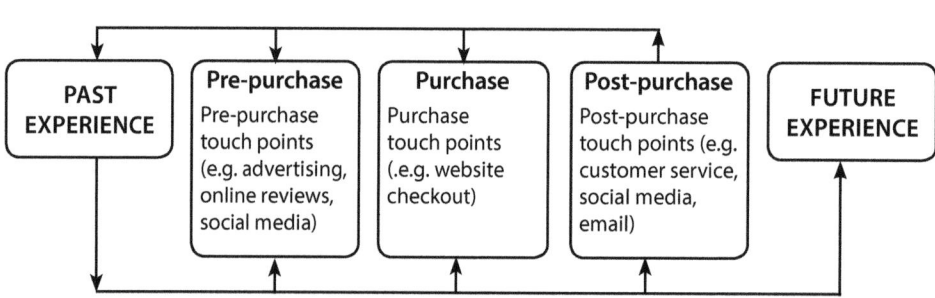

Figure 3.3: The Customer Journey, adapted from Lemon and Verhoef (2016).

Of course, even if a purchase is made online, the purchase process itself may not occur entirely online. The consumer may visit physical stores to try the product, before returning to an online channel to make the purchase. The behaviour of researching products in store, and purchasing online, is known as 'showrooming', and its opposite, 'webrooming' involves researching online, and purchasing in store (Flavián et al., 2016). So, as consumers choose to mix both online and offline channels, going back to the fundamentals underpinning behaviour (such as motivations for using different channels) can help inform marketing strategy. For instance, Hou and Elliott (2021) identify motivations for mobile shopping such as convenience seeking, bargain hunting, enjoyment seeking, perceived usefulness, and ease of use. One simple example related to the motivation 'bargain hunting' would be the use of sales promotions. For example, offering discount codes for mobile in-app purchases would be useful for those consumers. Similarly, given the motivation of convenience, allowing easier purchasing of the products, for example, by tapping on a mobile ad, offers advantage to those consumers. Such innovations offer advantage but, also, have a resource cost to marketers and consumers. Accessing more efficient means of engaging this process have facilitated the rise in new technologies and novel consumer spaces.

Consumers of digital technologies

New technologies, such as AI (Artificial Intelligence), and the 'Realities' of VR, AR, MR and XR (Virtual, Augmented, Mixed and Extended Realities) are increasingly prominent. Generative AI involves complex machine learning models trained on large amounts of data, which can generate content based on prompts from a user. Large language models such as ChatGPT can be used to create text content for marketing, whereas image generating tools such as DALL-E or Midjourney can be used to create images (Kshetri et al., 2023). In many cases, consumers may not be aware that the content they are seeing is AI generated. Nevertheless, evidence suggests that AI-created content tends to be perceived as higher quality than content produced by humans (Zhang & Gosline, 2023). At the same time, research suggests that increased use of AI would make 40% of consumers trust brands less (Ipsos, 2023). Indeed, individuals may perceive ChatGPT as 'creepy', negatively influencing intentions to continue using it (Baek & Kim, 2023) and some marketers are already seeing consumers push back against the removal of human contributions to offerings (Pulver, 2024). If interacting with AI tools can make some individuals feel uneasy then, by extension, AI-generated communications may produce similar effects, providing a dilemma for marketers. Additionally, as generative AI tools draw on past data to generate new content, this content may reflect biases inherent in past data. Piers (2024) identifies that ChatGPT text may reflect racial bias, whereas Sun et al. (2024) document the presence of gender bias in images generated by DALL-E, highlighting potential ethical issues with AI generated content.

Reality technologies are enabling new ways of interacting with consumers. Virtual reality offers an immersive, interactive virtual environment, whereas augmented reality creates a display of the real world, enhanced/overlayed with digital objects (Milgram & Kishino, 1994). Whilst these technologies have existed for decades, advancements in recent years have made them more broadly accessible. For instance, VR headsets are readily available at most price points, and AR creative tools are now available via smartphones. In turn, marketers are also increasingly using these technologies (Wedel et al., 2020). For consumers to engage with this type of marketing communication, they must use the technology, so it is useful to understand which needs the use of AR satisfies. Smink et al. (2021) identify gratifications such as entertainment, information, and innovation as drivers of satisfaction with AR. Whilst these gratifications are similar to those obtained from other media, these can nonetheless inform the design of AR-marketing. Developing entertaining, informative and novel AR-marketing should increase the likelihood of consumers engaging in the desired behaviour. Notably, however, Smink et al. (2021) also found that privacy concerns had a negative impact on AR preference for those who were not already users of AR, highlighting one of the downsides of AR use and a potential barrier to consumer adoption of these technologies.

Example

Coca-Cola's '#TakeATaste Now' campaign used AR technology as part of a digital out of home campaign, enabling consumers to interact with digital outdoor screens using their mobiles. By scanning the QR code on the screens, consumers could grab a virtual Coca Cola Zero bottle in their hands, facilitated by AR technology using their device cameras. The virtual bottle could then be redeemed physically in a Tesco shop.

Source: https://www.jcdecaux.co.uk/news/coca-cola-zero-sugar-launches-first-its-kind-interactive-ar-giveaway-campaign-inviting-fans

Consuming social media

Many consumers will have a presence within digital media via social media (an umbrella term for technologies that allow users to create and share content). These include social network sites (SNS), such as Facebook, YouTube, Wikipedia, WhatsApp, amongst many others. Whiting and Williams (2013) note that, amongst other factors, self-presentation drives users' satisfaction with social media. That is, the ability to present themselves and self-disclose as they wish is vital for these environments to be wanted and valued. Hence, an added complexity for marketers is that a consumer's adoption of, and engagement with brands and communications is visible to their friends, followers and others. Furthermore, consumers may exhibit different types of behaviours in relation to brands on social media. Muntinga et al., (2011) categorise these behaviours into consumption (reading posts or watching videos), contribution (commenting or participating in conversations) and creation (writing brand-related posts, creating videos, etc.). Although the first category reflects traditional patterns of communications from companies to consumers, contribution and creation behaviours mean that consumers can communicate with the brand itself, and with other consumers, as they expend time and effort to comment or create new content. Thus, on social media, the consumer is not simply a recipient of marketing communications but, rather they become marketers, repackaging meaning within brand messages before release to their own target audiences. They are also, therefore, subsequently constrained by the pervading social pressures of their own audiences, as these develop to become populous and multifarious (Marder et al., 2012).

There is variety in the social media platforms that consumers can be active on, with different platforms having different characteristics. For example, Reddit is structured around communities on specific topics, in which users can post and comment on others' posts, whereas TikTok is focused on short-form video content. Instagram began as an image-sharing platform but, similar to TikTok, also now focuses substantially on short-form video content.

These varying characteristics enable consumers to evidence different motives for their brand-related behaviours (consumption, contribution, creation) on different platform types (Buzeta et al., 2020). On profile-based platforms (e.g., Instagram), consumption behaviours are driven by entertainment motives, whereas on content-based platforms (e.g., Reddit), they are driven by information-seeking motives (Buzeta et al., 2020). Similarly, contribution behaviours are driven by remuneration motives (obtaining a reward or financial benefit) on profile-based platforms, but not on content-based platforms (Buzeta et al., 2020). These findings highlight how an understanding of motivations, in this case related to behaviours on social media platforms, can inform marketing communications, and in particular, creative strategies. For instance, informational message appeals that address product or service benefits may be more useful on content-based platforms such as Reddit, than on profile-based platforms such as Instagram, if the goal is to encourage views. Creative approaches such as storytelling, may in turn generate more views on Instagram, whilst rewards may enhance the number of comments on a brand's posts. Finally, as identified by Buzeta et al., (2020), empowerment motives (related to influencing others) drive creation behaviour across all platform types, suggesting they could be generally relevant to encourage consumers to create user-generated content. Interestingly, empowerment was also found to drive contribution and consumption behaviours (Buzeta et al., 2020), so it could be considered a general driver of brand-related behaviour on social media.

Whilst the context of consumption differs on social media compared to traditional consumption contexts, with additional behaviours for consumers to engage in beyond purchasing, a consideration of the underlying motives for these behaviours remains important for effective marketing communications.

Example

Sephora UK, a beauty retailer, promoted various giveaways on Instagram. For the launch of Rare Beauty products (a beauty brand created by actress and singer Selena Gomez) in Sephora UK stores, Sephora asked people to follow both its own and Rare Beauty's Instagram account and comment to "*Tell us what makes you feel rare*", in return for a chance to win a cosmetic set from the brand. This illustrates the use of rewards to encourage comment contributions from an Instagram audience, appealing to remuneration-related motives.

Source: https://www.instagram.com/sephorauk/reel/C4OY2_CsnZs/

Social media influencers are "*a new category of opinion leaders, with a position somewhere between celebrities and friends, that has emerged with the growth of social media opportunities*" (Belanche et al., 2021: 187). Influencers (as the name suggests) exert influence over the decisions of their social media audience, and this can be enacted through simple mentions or recommendations, or more elaborate product testing or reviews. Influencers present new opportunities for marketers, primarily through sponsorships in which influencers may be contracted to promote a product or service. However, as influencers are themselves consumers of products and services, they may also share recommendations without a financial remuneration, and some even specialise in objectively testing products. Their influence can also be linked back to well established consumer behaviour concepts, such as values. Consumers tend to follow influencers whose values and beliefs align with their own values, and when these influencers promote products which align with their image, the promotion is more likely to be successful (Belanche et al., 2021).

Summary

Consumers are considered fundamental drivers of marketing activity and this chapter has considered the value to marketing communications of understanding and explaining consumer choice. The nature of the consumer has been explored and subsequently located within the variety of contexts that form the marketing communications landscape. Key theoretical ideas including consumer values, motivations and involvement are presented and used as a basis to explain both the consumer's decision management and, also, their relationships with marketing communications. Figure 3.4 seeks to represent this process by placing these interconnected concepts as hierarchical foundations underpinning consumer choice.

3

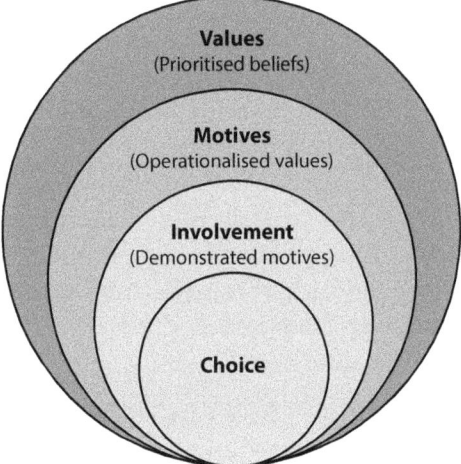

Figure 3.4: Relationship between values, motives, involvement and choice

The figure highlights the fundamental space occupied by values, which represent the core truths of individual identity – the reasons we are who we are. These values may be operationalised by our motives. That is, motives reveal our values to ourselves and others by signalling our liking and affiliation with certain goals and objectives. These motives shape our engagement with the marketing world in more tangible ways, by moderating our involvement with marketing offerings such as products and communications.

Consumers exist in various forms and occupy numerous spaces, places and times. For the marketer, the trick is perhaps to worry less about who consumers are but, rather, consider who they want to be. By embedding consumer values and motives within contextualised evaluations of involvement, marketing communications become usefully informed by the consumers. This allows for the co-creation of meaningful messages that will naturally occur within the spaces, places and times expected by those consumers.

For many, there may be an implicit assumption that all marketing communications are created for the purposes of persuading people to purchase products or to engage with services. Whilst this objective will undoubtedly drive much of the content of communications, there is an increasing realisation that communications are about more than persuasion. Whereas traditional methods of communication emphasise unidirectional approaches or, at best, cyclical approaches to understanding consumers' relationship with marketing communications, contemporary approaches (see Chapter 1) emphasise shared values and interactivity. Key questions, as noted previously, include whether we see consumers as different or similar and, if there are emergent patterns, how do marketers usefully manage these within mutually beneficial relationships?

Further reading

Dellaert, B. G., Shu, S. B., Arentze, T. A., Baker, T., Diehl, K., Donkers, B., ... & Steffel, M. (2020). Consumer decisions with artificially intelligent voice assistants. *Marketing Letters*, **31**, 335-347.

This article provides an overview of how Artificially Intelligent Voice Assistants (AIVAs) are transforming consumer decision-making processes. It explores the shift from traditional online purchases to AI-powered voice-based dialogues and offers propositions for further research. Additionally, it provides recommendations for marketing managers and policymakers on responding to AIVAs' impact on consumer decisions.

Faulds, D. J., Mangold, W. G., Raju, P. S., & Valsalan, S. (2018). The mobile shopping revolution: Redefining the consumer decision process. *Business Horizons*, **61**(2), 323-338.

This article explores how mobile devices are revolutionizing retail by shifting focus from purchase outcomes to influencing the entire consumer decision process. It identifies four foundational pillars that enable retailers to engage customers continuously and gain a competitive edge in the mobile shopping era.

O'Cass, A. (2000) An assessment of consumers product, purchase decision, advertising and consumption involvement in fashion clothing, *Journal of Economic Psychology*, **21** (5), 545–576.

This article provides a comprehensive overview of the concept of involvement and its various types. The authors propose an approach to conceptualizing and measuring four key types of involvement, designed to enhance understanding of consumer behaviour and improve marketing mix strategies.

Scherr, S. & Wang, K. (2021) Explaining the success of social media with gratification niches: Motivations behind daytime, nighttime, and active use of TikTok in China, *Computers in Human Behavior*, **124**. https://doi.org/10.1016/j.

chb.2021.106893

This article also uses a gratifications-based approach, this time exploring TikTok usage within Chinese users, and across temporal contexts of usage.

Whiting, A. & Williams, D. (2013) Why people use social media: a uses and gratifications approach, *Qualitative Market Research: An International Journal*, 16 (4), 362-369.

This article considers motives for social media engagement, framing undertaking within an established idea of uses and gratifications – that is, how people rationalise their needs for using social media, and their perceived benefits of those choices.

Review questions

1. Which of the following is NOT a stage in the consumer decision-making model:

   a) Information search

   b) Purchase decision

   c) Product testing

   d) Problem recognition

2. Which of the following is not a 'motivational conflict dualism':

   a) Approach-Approach

   b) Approach-Avoid

   c) Avoid-Avoid

   d) Avoid-Approach

3. Which of the following combinations are taken from Holbrook's (1999) typology of Consumer Values:

   a) Efficiency – Excellence – Class – Self-Esteem – Play – Aesthetics – Ethics – Religiosity

   b) Efficiency – Excellence – Status – Self-Esteem – Play – Aesthetics – Ethics – Spirituality

   c) Efficiency – Excellence – Status – Self-Esteem – Fun – Aesthetics – Morality – Spirituality

   d) Efficiency – Pride – Status – Self-Esteem – Play – Aesthetics – Ethics – Spirituality

4. This text notes four types of involvement: cognitive, affective, situational, and which other type?

   a) Temporary

   b) Enduring

   c) Permanent

   d) Transient

5. Taheri et al (2014) note key differences between the ideas of involvement and engagement. Which of the following is NOT a feature of engagement:

   a) Proactive relationship building
   b) Broad, two-way interactivity between consumers and brands/marketing
   c) Limited, one-way process, bounded within consumer's understanding
   d) None of these

6. According to Flavián et al. (2016), if a consumer researches their purchase online and subsequently purchases in a physical store they are engaging in …?:

   a) Webrooming
   b) Showrooming
   c) Showboating
   d) Webtailing

7. Within digital reality technologies, XR is an abbreviation of:

   a) Expedient
   b) Exaggerated
   c) Excluded
   d) Extended

8. Considering the different types of brand-related behaviours that consumers can engage in on social media, which of the following is a 'contribution' behaviour?:

   a) Watching videos of a brand
   b) Creating a product review video
   c) Commenting on a brand's post
   d) Reading a brand's post

9. Which of the following consumer journey touchpoints are controlled by the brand?

   a) An unsponsored YouTube video by an influencer
   b) A review posted by a consumer on their blog
   c) A video on the brand's YouTube channel
   d) A friend's negative opinion regarding the brand

10. This text notes that consumer decisions may be broadly mapped to which sequential ideas?

    a) Beliefs – Emotions - Behaviours
    b) Values – Motives – Involvement – Choice
    c) Pre-purchase – Purchase – Post-purchase
    d) Antecedent – Situational – Purchase – Post-purchase

Answers

The answers to these questions can be found at the back of this book, or at the Marketing Communications page at Goodfellow Publishers:

https://www.goodfellowpublishers.com

References

Baek, T. H., & Kim, M. (2023) Is ChatGPT scary good? How user motivations affect creepiness and trust in generative artificial intelligence. *Telematics and Informatics*, 83, 102030.

Bagozzi, R. (1978) Marketing as exchange: a theory of transactions in the market place. *American Behavioral Science*, **21** (4), 257-261.

Baudrillard, J. (1988) The system of objects, in M. Poster (Ed.) *Jean Baudrillard: Selected Writings*, Cambridge: Polity Press, pp 10-28.

Baxendale, S., Macdonald, E. K., and Wilson, H. N. (2015) The Impact of Different Touchpoints on Brand Consideration. *Journal of Retailing*, **91**(2), 235-253. https://doi.org/10.1016/j.jretai.2014.12.008

Belanche, D., Casaló, L. V., Flavián, M., & Ibáñez-Sánchez, S. (2021) Understanding influencer marketing: The role of congruence between influencers, products and consumers. *Journal of Business Research*, **132**, 186-195. https://doi.org/10.1016/j.jbusres.2021.03.067

Buzeta, C., De Pelsmacker, P., & Dens, N. (2020) Motivations to use different social media types and their impact on consumers' online brand-related activities (COBRAs). *Journal of Interactive Marketing*, **52**(1), 79-98. https://doi.org/10.1016/j.intmar.2020.04.004

Costello, J. P., & Reczek, R. W. (2020) Providers Versus platforms: marketing communications in the sharing economy. *Journal of Marketing*, **84**(6), 22-38. https://doi.org/10.1177/0022242920925038

Cova, B. & Cova, V. (2012) On the road to prosumption: marketing discourse and the development of consumer competencies, *Consumption, Markets and Culture*, **15**, 2, 149-168.

Desmond, J. (2003) *Consuming Behaviour*, Basingstoke: Palgrave-MacMillan.

Dichter, E. (1947) Psychology in market research, *Harvard Business Review*, **25** (4) 432-443.

Dijkmans, C., Kerkhof, P., Buyukcan-Tetik, A., & Beukeboom, C. J. (2015) Online conversation and corporate reputation: a two-wave longitudinal study on the effects of exposure to the social media activities of a highly interactive company. *Journal of Computer-Mediated Communication*, 20(6), 632-648. https://doi.org/10.1111/jcc4.12132

Dwyer, R., Schurr, P. & Oh, S. (1987) Developing buyer-seller relationships, *Journal of Marketing*, **51** (April), 11-27.

Festinger, L. (1954) A theory of social comparison, processes, *Human Relations*, **7** (2), 117-140.

Flavián, C., Gurrea, R., & Orús, C. (2016) Choice confidence in the webrooming purchase process: The impact of online positive reviews and the motivation to touch. *Journal of Consumer Behaviour*, **15**(5), 459-476. https://doi.org/10.1002/cb.1585

Galbraith, J.K. (1958) *The Affluent Society*, London: Pelican.

Gronroos, C. (2004) The relationship marketing process: communication, interaction, dialogue, value, *Journal of Business and Industrial Marketing*, **19** (2), 99-113.

Gutman, J. (1981) A means-end model for facilitating analysis of product markets based on consumer judgement. *Advances in Consumer Research*, **8**, 116-21.

Gutman, J. (1982) A means-end chain model based on consumer categorization processes. *Journal of Marketing*, **46**(2), 60-72.

Holbrook, M.B. & Hirschmann, E.C. (1992) The experiential aspects of consumption: Consumer fantasies, feelings, and fun, *Journal of Consumer Research*, **9** (2), 132-140.

Holbrook, M.B. (1999) *Consumer Value: A framework for analysis and research*, London: Routledge.

Hou, J., & Elliott, K. (2021) Mobile shopping intensity: Consumer demographics and motivations. *Journal of Retailing and Consumer Services*, **63**, 102741. https://doi.org/10.1016/j.jretconser.2021.102741

Hudson, S. & Hudson, D. (2006) Branded entertainment: a new advertising technique or product placement in disguise. *Journal of Marketing Management*. **22**(5-6), 489-504.

Ipsos. (2023) Public Poll Findings and Methodology, *Topline Ipsos Consumer Tracker Wave 81*. www.ipsos.com/en-us/news-polls/consumer-behavior-time-covid-19

Kotler, P., Keller, K.L., Brady, M., Goodman, M. & Hansen, T. (2016) *Marketing Management*. 3rd ed. Pearson.

Kshetri, N., Dwivedi, Y. K., Davenport, T. H., & Panteli, N. (2023) Generative artificial intelligence in marketing: Applications, opportunities, challenges, and research agenda. *International Journal of Information Management*. 75, 102716. https://doi.org/10.1016/j.ijinfomgt.2023.102716

Laaksonen, P. (1994). *Consumer Involvement: Concepts and research*. London: Routledge.

LaBerge, L., O'Toole, C., Schneider, J., and Smaje, K. (2020) *How COVID-19 has pushed companies over the technology tipping point—and transformed business forever*. McKinsey and Company. https://www.mckinsey.com/capabilities/ strategy-and-corporate-finance/our-insights/how-covid-19-has-pushed-companies-over-the-technology-tipping-point-and-transformed-business-forever#/

Laricchia, F. (2024) *Smartphones - statistics and facts*. Statista. https://www.statista. com/topics/840/smartphones/#topicOverview

Lemon, K. N., and Verhoef, P. C. (2016) Understanding customer experience throughout the customer journey. *Journal of Marketing*, **80**(6), 69-96. https://doi. org/10.1509/jm.15.0420

Marder, B., Joinson, A., Shankar, A. & Archer-Brown, C. (2012) Any user can be any self that they want so long as it is what they 'ought' to be: Exploring self-presentation in the presence of multiple audiences on social network sites. In Robinson, L. (Ed.) *Marketing Dynamism and Sustainability: Things change; things stay the same…*, Proceedings of the 2012 Academy of Marketing Science (AMS) Annual Conference, New Orleans, 621-626, Springer International Publishing.

Martin, D. & Schouten, J. (2014) Consumption-driven market emergence, *Journal of Consumer Research*, **40** (5), 855-870.

Milgram, P., & Kishino, F. (1994) A taxonomy of mixed reality visual displays. *IEICE Transactions on Information and Systems*, **77**(12), 1321-1329.

Muntinga, D. G., Moorman, M., & Smit, E. G. (2011). Introducing COBRAs: Exploring motivations for brand-related social media use. *International Journal of Advertising*, **30**(1), 13-46.

O'Cass, A. (2000) An assessment of consumers' product, purchase decision, advertising and consumption involvement in fashion clothing, *Journal of Economic Psychology*, **21** (5), 545–576.

Packard, V. (1957) *The Hidden Persuaders*, London; Penguin.

Piers, C. (2024) Even ChatGPT says ChatGPT is racially biased. *Scientific American*.www.scientificamerican.com/article/ even-chatgpt-says-chatgpt-is-racially-biased/

Pulver, A. (2024) London premiere of movie with AI-generated script cancelled after backlash, *The Guardian*, 16 June. https://www.theguardian.com/film/ article/2024/jun/20/premiere-movie-ai-generated-script-cancelled-backlash-the-last-screenwriter-prince-charles-cinema.

Reynolds, T.J. & Craddock, A.B. (1988) The application of the MECCAS model to the development and assessment of advertising strategy: A case study, *Journal of Advertising Research*, April/May, 43-54.

Rokeach, M. (1973) *The Nature of Human Values*, New York; Free Press

Rosengren, S. & Dahlen, M. (2015) Exploring advertising equity: how a brand's past advertising may affect consumer willingness to approach its future ads.

Journal of Advertising, **44** (1).

Ryan, D. (2014) *Understanding Digital Marketing: Marketing strategies for engaging the digital generation,* London; Kogan Page.

Schwartz, S.H. (1992) Universals in the content and structure of values: theoretical advances and empirical tests in 20 countries, in M. Zanna (Ed.) *Advances in Experimental Social Psychology,* **25**, 1–65.

Smink, A. R., van Reijmersdal, E. A., & van Noort, G. (2021) Consumers' use of augmented reality apps: prevalence, user characteristics, and gratifications. *Journal of Advertising,* *51*(1), 85-94. https://doi.org/10.1080/00913367.2021.1973622

Solomon, M. R. (2003) *Conquering Consumerspace: Marketing strategies for a branded world,* New York, Amacom.

Sun, L., Wei, M., Sun, Y., Suh, Y. J., Shen, L., & Yang, S. (2024) Smiling women pitching down: auditing representational and presentational gender biases in image-generative AI. *Journal of Computer-Mediated Communication,* **29**(1), zmad045.

Taheri, B., Jafari, A. & O'Gorman, K. (2014). Keeping your audience: Presenting a visitor engagement scale, *Tourism Management,* **42**, 321-329.

Taheri, B., Farrington, T., Gori, K., Hogg, G. & O'Gorman, K. (2017). Escape, entitlement, and experience: Liminoid motivators within commercial hospitality, *International Journal of Contemporary Hospitality Management.* **29** (4), 1148-1166.

The CMO Survey. (2023) *Managing Brand, Growth and Metrics - Highlights and Insights Report March 2023.* https://cmosurvey.org/wp-content/uploads/2024/03/The_CMO_Survey-Highlights_and_Insights_Report-March_2023-20240328-142707.pdf

Turner, J. C., Hogg, M. A., Oakes, P. J., Reicher, S. D. & Wetherell, M. S. (1987). *Rediscovering the Social Group: A self-categorization theory.* Oxford: Blackwell.

Vroom, V.H. (1964) *Work and Motivation.* Wiley.

Wedel, M., Bigné, E., & Zhang, J. (2020) Virtual and augmented reality: Advancing research in consumer marketing. *International Journal of Research in Marketing,* *37*(3), 443-465. https://doi.org/10.1016/j.ijresmar.2020.04.004

Whiting, A. & Williams, D. (2013) Why people use social media: a uses and gratifications approach, *Qualitative Market Research: An International Journal,* **16** (4), 362-369.

Zaichowsky, J.L. (1985) Measuring the involvement construct in marketing, *Journal of Consumer Research,* **12** (December), 341-352.

Zhang, Y., & Gosline, R. (2023) Human favoritism, not AI aversion: People's perceptions (and bias) toward generative AI, human experts, and human–GAI collaboration in persuasive content generation. *Judgment and Decision Making,* **18**, e41. https://doi.org/10.1017/jdm.2023.37

4 Marketing Communications Strategy

Babak Taheri

Like Alice in Wonderland, if you do not know where you want to get to, then you're likely to meander and have an adventure – fun perhaps but from a business perspective this would be a digression with a cost attached. Most enterprises operate in a world of the unknown and thus need explicit guidance to help reduce uncertainty as well as risk. Enterprises aim to promote innovation, facilitate decision making, and establish standards of quality to aid completion of work. In other words, enterprises want direction and help to focus towards a particular outcome. Along with controlling resources, strategy and planning do this.

Marketing strategy is broad in scope and looks at all the influencing factors, and considers both that which is known and that which is unforeseen – it asks the question 'why?' and seeks to understand competitive markets relative to "recognising and achieving an economic advantage that endures" (Wensley, 2008: 55). It therefore shapes and drives the plan towards the goal. The plan is the logical sequence of steps, or stages, towards a particular end. It asks the question: 'how?'. Together, marketing strategy and planning are the formalisation of an approach to marketing which provides the direction and says that goals and objectives form the basis of the marketing plan. As mentioned above, like Alice, the alternative is to digress and have a costly adventure! Therefore, where you are going needs to be articulated and communicated clearly to all to achieve success.

This chapter discusses how marketing communications strategy fits within marketing strategy. It also positions marketing strategy within the context of the firm's purpose and intent – its corporate strategy – and argues that there is no particular distinction between the parts of strategy as they are all interrelated and mutually dependent on each other. A structure for evaluating marketing communications strategy is given, and the chapter concludes with a suggested framework for marketing communications planning.

What is strategy?

Planning *or preparation* plus creating something "new and emerging which in effect becomes a reality" *or development* equates to strategy. Thus strategy, according to MacIntosh and Maclean (2015: 3) is:

> *"...the craft of collectively rising to a significant challenge and accomplishing more than might be reasonably expected as a result of self-knowledge, resolve, foresight, creativity and genuine capabilities cultivated over the medium to long term."*

What they are saying in effect, is that strategy is not just predetermined by means of crafting or preparing a plan to be acted upon by all, but that planning is only a part of what constitutes a successful outcome. Strategy also includes developing a platform which acts as a conduit for ideas, skills, creativity and fortitude, and that strategy acknowledges people's experience as well as key traits such as tenaciousness and willpower. One key point to capture from MacIntosh and Maclean (2015) is their focus on strategy being a process over time and that most importantly strategy includes people as *strategists*, and that this human element can make or break strategic direction, and consequently build value or destroy a firm's ability to make more value over time.

Take the case of the marketing director in the professional services sector – for example, in an accountancy firm where he has become 'frozen' in time. He is unmoving in his stance because he is convinced that his consumers would not use online search tools for information search (Frederiksen, 2013) so there is no reason to invest monies in this medium for marketing communication. That might be the case now but contexts change. And the environment for consumers searching for information on professional service firms can change too, so this manager needs to move with the times. This marketing director is frozen in time and is of the view that only at conferences and public speaking engagements will his consultancy business capture referrals which can be converted into business. Meanwhile, other more competitive professional service firms are innovating. They are using current marketing research data and more contemporary mediated communication platforms along with knowledgeable experts (agents) in order to capture new business.

A marketing director as a strategist would take a more innovative approach. He would release monies and make decisions relative to trialling new means and methods of communication. And he would want to interpret and reflect in order to remain as innovative and competitive as possible. He is 'cultivating capabilities' in the sense that MacIntosh and MacLean describe above.

If strategy is a function of planning and creativity, and is a process which has the strategist at its core, then the heart of strategic planning has to be research – both marketing research and consumer insight, and this is captured for input at both corporate and marketing level – that is prior to any planning for marketing communications. As such it does shape marketing communications and this is illustrated as a chart in Figure 4.1. This illustration depicts the different levels of strategy and shows the context and strategic contribution made by marketing communications, and as such forms the structure for this chapter.

Figure 4.1: The strategic contribution of marketing communications.

Source: adapted from Baker (2014), Crawford et al. (1983), and Johnson et al. (2008).

Strategic marketing management

Whilst corporate level strategy is concerned with the broad picture of the overall purpose and intent of the firm, strategic marketing management takes the view that you are much more likely to see the marketing function as having both a firm-based position and an operational one, because it attends to market places as well as marketing behaviour (Baker, 2014). In other words, marketing strategy integrates at all levels and refers to the key choices made on "*...products, markets, marketing activities, and marketing resources in the creation, communication and delivery of products that offer value to customers in exchanges with the organisation and thereby enable the organisation to achieve specific objectives*" (Varadarajan, 2010: 128). Acknowledging that marketing strategy in a firm is inter-linked at various levels (for example, business and marketing management) leads us to surmise that the firm deals, at its business level, with issues around what, where and how it will compete and with what. Therefore marketing planning involves the marketing mix – promotion, product, price, place plus process, physical evidence and people.

Marketing strategy, as outlined by Varadarajan above, is, therefore, an explanation of capabilities and results in the process of developing a 'road map' which is modern business parlance for a route to deliver outcomes or planning. Figure 4.1 illustrates how the components of strategy interlink with each other. Note that there are two levels of positioning – one which is the major thrust of positioning within marketing strategy and that is the framework of segmentation, target market and positioning (STP). Positioning within marketing strategy concerns (i) the market place and (ii) the image in our minds (Baker, 2014: 284/5). The second positioning concept (image) underpins marketing communications and is about positioning an 'image' in the mind of consumers which is achieved through communication tactics in the main. This is explained more fully in the structure for marketing communications below, which sets out the strategic contribution of marketing communications.

A structure for understanding marketing communications strategy

Strategy within the context of marketing communications relates to how a brand is 'positioned', and how this positioning of the brand has a preferred way of communicating with consumers, customers and stakeholders. *Tactics* relate to the communications mix which is designed to deliver the positioning strategy. Marketing communications *plans* relate to the promotional campaigns whose explicit intent is to convey and express the brand's marketing communication tactics and strategy (Fill, 2013). Therefore, marketing communications strategy is about the overarching theme and direction that the communications programme is going to take. How does the communications fit in with the rest of the company's strategic purpose and intent, and also its values, for instance? Also, for example, how will the communications flow in its delivery? Will it be a heavy burst of TV in August? It is also about identifying the target audience – who, what and how does this audience watch TV, for example – or are they on their holidays in August and less likely to watch TV? And what are we going to say? What are the key messages and themes if the target audience is young – how will they attend to the messages, and will it appeal to them in a compelling and memorable way? Underlining these questions are the key points of positioning an image (Baker, 2014) and the triad of audience, message and media (Dahlen et al., 2010). Taken together, a structure which Fill (2013) calls 'the four approaches', and which latterly he refers to as the '4 interpretations' (Fill & Turnbull, 2016:154), for planning a marketing communications strategy looks like this:

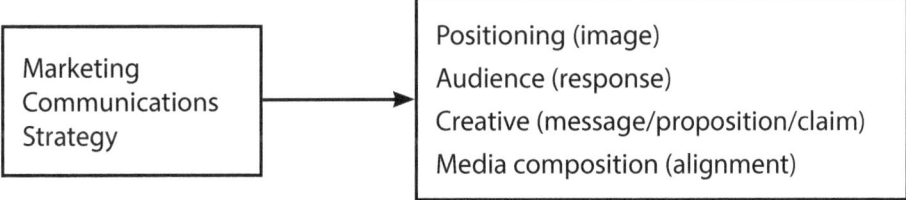

Figure 4.2: Four approaches to planning a marketing communications strategy.
Source: Adapted from Baker (2014), Dahlen et al. (2010) & Fill (2013)

Strategic planning for marketing communications

The strategic considerations for marketing communications, as outlined above in Figure 4.2, are therefore centred on how the target audience (TA) responds, the positioning both in the market place and in people's minds, the creative element by way of engagement with the audience, and in selecting and aligning media channels to suit. Each of these four modes of approach to planning for marketing communications is explained in turn.

The act of positioning and the position achieved

Positioning is a strategic activity which has two primary objectives according to Crawford et al. (1983):

1 To create a position for a product/service in the mind of the consumer. This position is made up of a bundle of consumer perceptions about the product/service relative to its competitors and many involve similarities and/or differences.

2 To set the tone for the marketing mix strategies that will communicate these perceptions and provide a common, unifying theme that is consistent across all marketing tools

A useful taxonomy for the positioning concept is put forward by Aaker and Shansby (1982) to explain and add clarity.

- Competition (differentiation)
- Segmentation (identifying features and associations which cause an overall impression)
- Image (creating relative perceptions and images).

Marketing communications draws on positioning at marketing strategy level (the positioning in the market place) on the one hand, and within marketing communications itself (Baker, 2014), positioning is about developing an image relative to perceptions and other images. Reis and Trout (2001) call it a *"battle for your mind"* urging all business managers to create a position in the prospect's mind. They emphasize advertising as the vehicle to gain relative image positioning, but arguably (Crawford et al, 1983) there are other marketing elements to consider, such as price and distribution, that can assist in forming perceptions.

Thus, prior to marketing communications, the 'battle' for the consumer's mind is done by segmentation. Target market selection is the identification of distinct group(s) who display common characteristics and who recall and respond to messages in a similar way. This suggests a fixed view of the target segments but it shouldn't be thought so. Targeting must also recognise that a consumer's congruity (resemblance or similarity to …) judgement about a marketing communications image can be formed with both actual (who I think I am) and ideal self-images (who I'd like to be) and thus affect consumer evaluation (the closer the segment group resembles the communication, the more positive is the message evaluation). This is more of an emotional take on segmentation and draws on a manager's knowledge captured from consumer behavioural science, so that communications are shaped around how consumers perceive themselves, leading to a greater likelihood of engagement. Positioning in the mind needs to be relatively strong so that your brand is top-of-mind and recall is more than good and better than the competition.

Therefore, within the context of marketing communications strategy, positioning is centred on how you want to be positioned in the minds of your consumers, customers and stakeholders. It's about visibility and recognition (Fill, 2013) from a people or consumer perspective, and that segmenting the market and identifying target segments are the *"prerequisites to successful positioning"* (2013: 150). It is important at this point in this discussion to link to Chapter 5, *Brands and Brand Communications*, and make a connection between positioning and its relation to the triangulation of the three brand Ps of promise, positioning and performance, all of which shape and drive marketing communications. The promise in marketing communications is the propositional claim which is based on marketing research and the creative 'big idea' (often translated into a strapline) whereby the core positioning and creative idea for advertising, and the look and appeal of the message can be translated across all platforms. (See Chapter 7 *Creativity in Advertising and Promotion* for more discussion on this topic.)

How different audiences respond

Marketing is an outside-in approach to business, and the consumer audience is the 'outside'. Within the organisation, in marketing communications terms, there may be many different types of audience, both on the outside and the inside, and those related to the organisation through investment, community, policy, family and agents/consultants, as well as suppliers, buyers, and co-creators of production – especially employees. The following exercise give insight into communicating with employees at British Airways. Three distinct groupings become clear: consumers, trade associates and stakeholders – all of whom require different types of communications especially in terms of *"what, where, when and how"*. According to Hughes & Fill (2008) they are:

- **Pull strategies** – to reach customers where the focus is on communicating directly with end-users (consumers and b2b)
- **Push strategies** – to reach members of the marketing channel where the aim is to move goods through these channels (trade and other intermediaries)
- **Profile strategies** – to reach all relevant stakeholders where the aim is to develop by building and growing long term relationships and to maintain a positive reputation

Pull and push marketing communications approaches to strategy are well known in the fundamentals of marketing knowledgem but not so the approach for profile where the core intention is to build reputation. This profile or stakeholder audience can influence the organisation and as such is more of an organisation-orientated activity and constitutes corporate communications. Corporate communications is the process that transforms corporate identity into corporate image and where public relations is the key element of the communications mix.

Case: Starbucks responds to a crisis

In 2018, Starbucks faced a significant external crisis when two African American men were arrested at a Philadelphia store for simply waiting for a friend. This incident sparked widespread outrage and accusations of racial bias against the company, severely damaging Starbucks' public image and affecting employee morale.

In response, Starbucks took decisive action to address both the internal and external fallout. The company temporarily closed over 8,000 stores across the United States to conduct racial bias training for nearly 175,000 employees. This training was designed to improve internal communication around issues of race and inclusivity, ensuring that all employees were equipped to handle similar situations appropriately in the future.

Externally, Starbucks launched a comprehensive public relations campaign to communicate their commitment to social justice and corporate responsibility. This included CEO Kevin Johnson appearing on various media platforms to apologize for the incident and outline the steps Starbucks was taking to prevent future occurrences.

The company also partnered with several advocacy groups and experts to develop and implement long-term strategies for promoting diversity and inclusion within the organization.

Source: Dahlstrom (2018)

Review questions:

1. Identify and explain whether external sponsorship is a push, pull or profile strategy when communicating with an audience?

2. Identify and explain whether internal engagement is a push, pull or profile strategy when communicating with an audience.

Message – developing a creative platform

The 'creative' interpretation of marketing communications strategy involves a creative idea which acts as a conduit for orchestrating communications across different types of platforms such as advertising, brand-led communications or participatory interactions (Cox et al/IPA, 2011). This can be seen in more detail in Figure 4.3:

Type of creative platform	Form	Expression
No level of integration:	Unorganised. May use one media channel and/or only one piece of marketing activity, e.g. website.	Unconnected.
Advertising-led integration: Getting your publics to attend to your product/service/idea either through paid or non-paid media using one idea.	Recognisable as 'matching luggage', i.e. look and tone is the same but message may be different.	Creative expression can vary over time and by message but share a strong executional idea, e.g. a celebrity.
Brand idea-led orchestration: Staged development from being advertising-led as above to fulfilling brand resonance – loyalty, attachment, community, engagement. (Keller, 2001a)	Conceptual and centred around brand characteristics. Tangible – functional attributes; intangible more emotional ideas, abstract	Deeper engagement, consistent and based loosely around a shared brand-idea.
Participation–led orchestration: Interactive	Centred around participation and experience.	Narrative, conversations including all forms of chat.

Figure 4.3: New models of marketing effectiveness by integration and orchestration. *Source:* Adapted from Cox et al./IPA, (2011:45-69) and Keller, (2001). See also Fill & Turnbull (2016: 344).

As Figure 4.3 points out, the four types of creative platform are expressed in different ways with differing levels of integration depending on communication and objectives as well as timeframes. What you do need is a core idea which can be transformed and explained across different types of media channels. Advertising is oftentimes referred to as the 'last remaining unfair competitive advantage' (IPA, 2007) and that is because it is one of the key variables that can make 'all other things unequal' through its influence in conveying a good idea. In the case of Honda's 'Power of Dreams' campaign which won a key industry award, the marketing director observed that the brand was gaining share in spite of not spending nearly the equivalent of other big brands (£20 million less than major competitors). The brand attributes this to the advertising campaign which delivered on brief – it reached those *"three important parts of the human being: the heart, the head and the wallet"* (2007: 2).

The creative idea is expressed through a promise which is more than a tagline – it is a proposition which holds all the values associated with the brand and as pointed out above, the claim which makes it different. This customer-focused value proposition provides the rationale for the branding being efficient and effective (Kotler et al., 2016; Keller, 2013). And take note that the claim made by this proposition is underpinned with marketing research and has to be proven to the industry advertising ombudsman, known in the UK as The Advertising Standards Authority. This gives the advertising and brand legitimacy to orchestrate its promise either implicitly or explicitly. For example, L'Oreal's 'Because you're worth it' is implicitly stated and expresses the essence of the brand eliciting a response of 'yes, maybe I am worth it' or 'damn right I am' depending on your self-esteem on the day. This is because an advertising promise translated in whatever type, size and weight of campaign, sets customers' expectations about the kinds of interactions they are going to have with you. An explicit message of "You should've gone to Specsavers" has an underlying promise of you'll be in 'safe hands' because of our experts so you can trust us for spectacles! In summary, a promise is a single-minded proposition which 'hooks' in the consumer by commanding attention and if, as a proposition it is value-laden, expressed and positioned correctly, it will springboard your advertising and therefore garner success. More on creative appeals is discussed and explained in Chapter 7, *Creativity in Advertising and Promotion*, when we can ask this question: how does a simple proposition for Sony Television "Delivers colour like no other", lead to half-a-million rubber balls being let loose on the hills of San Francisco?

Media –composition and alignment

How media is composed by way of planning and selection involves an understanding the following:

- *Frequency* of messages (how often do I need to talk to my audience to be effective);
- *Reach* (to whom am I going to talk and what is the likelihood of a response;
- The *media* channels identified for selection (the intermediate means and methods of enabling communications to flow either singularly or two-way)
- *Message* or the creative appeal which will compel the audience to do something such as respond (or just be aware of the brand and communication).

Taking all these factors into account enables a composition strategy where all the chosen media, loadings and timings are combined in such a way as to maximise effectiveness.

Scheduling

Scheduling includes planning for media selection. For example, a frequency strategy would be where the schedule may appear to be either intermittent or continuous. An *intermittent* decision looks like there are periods of intense activity (for example seasonal products like garden products and also travel) whereas a *continuous* stance (for example utility type products) is where there is a continuous pattern of messaging, thus gaining increased exposure. Exposure to the communications is key because it is likely that the consumer will move along the brand recognition continuum where the ultimate objective is for consumers to have a strong resonance with the brand so that the relationship is intense and so developed that it is a full relationship of loyalty, attachment, engagement and community.

It is also possible to plan a schedule which is both continuous and intermittent. For example, *pulsing* is where there is advertising which is continuous but also where there are moments of increased activity such as the holiday industry. In the UK, Thomas Cook advertisements appear regularly in the media under the guise of brand-led communications where 'awareness' of the brand is the key communications objective, but during January to April, there is intense activity in all media, but especially on TV and in digital media, sending out a message which is more advertising-led, with special offers for families for instance. The actual holiday bookings are for July and August but with all UK schools taking their annual holidays in the peak summer months, it therefore means that the company can advertise early for the holiday hotspots and increase revenue through deposits in the earlier part of the year which is unseasonal. This in turn leads to better planning for airline routes, airline seats and hotel beds along with resources to manage the service during the peak months.

Reach

Reach is important because it tells you the number of exposures your marketing communications is likely to reach given the size of the population that is likely to see your efforts during a given time period. Having identified the target audience, maximum coverage of that segment is the key objective of media and an important consideration is not to duplicate, which is an ineffective use of resource – that is, perhaps your money and effort are better used elsewhere on something more productive! Managers also need to be aware of the way media agents and consultants measure exposure. For example, the standard measure used by agencies is

OTS (the number of people who have the opportunity to see) and not an absolute figure of those that do see it. And in digital media, the complexity of analysis and schedule design means there is a different way of looking at metrics (See Chapter 8, *Digital Marketing*, for more information on metrics).

Thus the media manager aims not to overload the audience so as to be ineffective but to load the audience enough to take effect. To achieve a balance in composition, credibility needs to be given to the content of the creative piece – the way the message is put together, how it will be conveyed and to whom will it appeal to most. And whilst it is important to understand that communications flow can be unidirectional or bidirectional, it is equally important to acknowledge the role of speed, for example in digital media, and the social interactions consumers make and enjoy, so that the brand may develop a lasting relationship which is more collaborative and thus deeper and more long term, in contrast to exchanges which are short and more likely to be forgotten sooner.

Planning marketing communications

Having understood the structured four ways or approaches – in other words the strategic means to designing a plan for marketing communications strategy (Positioning, Audience, the Creative, and Media composition), and where marketing communications fits into the role of marketing management within the context of the corporate firm, it leaves the practitioner to develop and design a plan for marketing communications. This aims to convey the context in which communications takes place, and the drivers that shape the design of the development process, for example the four approaches to planning for marketing communications, along with how the communications will be conveyed, and further explain the intention regarding interpretation of the marketing communications. This expression of a proposal or plan therefore provides cohesion amongst management and stakeholders in order to minimise errors and maximise efficiency and effectiveness.

A suggested illustration adapted from Fill's (2013:161) Marketing Communications Planning Framework (MCPF), and Smith's 1993 SOSTAC Planning System - Situation, Objectives, Strategies, Tactics, Action and Control (Smith & Zook, 2012:226) is visualised in Figure 4.4.

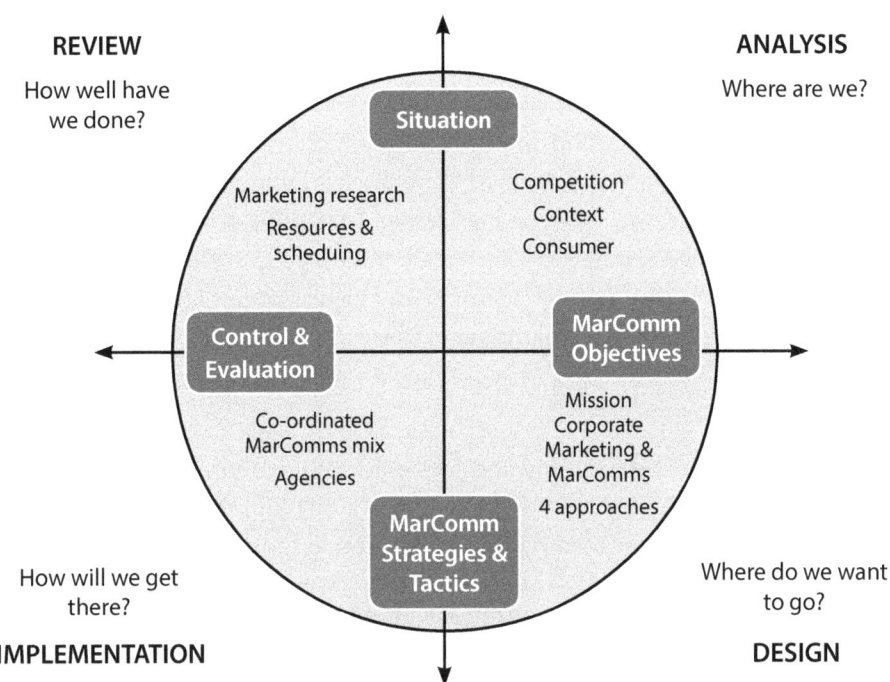

Figure 4.4: A marketing communications plan.

The illustration outlines the component parts of a marketing communications plan. The four corners of the diagram highlight the development phases so that the first phase is analysis, followed by design, implementation and finally control. The text outside of the ring tells us what the different phases are trying to achieve and the points of the circle depict the four structures of the marketing communications plan: the situation, marketing communication objectives, marketing communication strategies and tactics and, lastly, control and evaluation. The reference texts inside the ring list the sub-texts of the marketing communications plan. For example, you can clearly see where the four approaches of Positioning (image), Audience (response), Creative (message & appeals) and Media composition (alignment) are placed following Objectives and before Tactics Key points to note are that the marketing communications plan does not have any discrete parts as such. Most of the parts are inter-linked – some more so than others, but most are interdependent. For example, consumer insight and marketing research highlight the circular nature of marketing communications planning.

Summary

The marketing communications plan provides a framework for the direction of marketing communications and is a critical component of the communication process. If it is too abstract and deemed to be unclear, then it is highly likely that the subsequent activity will also be ineffective. Marketing communications also needs to be considered relative to other strategies because most levels of strategy are integrated and emerge through learning and experience, so that due reflection and review can feed into future planning cycles.

Further readings

Caemmerer, B. (2009) The planning and implementation of integrated marketing communications. *Marketing Intelligence and Planning*, **27** (4), 524-538.

This journal article is an exemplar of application in the design, development and delivery of a real product launch by French car firm Renault as it redesigns its marketing communications programme in order to engage and communicate with the German market.

Campbell, J. (2012) 'How W+K's campaign for Honda was made', Creative Bloq, 20 September. https://www.creativebloq.com/advertising/power-dreams-11135302.

This blog provides a detailed overview of Honda's "The Power of Dreams" campaign, showcasing innovative advertising strategies. It highlights how creativity and storytelling align with brand values to create successful marketing. The blog also offers insights into the behind-the-scenes processes of creating memorable advertisements.

Shankar, V., Grewal, D., Sunder, S., Fossen, B., Peters, K., & Agarwal, A. (2022). Digital marketing communication in global marketplaces: A review of extant research, future directions, and potential approaches. *International Journal of Research in Marketing*, **39**(2), 541–56.

This journal article by Shankar et al. (2022) provides a comprehensive review of digital marketing communication in four major duads, B2C, B2B, C2C, C2B along four major components: goals; channels, media, and platforms; content; and response. It highlights key research gaps and questions, emphasizing the need for managers to formulate effective digital marketing strategies in both local and global contexts.

Key, T. M., & Czaplewski, A. J. (2017). Upstream social marketing strategy: An integrated marketing communications approach. *Business Horizons*, 60(3), 325–333.

This article offers how marketers can develop a social media marketing strategy to offer upstream audience. The concept of 'upstream' pertains to individuals and entities who influence the societal and environmental framework, including politicians, policymakers, civil servants, decision-makers, regulators, managers, educators, and the media.

Holt, D. (2016). Branding in the age of social media. *Harvard Business Review*, 94(3), 40-50.

This seminar article explains the importance of understanding and applying cultural branding, in which brands collaborate with the power of culture to engage consumers. It serves as an alternative to traditional branded content.

Review questions

1. Strategy, according to MacIntosh and Maclean (2015) is a function of:

    a) Planning, creativity and people
    b) Creativity, strategic planning and no people
    c) Strategic planning, people and competition
    d) Competition, creativity and planning

2. Marketing research and consumer insight help shape marketing communications by:

    a) Helping to design and develop a brand's marketing and managerial communications
    b) Helping to uncover and develop the big ideas to propel a brands creative communications
    c) Helping to drive the communications to perform through having a promise, and being positioned correctly.
    d) All of the above

3. Strategic Marketing Management (SMM) integrates strategic management, with marketing communications strategy by means of appropriate goals that:

    a) Highlight the direction the marketing communications is to take
    b) Highlight the direction the brand positioning is to take
    c) Highlight the direction the strategic positioning is to take
    d) Highlight the direction of the segmentation and target audience.

4. Strategic Management and Strategic Marketing Management (SMM) drive marketing communications strategy by shaping the marketing mix which is known as the :

    a) Just the 4 Ps
    b) Only 1 P
    c) All 7 of the Ps
    d) All the Ps except people

5. Marketing communications strategy is centred on an understanding of:

   a) Consumer audiences, media composition, brand positioning and market development

   b) Brand positioning, stakeholder audiences, the creative platforms and media composition.

   c) Market development, government audiences, creative platform and brand positioning

   d) Creative platform, media composition, the company's positioning and stakeholder audiences

6. Positioning, in marketing communications strategy, is how you want to be positioned in the minds of:

   a) Consumers, customers and stakeholders.

   b) Community, customers and stakeholders

   c) Customers, employees and consumers

   d) Caretakers, consumers and community

7. There are three distinct audience groupings in marketing communications strategy which are:

   a) Profile, pull and play

   b) Pull, play and profile

   c) Pull, push and profile

   d) Play, ploy and pull

8. The 'big idea' in marketing communications strategy is where the creative idea acts as a platform for:

   a) Advertising, brand and participatory communications

   b) Advertising, brand and interactive contradictions

   c) Advertising, brand and participatory commiserations

   d) Advertising, brand and interactive configurations

9. Media composition includes:

   a) Frequency, reach, creative content & media channels

   b) Frequency, creative reach, contact and media channels

   c) Frequency, reach and content, and creative channels

   d) Frequency, channels of reach, creative content and media

10. A basic marketing communications plan consists of elements that include:

   a) Where are we? Where do we want to go? How will we get there? And How well have we done?

   b) Situational audit, objectives, strategies, tactics and review

   c) Analysis, design, implementation and control

   d) All of the above

Answers

The answers to these questions can be found at the back of this book, or at the Marketing Communications page at Goodfellow Publishers:

https://www.goodfellowpublishers.com

4

References

Aaker, D. & Shansby, J.G. (1982) Positioning your product. *Business Horizons*. May/June

Baker, M.J. (2014) *Marketing Strategy and Management* (5ed). Palgrave McMillan.

Bashford, S. (2011) British Airways buildingbrand inside. *Marketing*. Haymarket Publications Ltd., http://www.marketingmagazine.co.uk/article/1081775/british-airways-building-brand-inside [accessed 20.06.2015]

Cohen, W. (2005) *The Marketing Plan*. John Wiley and Sons. NJ. USA.

Crawford, D.M., Urban, D.J. & Buzas, T.E. (1983) *Positioning: a conceptual review and taxonomy of alternatives*. Working Paper No 354. The University of Michigan.

Cox, K., Crowther, J., Hubbard, T. & Turner, D./IPA (2011) *New Models of Marketing Effectiveness: from integration to orchestration*. IPA/WARC, London. With thanks to Brian Coane, Chair IPA Scotland for access and usage.

Dahlen, M., Lange, F. & Smith, T. (2010) *Marketing Communications: a brand narrative approach*. John Wiley & Sons Ltd.

Dahlstrom, L. (2018) 'Beyond May 29: Lessons from Starbucks' Anti-Bias Training and What's Next', Starbucks Stories, 29 May 2018 [Blog]. Available at https://stories.starbucks.com/stories/2018/beyond-may-29-lessons-from-starbucks-anti-bias-training-and-whats-next/ (Accessed 4 June 2024).

Fill, C. (2013) Marketing Communications: Brands, Experiences and Participation. Pearson.

Frederiksen, L. (2013) Online marketing for professional services: how to use online marketing to drive growth and profits. http://www.hingemarketing.com/blog/story/online-marketing-strategy-gone-wrong [accessed 16.6.2015]

Hughes, G. and Fill, C. (2008) *The Official CIM Coursebook : Marketing Communications*. The Chartered Institute of Marketing. Elsevier Ltd., Oxford. UK.

IPA (2007) *Judging Creative Ideas*. Institute of Practitioners in Advertising. http://www.ipa.co.uk/Document/judging-creative-ideas-best-practice-guide.

Johnson, G., Scholes, K. & Whittington, R. (2008) *Exploring Corporate Strategy*. 8/ed. Pearson Education.

Keller, K.L. (2001). Building customer-based brand equity: A blueprint for creating strong brands. *Marketing Management*. July/August: 15–19.

Keller, K.L. (2013). *Strategic Brand Management: Building, measuring and managing brand equity*. 4th ed. Pearson.

Kotler, P., Keller, K.L., Brady, M., Goodman, M. & Hansen, T. (2016) *Marketing Management*. 3rd ed. Pearson.

MacIntosh, R. & Maclean, D. (2015) *Strategic Management: Strategists at work*. Palgrave Macmillan.

Reis, A. and Trout, J. (2001) *The Battle for your mind – how to be seen and heard in the overcrowded marketplace*. McGraw-Hill. USA.

Smith, P.R. and Zook, Ze (2012) *Marketing Communications: integrating offline and online social media*. 5/ed. Kogan Page.

Varadarajan, R. (2010) Strategic marketing and marketing strategy: domain, definition, fundamental issues and foundational premises. *Journal of the Academy of Marketing Sciences* **38**, 119-140.

Wensley, R. (2008) The basics of marketing strategy, in Baker, M.J. and Hart, S.J. (eds) *The Marketing Handbook*. Elsevier Ltd., pp 55-80.

5 Branding and Brand Communications

Ross Curran and Babak Taheri

Brands

Brands have been used as an effective method of marking craftsmen's output from at least the Middle Ages. Brands are defined by the American Marketing Association (AMA) (1960) in their widely used definition as:

> *"...a name, term, sign, symbol or design, or a combination of them, intended to identify the goods or services of one seller or group of sellers and to differentiate them from those of competitors."*

Following the AMA definition, a brand consists of various elements, which could include combinations of names, signs, terms, symbols, URLs, and even employees (DuBois et al., 2014). In more recent times, developing technology and increasingly competitive markets have ensured that brands have evolved from basic marks of quality, to conduits of values, ideas, and sophisticated personalities (Aaker, 1997) allowing marketers new ways to connect with their customers, and stand out from the competition. It should be noted that products and brands are not necessarily the same thing. While products can refer to anything that may satisfy needs or wants, and can include things such as laptops, banking services, or charitable assistance; a brand is the addition to the product of elements that make it stand out from competition, or differentiate it. For example, an Apple or Dell logo conjure up very different perceptions of the laptop product, its typical users, and the tasks it can be used for. Likewise, although one type of car manufacturer (e.g., Volvo) is functionally very similar to another (e.g., Ford), the brand, or logo adorning it. influences the perceptions consumers subsequently hold (often Volvo is strongly associated with safety). Consequently, branding affects consumers' perceptions of a product or service and allows them to associate products with certain attributes (e.g., trust, reliability, safety and fun).

Fill (2013) suggests successful brands incorporate three elements: promises, positioning and performance. Brands can therefore be seen as promises, underpinning their perceived positioning by stakeholders and resulting expectations. Where these promises and expectations converge, brand performances are the result. Figure 5.1 below illustrates this process.

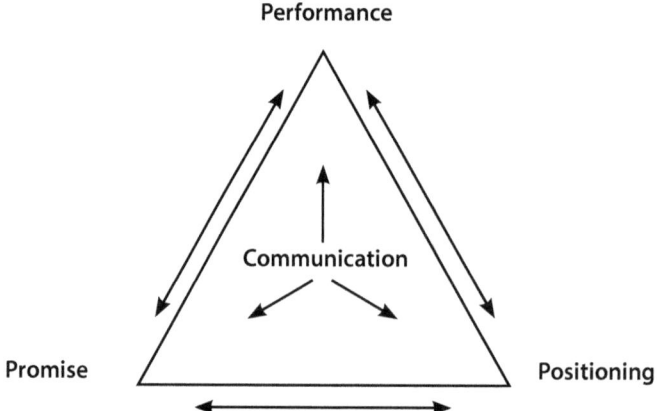

Figure 5.1: 3 Brand Ps

As Figure 5.1 shows, communication is critical as it is shaped and driven by the interaction of the three brand Ps. Communication variously conveys the brand promise, and accurately positions the brand, whilst encouraging its successful performance.

Brands can be manufacturer, or own-label brands. *Manufacturer brands* are developed and controlled by the producer of the product or provider of the service, whereas *own-label brands* (also called distributer/retailer brands) are developed and controlled by distributors. For example, Coca-Cola is a manufacturer brand, where the manufacturer retains responsibility and control over marketing. Large supermarkets may wish to enhance their retail revenue by developing an own-label cola drink, or in other words, an own-label brand. While generally these brands are priced as a cheaper alternative for consumers, they can be positioned as high quality, luxuries, or indeed healthier alternatives (such as Marks & Spencer's *Count on Us* range). To combat the rise of own-label brands, so called *fighter brands* are emerging. Fighter brands are additional manufacturer brands developed specifically to compete with own-label or competing brands, often in the form of a lower price alternative to the primary manufacturer brand, but also as a defensive competitive strategy. In the airline industry for example, to combat increasing competition from low-cost airlines such as Ryanair, British Airways ultimately unsuccessfully, launched its own low-cost airline under the 'Go' brand. Traditionally branding has focused on external stakeholders (Aurand et al., 2005), but growing evidence suggests brands have significant internal influence, and affect employees of their host organisation (Schlager et al., 2011). There are also *licensed brands* (i.e., a brand produced by a company under authorisation from the owner for a fee) and *pure play* brands (i.e., a brand which can offer manufacturer and own-label brands).

Table 5.1: Benefits attributable to brands

Benefit	Description	Example
Brand extensions	Strong core brand allows for subsequent brand extensions to retain positive associations towards the core offering.	Coca-Cola (core brand) and Diet Coke, Cherry Coke, Coke Lemon as brand extensions.
Trust	Products or services functionally on an equal footing, with high economic cost to the consumer, render trust important to the purchase decision. Trust is particularly important in online transactions (Grabner-Kraeuter 2002).	Coca-Cola's Dasani bottled water betrayed consumer trust when questions were raised about its source.
Quality guarantee	Aids consumer purchase decisions by indicating the level of quality the consumer should expect.	BMW cars are generally expected by consumers to be better quality than Ford, or Vauxhall, however this assertion is often solely based upon the brand.
Consumer perceptions	Successful brands can yield a positive influence on consumer perceptions through the perceptions the consumer gains from the brand.	Sports Direct owns several previously independent brand names such as Slazenger, Dunlop and Donnay. Despite changes in ownership, the brands continue to generate strong sales.
Barrier to competition	Although newly entering brands may be functionally superior to established brands, a strong brand with positive perceptions render it difficult for new brands to compete.	Virgin's attempts to take on Coca-Cola and Pepsi and launch its own Virgin Cola product failed due to the prevailing strength of the established brands.
Higher profits	Market-leading brands can command a higher price than weaker ones. Furthermore, they often benefit from established supply and sales networks, thus accruing economies of scale.	Kellogg's can command a price premium, due to the perceived added-value it offers consumers.
Increased company value	Strong brands can become valuable assets, and can add significantly to the value of a company.	Apple and Google's brands add significant financial value to such companies.

Developing and maintaining strong brands is time-consuming, costly, and requires high levels of commitment from organisations (Aaker, 2000). However, if cultivated properly, the benefits to an organisation can be enormous and not just limited to increased financial return. Table 5.1 illustrates the potential benefits brands can bring organisations.

As Table 5.1 shows, the benefits of strong brands are vast (Keller, 2002). Ultimately, as well as illustrating the primary offering of an organisation, they influence purchase decisions, reduce perceptions of risk, elicit trust, and promise a certain level of quality (De-Chernatony and Dall'Olmo Riley, 1998).

Brand strategies used by organisations and the planning process involved are now considered.

Exercise

Examine the packaging of your favourite branded product. What messages do you think the marketers are trying to convey? Are there several? Is there one? Who do you think the messages are intended for? In your opinion, are they effective? Do you think you are the type of person who is 'meant' to buy that brand?

Branding strategies and planning

Developing successful brands requires careful planning and consideration, resulting in the implementation of brand strategies. To be successful, organisations must be fully committed to investing in their brands over the long-term. The initial decision concerning brand strategy is in regard to whether to develop a brand at all. Some specialist, and industrial, products remain unbranded, although this is uncommon, as it can avoid burdening organisations with costly branding processes, nevertheless, this is increasingly rare and most products are branded to some extent. Second, an organisation must decide on the most suitable overarching brand strategy. The choice of brand strategy will be guided by the current situation, and aims, of an organisation. Several brand strategy options applicable to organisations marketing a *single brand* are described in Table 5.2.

Table 5.2: Basic brand strategies for single brand cases

Brand strategy	Use	Example
Line extension	One brand name is used for all new product introductions.	Ben & Jerry's use this strategy across their range of ice-cream flavours.
Brand extension	Where current brands are applied to products in different categories.	Ferrari, famous for manufacturing cars, uses this strategy in its clothing range.
Multi-brands	When various brands are used for various products and ranges.	Consumer goods company Unilever deploy this strategy amongst their diverse brand catalogue which includes male shower-gel Lynx, and Hellman's Mayonnaise.

Line extensions, as described in Table 5.2, are frequently used by marketers, and can aid an organisation's competitive position in several ways; through occupation of shelf-space that would otherwise be used by competitors, targeting a niche subgroup of consumers more effectively, and encouraging a dyadic flow of positive feeling between the new brand extension and its parent brand, potentially boosting sales across the brand portfolio (Reddy et al., 1994). Line extensions can also have negative impacts such as dilution of meaning in the minds of consumers regarding the attributes of a brand. Furthermore, there is the possibility that a brand extension, rather than winning market share from competition, takes sales away from the parent brand, negatively affecting an organisation's bottom line. Finally, unsuccessful brand extensions can have negative impacts upon the parent brand, for example, if a new brand extension become embroiled in controversy or was deemed to be of unacceptable quality, negative perceptions could adversely impact the parent brand's sales.

Brand extensions as described in Table 5.2 allow organisations to introduce new products or services at reduced risk, as they can 'piggy-back' upon the positive attitudes towards the original brand. Another advantage is the reduced cost associated with this approach as opposed to launching an entirely new and untested brand. Conversely, there are significant risks to the parent brand of brand extensions. First, if unsuccessful, the extended brand may damage the standing of its parent. Second, where brand extension is confusingly applied to products or services entirely unconnected to the parent brand, the meaning and essence conveyed by the parent brand can be diluted. Organisations using this strategy have to ensure the same core values of the brand are received by consumers across the portfolio, consequently, *corporate branding* is increasingly deployed (Knox & Bickerton, 2003). Here, one company brand pervades the range of products/services it offers. Corporate branding also allows for savings in advertising and branding costs, while mitigating the risk of new product/service launches. However, when damaged, it can be difficult to change. Furthermore, corporate branding is less useful at tapping niche sub-groups of the market and tends to be constrained to holding only a broad appeal (Knox & Bickerton 2003). For example, Sony used corporate branding across both its range of televisions and its range of MP3 players.

Multi-branding, as noted in Table 5.2, allows organisations to have several distinct, strong, branded product ranges in various markets. Multi-branding is often used in conjunction with brand extensions and can reduce overall risk to an organisation should one of its brands gain a negative reputation, and allow for more complex targeting of market segments. However, it can be very costly and prevents products from accruing cross-brand benefits.

Dual branding strategies involve organisations incorporating more than one brand into their product/service. Typically, one of three dual branding strategies are deployed, these are described in Figure 5.2.

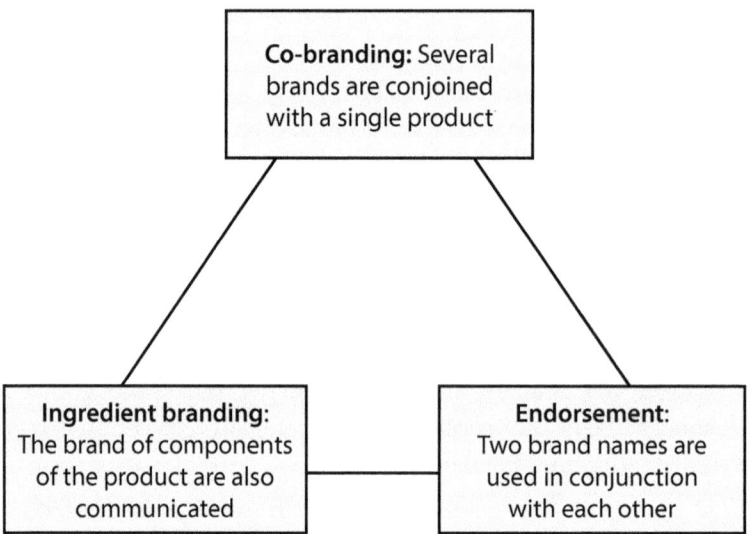

Figure 5.2: Multiple-brand strategies

Figure 5.2 describes co-branding, ingredient, and endorsement brand strategies. *Co-branding* pertains to the incorporation of two or more brands together in the marketing of a product, for mutual benefit. For example, All Nippon Airways (ANA) has announced plans incorporating the Star Wars brand into the livery of one of its aircraft (ANA, 2015). This benefits both parties, providing publicity for an upcoming Star Wars film while also supplementing the image of ANA as a modern, dynamic, quirky airline. Like most branding strategies, co-branding can result in negative as well as positive perceptions of one brand affecting the other, however prevailing research suggests stronger support of a net beneficial effect (Washburn et al., 2000).

With *ingredient* branding, airlines also provide a good example. By maintaining, and often explicating strongly their aircraft manufacturer brands, (e.g. through the Dreamliner moniker) ANA benefits from the notions of modernity and comfort the brand exudes. Similarly British Airways and Air France benefitted from the notions of style and sophistication inherent in the Concord brand. Consider boarding an aircraft for a respected airline that was embellished with Ilyushin Il-62 (a Soviet-made passenger jetliner still used by many airlines today), perhaps this would elicit feelings of apprehension, hence, ingredient branding can yield either positive or negative effects (Desai and Keller 2002).

Finally *endorsement* branding, whereby an organisation applies two brands to a product, straddles the area between the concepts of multi-branding and brand extensions (Saunders & Guoqun, 1997). For example, car manufacturers such as Volkswagen use endorsement branding when marketing their Golf range. The Golf brand conveys particular values and attitudes that appeal to certain market segments. The Golf brand benefits from the perceptions of quality and style traditionally associated with Volkswagen, while allowing Volkswagen to target various markets via other models and brands. For example, Volkswagen's coupe, the Scirocco, conveys different messages towards a different market segment than Volkswagen's MPV, the Touran. Nevertheless, both of these brands benefit from the overall Volkswagen brand suggestive of quality and style.

The brand strategies presented above are not intended to be exhaustive, but instead broadly representative of the most common brand strategies being applied. What is important to understand, is the frequency with which brand strategies are variously combined and tailored by organisations to best suit their needs. Ultimately, implementing the perfect brand strategy is a balancing act, there will always be benefits and drawbacks and the need to continually adapt a strategy to an increasingly cynical marketplace.

Exercise

Consider a car manufacturer, a sports clothing brand, and your local supermarket. What brand strategies do companies in these different sectors apply? Are different strategies appropriate for different sectors?

Brand image

Evolving from the field of psychology, and predicated upon a growing acceptance that products hold important existential as well as physical value to consumers (Gardner & Levy, 1955), brand image has emerged as an essential marketing concept, and an important contributor to brand equity. Brand image can be viewed as a multi-dimensional concept, a summation of consumer perceptions towards a brand derived from their personally held associations (Hsieh et al., 2004).

In other words, brand image is about consumers not only buying a physical product, but also purchasing the brand image associated with it. These associations can be formed in numerous ways, both through traditional marketer-controlled techniques (e.g., advertising, promotions, price, product design) as well as via less conventional methods including:

- Direct experience and interaction with the brand
- Information conveyed by media sources
- Personal inferences made by individuals
- Associations between brands and particular people, places or events.

To generate a successful brand image, marketers have to be aware of the influence of these information sources, and control them where possible. Consider the brand image of the oil giant BP. BP invest large sums into marketing activity, which has generally allowed BP to avoid having a negative brand image. However, the Deepwater Horizon accident of 2010 caused significant harm to the brand image of BP; this incident was generally out of their control and unforeseen. Marketers must try and plan in advance for the worst, to devise strategies for dealing with brand image damaging events. Similarly, many companies have taken to court and sued individuals or media organisations for making public aspersions regarding a company, consequently acting as an effective deterrent to subsequent action.

Benefits of brand image

Successful brand image should be distinctive, positive in nature, and immediately recognisable. Brand image has been shown to positively affect consumer purchase decisions (Dolich, 1969), and to capitalise upon the growing value of the symbolic, rather than functional value of products (Levy, 1959). Ultimately, creating and projecting a successful brand image increases the likelihood of consumers buying into a brand (Hsieh, 2002; O'Cass & Grace, 2004). Brand image can manifest through three types of benefit: functional, emotional, and rational.

- *Functional* benefits communicate to the consumer the benefits of using one brand over another, for example, whether one brand of washing powder cleans clothes more effectively, at lower temperatures, and makes them smell fresher for longer.
- *Emotional* benefits reflect how the brand image makes the consumer feel when consuming a product, for example purchasing Body Shop products may, on an emotional level allow consumers to identify with environmental and ethical causes, consequently satisfying them.

- Finally, *rational* benefits of brand image concern the consumer's assessment of the difference between one brand and its competition.

Brand attributes are a holistic, all-encompassing evaluation consumers have of a brand. Ultimately, brand image is becoming increasingly important, an idea reinforced by Levy (1959) who has previously stated:

> *"If the manufacturer understands that he is selling symbols as well as goods, he can view his product more completely."* (p. 124)

Levy's foretelling of the importance of brand image, and the symbolic rather than the functional elements of products has become increasingly relevant.

Exercise

Consider the low-cost airline Ryanair. Explore the company's adverts on YouTube; examine its website; and use the internet to understand the flying experience its passengers receive. Now describe the brand image of Ryanair. Is it consistent? Is it clear? Is it distinctive? Also consider how the airline can use non-traditional marketing methods to protect and project its brand image further.

Brand equity

The proliferation of the brand equity concept has developed in tandem with an increasing appreciation of the power brands hold (Keller, 2002). Nevertheless, despite general acceptance of the benefits, e.g. increased stock prices (Simon & Sullivan, 1993), improved long term cash flow (Srivastava & Shocker, 1991), and the ability to command premium prices (Keller, 1993), there is debate as to what brand equity is, and crucially, how best to measure it.

Understanding brand equity's interaction with different stages of the marketing process emphasises both the concept's importance, as well as the cyclical nature of marketing. Figure 5.3 below conveys the influence brand equity holds. Initial marketing activity (product development, pricing, distribution decisions, and promotional activity) along with the implementation of appropriate brand strategies contribute towards brand equity (Yoo et al., 2000). The development of brand equity consequently increases value for both the organisation and the customer, value that then feeds back to the marketing activity stage and influences the process all over again, while generating sustainable competitive advantage (Bharadwaj et al., 1993). The process can be described as cyclical, as marketing managers should constantly be seeking to elevate, and subsequently benefit from enhancing the value of brand equity.

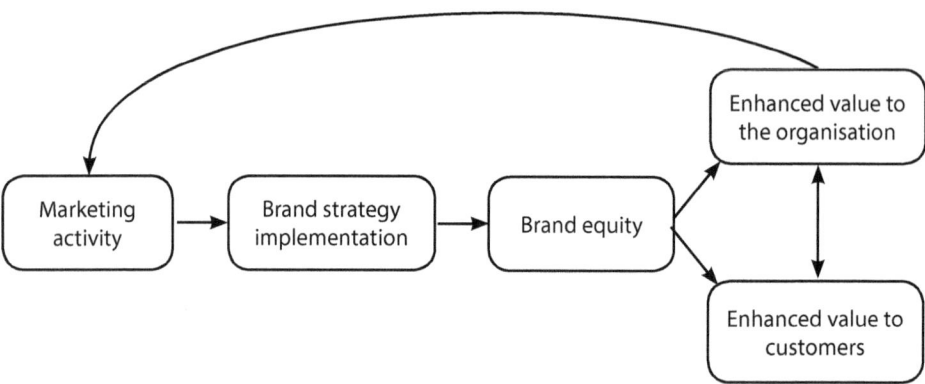

Figure 5.3: Marketing process. Adapted from Yoo et al. (2000)

Brand equity has been generally defined as *"…the marketing effects uniquely attributable to the brand"* (Keller, 1993: 1). Farquhar (1989) suggested the financial added-value to a product constituted brand equity, whereas Swait et al. (1993) consider brand equity to be the internal valuation consumers hold of a brand competing against other brands, compared to a non-competitive market. Feldwick (1996) offers an attempt at a universal definition of brand equity whereby it is a construct of brand value (evaluated through accounts and financial monitoring), brand strength (evaluated through consumer-brand attachment), and brand description (attitudes held by customers towards a brand). Subsequently, other researchers have variously suggested further elements, and definitional debates continue. Nevertheless, there is a general consensus of the benefits amid continuing attempts to develop it. Farquhar (1989) identified three approaches to generating, and increasing brand equity; to build, buy, or borrow it. These are explained in Table 5.3.

As Table 5.3 shows, there are several different approaches to acquiring brand equity. The most appropriate depends on the competitive environment, the strengths and abilities of the organisation, and the target customer base. Different markets will be more receptive to different techniques. Once organisations have established brand equity, to realise its value and derive the financial benefits it brings requires some form of measurement.

Table 5.3: Obtaining brand equity: Adapted from Farquhar (1989).

Strategy	Description	Example
Building brand equity	Building a strong brand through developing positive brand evaluations and well-received brand attitudes, whilst ensuring the projection of a strong brand image.	Apple have steadily enhanced their brand equity over a long period of time, honing and adjusting their brand to enhance reception, furthermore, they have been consistent in the image they project.
Buying brand equity	Acquiring a company, and gaining ownership of its products and brands can also develop brand equity. Obtaining licenses to incorporate other brands into a product is a variation of this approach.	Sports Direct purchased several brands such as Donnay and Karrimor, acquiring their brand equity. Walt Disney license many of their characters to external companies to produce products.
Borrowing brand equity	Brand extensions can allow products to 'borrow' the positive attributes consumers hold towards a brand when applied to a new product.	Mars use this approach across their range, for example, applying the Mars logo to their ice-cream range, as well as the core Mars bar product.

Measuring brand equity

The need to accurately measure brand equity has become increasingly important with growing awareness of the added-value derived through its possession. Academia has lagged behind industry in this area, driven by desire to attain the benefits of brand equity, industry has focused on placing a monetary value on brands, often calculated from a financially biased perspective, leading to brands commonly being assessed on financial, rather than overall marketing value (Pappu et al., 2005). Interbrands, one of the world leading brand consulting firms, compile its own best brand value list every year; the 2023 top ten valuable brands are:

Table 5.4: Top ten valuable brands in 2023. Source: Interbrands (2023)

Global rank	Brand	Brand Value ($bil)
1	Apple	502.68
2	Microsoft	316.66
3	Amazon	276,929
4	Google	260.26
5	Samsung	47.91.41
6	Toyota	64.50
7	Mercedes-Benz	60.414
8	Coca-Cola	58.05
9	Nike	53.77
10	BMW	51.16

Table 5.4 presents the ten highest valued brands according to Interbrands. Such lists can be influential to prospective shareholders, owners, and competitors, however, they represent the product of industry, where the emphasis invariably rests on the bottom line. Academic attempts have been advanced through the introduction of the five brand equity areas requiring measurement. These are described by Aaker (1996) as measures of loyalty, quality and leadership, brand associations, and measures of differentiation, brand awareness, and market behaviour measures. Aaker (1996) suggests that to be effective, brand equity measures should meet several criteria. They first should represent an accurate conceptualisation of the concept, evaluating it in its entirety. Additionally, measures of brand equity should be credible in the eyes of practitioners, ultimately resulting in valuable, actionable information. Furthermore, effective measurement of brand equity should be responsive, non-static, and thus a true reflection of changes in the marketplace. Finally, effective measures should have general applicability across an organisation's brand portfolio, consequently generating scope for useful comparisons between brands, thus allowing for strategic decisions to be made. Ultimately, owing to the multi-dimensionality of the concept, and influence of context upon it, the development of very complex, universal measures of brand equity is a Sisyphean cause (Barwise, 1993). Nevertheless, attempts continue with arguable rates of success.

Finally, Keller (2014) identifies four implications of marketing programs to build, measure, and manage brand equity, including:

- Identifying and developing brand plans (i.e., a clear understanding of what the brand is to represent and how it would be positioned with respect to competitors);

- Designing and implementing brand marketing programs (i.e., the marketing activities and supporting marketing programs and the way the brand is integrated into them e.g., pricing strategy and product strategy); also other associations indirectly transferred to the brand as a result of linking it to some other entity (e.g., country of origin);

- Measuring and interpreting brand performance (i.e., to manage brands profitably, managers should successfully design and implement a brand equity measurement system); and finally

- Growing and sustaining brand equity (i.e., understanding how branding strategies should reflect corporate concerns and be adjusted, if at all, over time or over geographical boundaries or multiple market segments).

Consider the Interbrand list of global brands. Are you surprised by any of the brands' position? Use examples to describe the benefits those organisations can accrue through their strong brand equity.

Brand positioning and repositioning

Having developed an effective, attractive brand, implemented it effectively with an appropriate strategy and brand image to derive the benefits of brand equity, organisations will, in order to maximise the likelihood of success, position their brands. Furthermore, in response to competition, organisations successful over the long-term will be required to engage in repositioning activities on an on-going basis.

5

Brand positioning

Brand positioning is concerned with the transmission of information to consumers and stakeholders, influencing how they perceive a brand in relation to other competitors, and the resulting position they believe the brand holds in the market. In essence, brand positioning has little to do with the physical attributes of the product, but rather the perceptions held within the mind of the consumer regarding that product (Hassan & Craft, 2012). The challenge for marketers then, is to ensure consumers position the brand favourably. The brand positioning concept is not restricted to branded products, but can equally apply to services, organisations as a whole (private, public and third sector), as well as destinations. However, it should be noted that the added complexity of managing multiple stakeholders renders organisational and destination positioning more complicated. For example, consider the stakeholders (e.g. local population and businesses, politicians, foreign owned tourism companies .) involved in positioning a destination brand; clearly then, the complexity involved in brand positioning is to some extent dependent upon the context in which it occurs.

Ultimately, the success of positioning activity is determined by the results of market segmentation and target marketing. Further, positioning activity should be commensurate with an organisations wider promotional objectives.

How it works

There is no generalizable, tick-box approach to successfully positioning a brand, nevertheless, as well as the experience and knowledge of the strategists involved, there are several considerations as well as useful tools that could be used to inform brand positioning decisions.

Marketers must evaluate the positioning undertaken by the competition, possibly necessitating consumer research. Based on this evaluation, marketers must next develop an actionable and realistic plan to position their brand. Finally, marketers must implement a positioning plan, before committing to on-going monitoring of consumer perceptions (Fill, 2013). A foundation stage of the process is evaluating competition, and creating a perceptual map represents a useful way to achieve this. A perceptual map conveys how consumers view the attributes of a brand in relation to its competition (Kim & Agrusa, 2005). For example, Figure 5.4 below illustrates possible perceptual map attributes in the squash racket market.

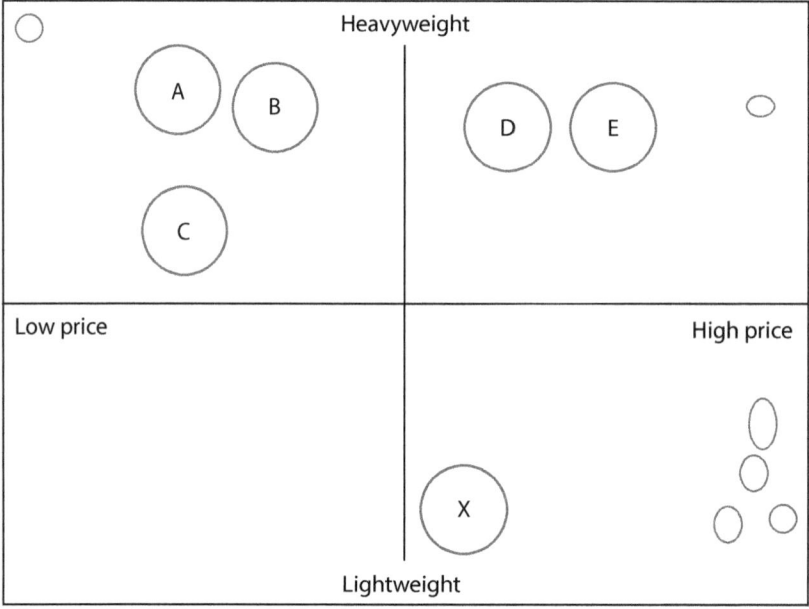

Figure 5.4: Perceptual map for a squash racket

The perceptual map above positions various products (in this case squash rackets) based upon consumer perceptions of selected attributes (in this case the weight and price of the racket). Based on Figure 5.4, we can see that products A, B and C are all positioned in the heavyweight, low price quadrant of the map. These three products are clustered in quite a crowded quadrant, thus, we can see that there is quite strong competition in this area. The high price, lightweight area is also quite crowded, consequently, marketers could consider that product X is located in an area of potential success. Note that product E is in a risky position, it offers a similar weight racket for a higher price than product D, consequently, it may be a likely candidate for repositioning. Creating perceptual maps provides marketers with valuable insight into the minds of their prospective consumers, allowing them to adjust aspects of brands to enhance perceptions as necessary. Furthermore, mapping allows marketers to distinguish unique and shared attributes of their brand with the competition. Finally, it can inform marketers of the most suitable positioning strategy to employ (Fill, 2013).

Positioning strategies

Positioning a brand in an optimum location within the consumer's mind, or perceptual map, is ultimately a reflection of the brand itself, its core values, and its core meaning. In order to utilise brand positioning, marketers must select and deploy the most appropriate strategy, conscious of the influence marketing strategy holds over consumer perceptions, for example, emphasising low price will affect consumer perceptions related to price. Table 5.5 offers description of some brand positioning strategies.

Table 5.5: Brand positioning strategies

Strategy	Description	Example
Price	Easily influenced by marketers. A low pricing strategy ensures customers are likely to perceive brands as lower quality, higher price generally leads to high quality perceptions. Price is not always appropriate where quality is not accurately reflected.	Aldi and Lidl position themselves as low-cost alternatives to established supermarkets. Waitrose and Marks & Spencer Food use price to indicate perceived quality. Morrison's attribute recent poor performance to holding neither a low nor high price position.
Product	Commonly used approach whereby marketers exert complete control. Product/service benefits are emphasised in relation to competitors' offerings.	The automotive industry uses this strategy, Alfa-Romeo emphasise their Italian roots, and the design and style of their cars; Volvo emphasise safety benefits.
Use	Marketers indicate to consumers when to use a brand, consumers then associate the brand with particular activities, times, events, etc.	Lucozade attempt to position their brand through use, striving to make their drink synonymous with sport and fitness.

Class dissociation	Used in crowded markets, brands position themselves by proclaiming to be different from competitors, establishing distinction messages.	In Japan, Happoshu is a variety of low-malt, low-priced beer. Consequently, brewers of high malt, traditional beer emphasise this purported authenticity, and superiority to dissociate themselves from lower malt content varieties.
User	Through communicating the 'typical' users of a brand, marketers can create a brand consumers aspire to associate with.	Popular perfume adverts generally include attractive models of an age similar to the target market and convey ideals of elegance, class and sophistication that consumers will be sympathetic to.
Competitor	Considered high risk, directly positioning a brand against a competitor is a combative strategy.	Rarely used, political parties frequently challenge competitor parties openly and publicly.
Heritage	Imbuing brands with heritage can have powerful results. It can enhance trust and contribute prestige to a brand, it is also difficult to imitate.	Charity brands such as the Scouts or Marie Curie possess a strong heritage, which can increase donor trust and enhance volunteer satisfaction (Curran et al., 2016).
Benefit	Marketers communicate the main advantages of their brand over competitors.	Washing powder brands frequently use benefit branding, emphasising how much whiter their product makes clothes compared to others.

The strategies presented in Table 5.5, represent merely a sample of approaches marketers can use to position a brand. Inevitably, marketers will use aspects of some strategies, combined with elements of others, resulting in the application of complex strategies, targeting nuanced segments of the market. Finally, Keller (2014) suggests four ways of identifying and establishing brand positioning:

1 Basic concepts (who the target is; who the main competitors are; how the brand is similar to these competitors; how the brand is different from them),

2 Target market (i.e., market segmentation),

3 Nature of competition (i.e., competitive analysis)

4 Points-of-parity (PoP) (i.e., attributes or benefits that consumers strongly associate with a brand, positively evaluate, and believe) and points-of-difference (PoD) (i.e., attributes shared with other brands; what are the conditions your brand must have?).

Repositioning

Critical to maintaining the long-term success of a brand, and ensuring it remains relevant to constantly changing consumer tastes, attitudes, and concerns, while continuing to be superior in some sense to competition, is the process of repositioning (Simms & Trott, 2007). In many cases, through constantly reinforcing images and brand benefits, repositioning can be unnecessary. Nevertheless, more so than ever before, technology is rendering markets increasingly fluid and dynamic, often necessitating repositioning to maintain strong market positions. However the process is often expensive and fraught with danger. For example, UK postal service Royal Mail was facing increasing competition from private delivery firms, and offering services considered to be much extended and removed from the organisation's original offerings. Consequently, to maintain a strong position in the market, Royal Mail was rebranded and positioned as 'Consignia', a supposedly more modern, dynamic, efficient organisation. The repositioning, despite being subjected to substantial prior market research, was a costly failure, and ultimately the name reverted back to Royal Mail. Repositioning can also apply to destination brands, for example the area of Govan in Glasgow has a reputation of social deprivation, however, through the costly and time-consuming process of establishing several cultural tourist offerings in tandem with development of the area's reputation and economy, there are increasing numbers of visitors (Butler et al., 2013). Ultimately, repositioning is vital to maintain market dominance, yet fraught with danger. Even armed with sophisticated market research analysis, repositioning often ends badly, it is costly, time-consuming, and high risk.

5

Exercise

Create perceptual brand maps for the following markets: Toothpaste, supermarkets, and laptop computers.

Conclusions

Now, more than ever before, marketing is complex, sophisticated, and nuanced. Through rapid developments in technology, marketers can gather information and target segments of markets that were previously undistinguished. Furthermore, globalisation and logistical interconnectedness have increased overall market size. To realise the opportunities this presents, developing the correct brand, delivered using appropriate and effective strategies is increasingly important. This evolution has not been one sided however; consumers too, are increasingly benefitting from the technology, and the information revolution to inform their consumption decisions within ever more crowded markets. As an outcome of these developments, brand equity has risen to prominence in determining the overall value and success of organisations. Building it is an immense challenge, but truly successful organisations understand the importance of maintaining it through constant evaluation.

Further reading

Dobni, D., & Zinkhan, G. M. (1990). In search of brand image: A foundation analysis. *Advances in Consumer Research*, **17**(1), 110-119.

> This paper explores the concept of brand image. Through analysis of a wealth of prior, conflicting brand image research, the authors highlight the complexity, and malleability of the concept and attempt to provide clarity. As an outcome, the paper presents what its authors see as the main elements of brand image.

Foroudi, P., Jin, Z., Gupta, S., Foroudi, M. M., & Kitchen, P. J. (2018). Perceptional components of brand equity: Configuring the symmetrical and asymmetrical paths to brand loyalty and brand purchase intention. *Journal of Business Research*, 89, 462–474.

> This research paper investigates the impact of brand perception on brand loyalty and brand purchase intention using a mixed method approach. The authors examine the combinations of various perceptional elements of brand equity.

Parris, D. L., & Guzmán, F. (2022). Evolving brand boundaries and expectations: Looking back on brand equity, brand loyalty, and brand image research to move forward. *Journal of Product & Brand Management*, **32**(2), 191–234.

> This paper provides a systematic literature review of three main brands concepts and offer an evolved definition for each of them that acknowledges the dynamic nature of them and in *"the era where brands are expected to be socially and socio-politically conscious."*

Pina, R., & Dias, Á. (2021). The influence of brand experiences on consumer-based brand equity. *Journal of Brand Management*, **28**(2), 99–115.

> This paper explores the impacts of different dimensions of brand experience on consumers' brand equity dimensions: awareness, loyalty, and perceived quality.

Swaminathan, V., Sorescu, A., Steenkamp, J.-B. E. M., O'Guinn, T. C. G., & Schmitt, B. (2020). Branding in a hyperconnected world: refocusing theories and rethinking boundaries. *Journal of Marketing*, **84**(2), 24–46.

> This paper examines the shift in branding in today's hyperconnected world where traditional corporate brands are competing with new brand entities including smart brands (e.g., Alexa), idea brands (e.g., #MeToo), platform brands (e.g., AirBnB), and person brands (e.g., Kim Kardashian). They provide a framework to rethink the role and functions of brands, brand (co) creation process, and brand management.

Tasci, A. D. (2020). A critical review and reconstruction of perceptual brand equity. *International Journal of Contemporary Hospitality Management*, **33**(1), 166–198.

In this paper, the authors delve into the multifaceted realm of brand equity, specifically focusing on customer-based brand equity (CBBE). Their objectives include distinguishing between financial and perceptual brand equity, analysing deviations from original conceptualizations, and exploring the structural relations of common CBBE components.

Review questions

1. What answer below best describes what constitutes a brand?

   a) Name, signs, symbols, employees, URLs etc
   b) The balance sheet of an organisation.
   c) The brand is what consumers perceive an organisation to be like.
   d) The brand is the strategy the managers decide to adopt.

2. How can brand equity be developed in an organisation?

   a) Building brand equity through investing in the brand and using appropriate strategies.
   b) Buying brand equity through a takeover of a strong brand, or through gaining a license to use an established brand on your products.
   c) Borrowing brand equity, using brand extensions.
   d) All of the above.

3. Select the statement that best describes brand positioning?

   a) It is when brands are shipped from the factory to be nearer the customer.
   b) Brand positioning is the position the brands occupy in the shop. For example, near the checkout, or at the back of the shop.
   c) It is the transmission of information to consumers and stakeholders, influencing how they perceive a brand in relation to other competitors, and the resulting position they believe the brand holds in the market
   d) It is when a previously expensive brand, is changed to become a low-cost, value brand.

4. Brand heritage can be a strong advantage to an organisation, it is difficult for competition to imitate and can elicit strong feelings of trust.

   a) True
   b) False

5. How many brand attributes can a perceptual map consider?

   a) Only one
   b) Two
   c) At least three
   d) Five or more

6. What statement below best describes brand repositioning?

   a) Fraught with danger and risk.
   b) A concept that is ongoing and cyclical in nature.
   c) Requires constant evaluation of the brand, and is thus costly.
   d) All of the above.

7. A supermarket produced cola drink would best be described as what type of brand?

   a) Ingredient brand.
   b) Own-label brands.
   c) Multi-brands.
   d) Competitor brands,

8. What statement best describes some benefits of brands?

   a. They act as a barrier to competition, create higher profits, and increase trust.
   b. They ensure the consumer is aware of increased value of a brand.
   c. They make it easy for consumers to return a product if it is faulty.
   d. They ensure the consumer does not remember negative aspects of a brand.

9. Positioning a brand in an optimum location within the marketers mind, is ultimately a reflection of the brand itself, its core values, and its core meaning.

   a) True
   b) False

10. Identify the most appropriate statement describing benefits of brand equity:

   a) Increased stock prices.
   b) Improved long term cash flow.
   c) Allows firms to command premium prices.
   d) All of the above.

Answers

The answers to these questions can be found at the back of this book, or at the Marketing Communications page at Goodfellow Publishers:

https://www.goodfellowpublishers.com

References

Aaker, D. (2000) *Building Strong Brands*, New York: Simon and Schuster.

Aaker, D. A. (1996) Measuring brand equity across products and markets, *California Management Review*, **38**(3), 103.

Aaker, J. L. (1997) Dimensions of brand personality, *Journal of Marketing Research*, **34** (3), 347-356.

ANA (2015) ANA Unveils Star Wars R2-D2 Livery for the 787-9 Dreamliner Aircrast The First and Only Passenger Aircraft to Feature a Star Wars Character, http://www.ana.co.jp/eng/aboutana/press/2015/150416.html [Accessed 30/04 2015].

American Marketing Association (AMA). (1960) *Marketing Definitions: A glossary of marketing terms*, Chicago IL: AMA.

Aurand, T. W., Gorchels, L. & Bishop, T. R. (2005) Human resource management's role in internal branding: an opportunity for cross-functional brand message synergy, *Journal of Product & Brand Management*, **14**(3), 163-169.

Barwise, P. (1993) Brand equity: snark or boojum?, *International Journal of Research in Marketing*, **10**(1), 93-104.

Bharadwaj, S. G., Varadarajan, P. R. & Fahy, J. (1993) Sustainable competitive advantage in service industries: a conceptual model and research propositions, *The Journal of Marketing*, **57**, 83-99.

Butler, R., Curran, R. & O'Gorman, K. D. (2013) Pro-poor tourism in a First World urban setting: Case study of Glasgow Govan, *International Journal of Tourism Research*, **15**(5), 443-457.

Curran, R., Taheri, B., MacIntosh, R. & O'Gorman, K. (2016) Nonprofit brand heritage its ability to influence volunteer retention, engagement, and satisfaction. *Nonprofit and Voluntary Sector Quarterly*, **45**(6), 1234 –1257, doi:10.1177/0899764016633532.

De-Chernatony, L. & Dall'Olmo Riley, F. (1998) Defining a 'brand': Beyond the literature with experts' interpretations, *Journal of Marketing Management*, **14**(5), 417-443.

Desai, K. K. & Keller, K. L. (2002) The effects of ingredient branding strategies on host brand extendibility, *Journal of Marketing*, **66**(1), 73-93.

Dolich, I. J. (1969) Congruence relationships between self images and product brands, *Journal of Marketing Research*, **6**(1), 80-84.

DuBois Gelb, B. & Rangarajan, D. (2014) Employee contributions to brand equity, *California Management Review*, **56**(2), 95-112.

Farquhar, P. H. (1989) Managing brand equity, *Marketing Research*, **1**(3), 24-33.

Feldwick, P. (1996) What is brand equity anyway, and how do you measure it?, *Journal of the Market Research Society*, **38**(2), 85-104.

Fill, C. (2013) *Marketing Communications: Brands, experiences and participation,* Pearson Higher Ed.

Forbes (2015) The World's Most Valuable Brands, available: https://www.forbes.com/sites/kurtbadenhausen/2015/05/13/the-worlds-most-valuable-brands-2015-behind-the-numbers/#5090dbbc5106 [Accessed 2 May 2015].

Gardner, B. B. & Levy, S. J. (1955) The product and the brand, *Harvard Business Review,* **33**(2), 33-39.

Grabner-Kraeuter, S. (2002) The role of consumers' trust in online-shopping, *Journal of Business Ethics,* **39**(1-2), 43-50.

Hassan, S. S. & Craft, S. (2012) Examining world market segmentation and brand positioning strategies, *Journal of Consumer Marketing,* **29**(5), 344-356.

Hsieh, M.-H. (2002) Identifying brand image dimensionality and measuring the degree of brand globalization: a cross-national study, *Journal of International Marketing,* **10**(2), 46-67.

Hsieh, M.-H., Pan, S.-L. & Setiono, R. (2004) Product-, corporate-, and country-image dimensions and purchase behavior: a multicountry analysis, *Journal of the Academy of Marketing Science,* **32**(3), 251-270.

Interbrand (2023) Best Global Brands. (n.d.). Interbrand. Retrieved 17 July 2024, from https://interbrand.com/best-global-brands/

Keller, K. L. (1993) Conceptualizing, measuring, and managing customer-based brand equity, *The Journal of Marketing,* **57** (1), 1-22.

Keller, K. L. (2002) Branding and brand equity, In: Weitz, B. and Wensley, R. ed. *Handbook of Marketing,* Sage, pp. 151-178.

Keller, K.L. (2014). *Strategic Brand Management: Building, measuring, and managing brand equity,* 4th ed., London: Pearson

Kim, S. S. & Agrusa, J. (2005) The positioning of overseas honeymoon destinations, *Annals of Tourism Research,* **32**(4), 887-904.

Knox, S. & Bickerton, D. (2003) The six conventions of corporate branding, *European Journal of Marketing,* **37**(7/8), 998-1016.

Levy, S. J. (1959) Symbols for sale, *Harvard Business Review,* **37**(4), 117-124.

O'Cass, A. & Grace, D. (2004) Exploring consumer experiences with a service brand, *Journal of Product & Brand Management,* **13**(4), 257-268.

Pappu, R., Quester, P. G. & Cooksey, R. W. (2005) Consumer-based brand equity: improving the measurement – empirical evidence, *Journal of Product & Brand Management,* **14**(3), 143-154.

Reddy, S. K., Holak, S. L. & Bhat, S. (1994) To extend or not to extend: Success determinants of line extensions, *Journal of Marketing Research,* **31**, 243-262.

Saunders, J. & Guoqun, F. (1997) Dual branding: how corporate names add value, *Journal of Product & Brand Management,* **6**(1), 40-48.

Schlager, T., Bodderas, M., Maas, P. & Cachelin, J. L. (2011) The influence of the employer brand on employee attitudes relevant for service branding: an empirical investigation, *Journal of Services Marketing,* **25**(7), 497-508.

Simms, C. & Trott, P. (2007) An analysis of the repositioning of the "BMW Mini" brand, *Journal of Product & Brand Management,* **16**(5), 297-309.

Simon, C. J. & Sullivan, M. W. (1993) The measurement and determinants of brand equity: a financial approach, *Marketing Science,* **12**(1), 28-52.

Srivastava, R. K. & Shocker, A. D. (1991) *Brand Equity: A perspective on its meaning and measurement,* Marketing Science Institute.

Swait, J., Erdem, T., Louviere, J. & Dubelaar, C. (1993) The equalization price: A measure of consumer-perceived brand equity, *International Journal of Research in Marketing,* **10**(1), 23-45.

Washburn, J. H., Till, B. D. & Priluck, R. (2000) Co-branding: brand equity and trial effects, *Journal of Consumer Marketing,* **17**(7), 591-604.

Yoo, B., Donthu, N. & Lee, S. (2000) An examination of selected marketing mix elements and brand equity, *Journal of the Academy of Marketing Science,* **28**(2), 195-211.

5

6 Integrated Marketing Communications

Kitty Shaw

If a brand like Apple supported a campaign about the impact on society of people spending too much time on their laptops and phones, or launched a very basic mobile phone would you think this was strange? This is because Apple has a very clear market positioning based on providing cutting edge technology products, which enhance people's lives. This positioning is evident in everything from its sleek product design to all of its marketing and customer communications across multiple channels. All of their communications are integrated to support their market positioning and brand values. This chapter discusses integrated marketing communications, why it is important for businesses and how to go about delivering an integrated approach. The chapter also looks at the challenges of doing so and the future of integration. It links to the case study on Standard Life plc, which is included in Chapter 11.

Integrated marketing communications is commonly abbreviated to IMC and this chapter will use this shorthand.

Defining integrated marketing communications

The term 'integrated marketing communications' was first coined in the 1990s and captured the need for marketers to co-ordinate their communications better, both across their different audiences or stakeholder groups, and their communications channels and promotional tools. Organisations may have worked with a number of specialist creative agencies or intermediaries for different elements of their promotional mix, including advertising, direct mailings, public relations and sponsorship, while customer service communications were handled by another part of the organisation. IMC is about ensuring that all of these elements are joined up and present a unified positioning and image across all communications – both internal and external.

However, IMC is about more than the tactical alignment of messages and colour schemes across different communications channels, media and audiences. It is a strategic management process, driven by corporate and marketing strategy. IMC involves all of the organisation's communications being driven by and supporting corporate and marketing objectives. Kotler (2000: 542) defines IMC as *"the concept under which a company carefully integrates and co-ordinates its many communications channels to deliver a clear, consistent and compelling message about the organization and its products."* Kotler's definition highlights the objective of IMC – to deliver clear and compelling messages, through whichever communications channels and media the organisation uses, across its multiple audiences.

IMC does not mean that exactly the same messages, images and so on have to be used across all audiences, channel and media, but that all communications support and reinforce the same messages about the organisation, its products and services. From a customer perspective this means that the organisation needs to consider all of the touch-points a customer might have with the organisation and its products and services, and ensure that it delivers consistent positioning through all of these. Figure 6.1 illustrates the broad range of touch-points a consumer might have with an organisation such as Standard Life, and the multiple opportunities or threats that these present to the organisations planned messaging and positioning. IMC is about ensuring that the organisation does everything it can to ensure that each of these touch-points is an opportunity rather than a threat to the organisation.

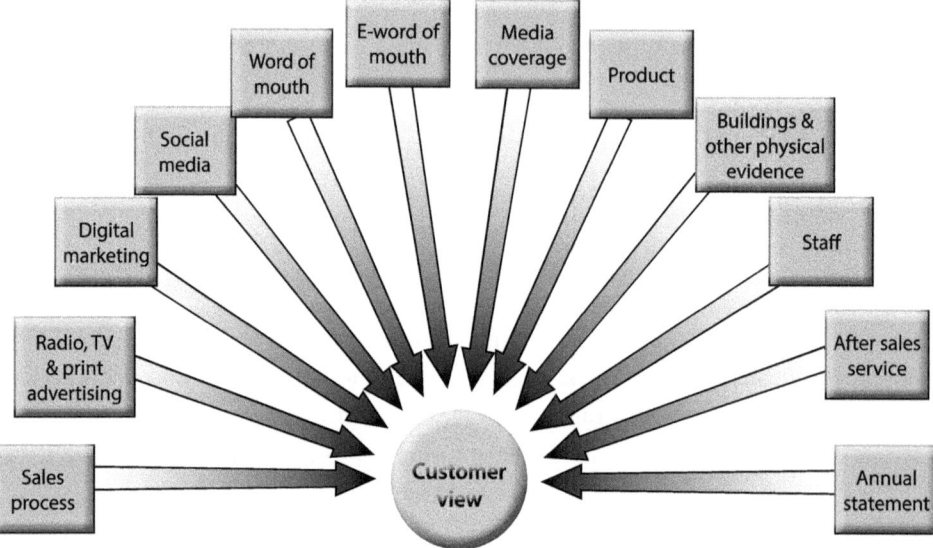

Figure 6.1: Customer touch-points

An important skill in managing IMC, is understanding the needs of each of the organisation's multiple key audiences and being able to translate the positioning and messaging derived from marketing strategy into communications, which are meaningful for each audience. In this way, the IMC approach is linked to the extent to which organisations are market-driven, as those organisations which are most focused on responding to the needs and developments of the outside world and their external stakeholders are best able to produce IMC (Reid, 2005). For any communications initiative, the company must determine which are its key audiences and develop messaging relevant to them through the channels and media which are appropriate and effective for reaching that particular group.

The following definition from the Chartered Institute of Marketing (CIM) emphasises the role of IMC in building relationships with the organisations various audiences.

> *"IMC can represent both a strategic and tactical approach to the planned management of an organisation's communications. IMC requires that organisations coordinate their various strategies, resources and messages in order that they enable meaningful engagement with target audiences. The main purposes are to develop a clear positioning and encourage stakeholder relationships that are of mutual value."* (CIM, 2015)

This definition stresses the role of IMC in providing a clear positioning for the organisation to help customers to understand what the business stands for.

IMC involves managing the organisation's communications across all of its communications tools. These might include some of those shown in Table 6.1.

Table 6.1: The tools of IMC. Adapted from Keller, 2001:820

Advertising	Print, TV, radio, cinema, outdoor
Direct marketing	Hardcopy, email and social media
Sales promotions	Email, in store,
Public relations	Communications with media, regulators and other stakeholders
Point of sale	Livery, staff appearance, look and feel
Sponsorship & event marketing	Celebrities, sports, arts and cause related
Personal selling	Face to face, telephone, email
Customer communications	Post sale servicing and information
Web presence	Website, social media activity, content marketing

Table 6.1 illustrates that there are several tools that marketers can use and that need to be considered in evaluating an IMC approach. Everything from advertising to sponsorship and the look and feel of an organisation can be used to support an IMC approach. At the same time, any of these elements can undermine an IMC approach if they are not aligned to support the organisation's core positioning and values.

To summarise, the key features of IMC are that it:

- is an audience driven approach to communications;
- is a strategic process;
- encompasses all touch-points for customers and other stakeholders;
- presents a single voice for an organisation's positioning and values; and
- aids relationship building by helping customers to understand what the organisation stands for.

The IMC planning process

The integrated marketing planning process needs to be driven by the organisation's strategic marketing plan and brand strategy, which in turn are driven by the overall strategic priorities of the organisation. If for example the high level strategy is for growth, then this will influence the communications objectives, positioning and messaging used. Figure 6.2 illustrates the IMC planning process.

In Chapter 4 we discussed the marketing communications strategy as part of the strategic marketing plan, which in turn is driven by corporate level strategy. Figure 4.2 illustrates that the elements of a marketing communications strategy are positioning, audience(s), creative and media. Delivering IMC means ensuring that all communications and customer touch-points support and reinforce the positioning determined in the strategic marketing plan; that they are in line with the needs of target audiences in terms of messaging; and that channels and media used are in line with audience needs and preferences. Figure 6.2 illustrates how this marketing planning process discussed in Chapter 4 flows through to deliver integrated communications programs, which support high level corporate and marketing strategy.

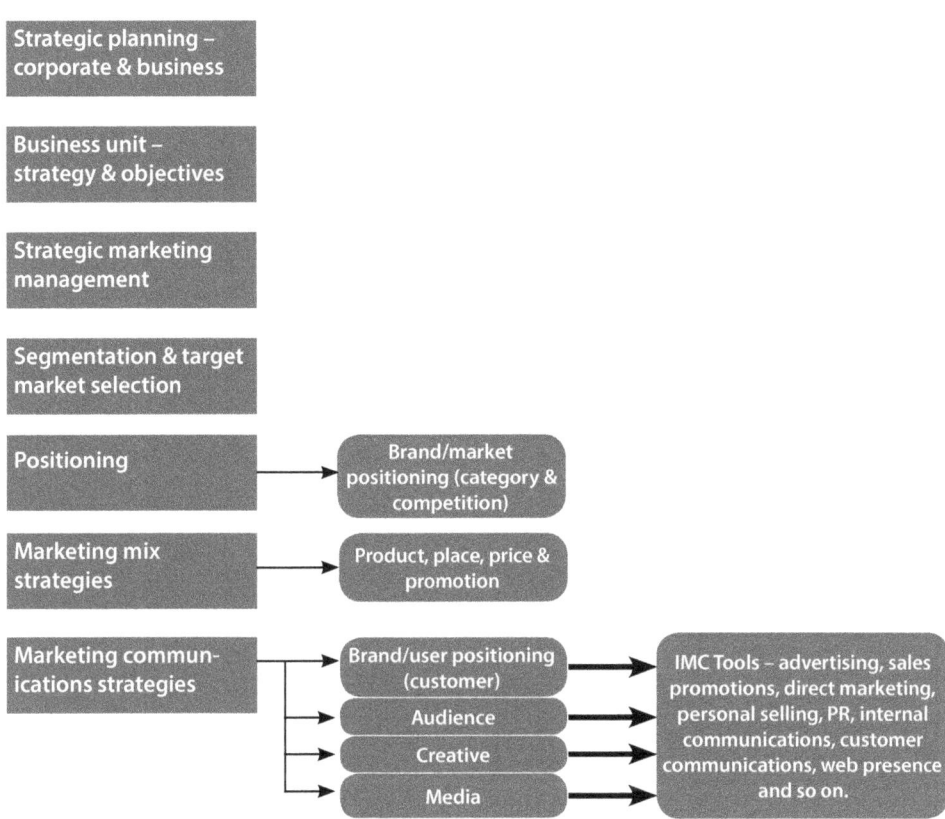

Figure 6.2: Integrated marketing communications as a strategic process

In the case study on Standard Life Plc. in Chapter 11 a clear link can be seen between the corporate objectives, the communications objectives and how these are then worked through to key messages and propositions for key stakeholder groups. In Standard Life's case a broad range of stakeholders are identified as is illustrated by Table 6.2.

Table 6.2: The multiple stakeholders of Standard Life plc.

Customers /clients	Segmented by product and distribution channel
Distributors	Independent financial advisers , workplace consultants
Prospective customers	Segments targeted for growth
Shareholders	Institutional and individual
Employees	Segmented by location, function and level
Media	National press, trade press, online news channels (trade and consumer), radio & TV
Other	Joint venture & strategic partners , UK Government & regulators, overseas governments & regulators

A model for planning and evaluating an IMC approach is provided by Kliatchko (2008). Reflecting recent thinking, Kliatchko's model stresses that the foundation of IMC is an approach to business planning and strategic management which is driven by a deep understanding of the needs of the organisation's multiple stakeholders. Where an organisation is focused from the top on the needs of its customers and other stakeholders, senior management are responsible for promoting a corporate vision and ensuring that the business is organised to deliver this vision. Kliatchko identifies '4 Pillars' of communication that need to be managed to produce effective IMC These are *stakeholders, content, channels* and *results*. The model, which is illustrated in Figure 6.3, is a useful framework to help guide and assess communications integration.

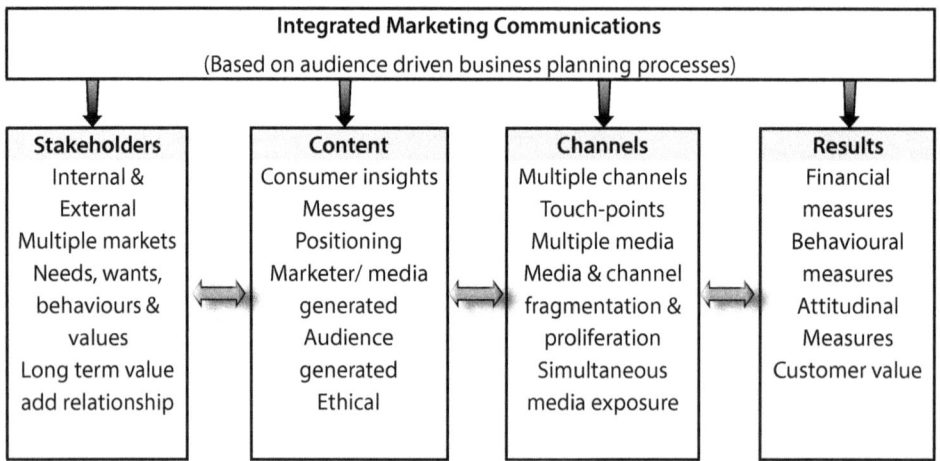

Figure 6.3: Kliatchko's 4 Pillars of Integrated Marketing Communications, Adapted from Kliatchko (2008)

Stakeholders

The Stakeholder pillar encompasses all of the organisation's multiple audiences, from customers to staff and shareholders amongst others, and requires the organisation to build a detailed understanding of their needs, behaviours, values and attitudes. This will range from understanding the targeted customer segments, in terms of their media habits and preferences, to knowing which trade press or social media sites are most likely to influence their opinions and behaviours. The Standard Life case study helps to illustrate this. Within the communications strategy, the overall communication purpose is defined as: *"To enhance Standard Life's brand and corporate reputation through stakeholder engagement and advocacy".* This stresses the importance to Standard Life of engaging with a number of stakeholders in order that they might become advocates, but also the need to integrate communications across stakeholders. The communications strategy then goes on to show how the group's positioning translates into a proposition for each of its key stakeholders, but all of these individual stakeholder propositions link back to and support the company's communications objectives. Similarly in planning communications for a specific event, such as the acquisition discussed, a key element of the communications plan is identifying all of the relevant stakeholders and their communications needs.

Content

The Content pillar encompasses all communications about the organisation, including messages produced by the company, as well as what others write about the company in the media, and customer views of the company posted on social media. Thus the integrated approach needs to take account of an *Interaction Model of Communications* (Baines & Fill, 2014: 355), where consumers themselves integrate messages from multiple sources, including the media and their interactions with other consumers, in forming their opinions of a company. An example of this is the retailer Marks and Spencer's 'Plan A', which is a strategic focus on sustainability across the business, defined as *"our way to help protect the planet – by sourcing responsibly, reducing waste and helping communities"* (Marks & Spencer, 2016). Plan A is central to the company's strategy and is evidenced and supported across several of company's communications, from in-store displays promoting Plan A, charging for plastic bags to discourage their use, and its "Schwopping" campaign in partnership with the charity Oxfam, which encourages customers to donate unwanted clothes, so that they can be re-used, sold or recycled. Plan A is a consistent theme, which flows through and underscores much of the content of the company's communications. In the same way, the key messages in the Standard Life communications strategy such as *"helping customers plan for the future"* underpin much of its content.

Channels

Kliatchko's third pillar, Channels covers all of the company's communications tools, such as TV, radio, social media, but also includes all other touch-points for the company's multiple stakeholders. Figure 6.1 illustrates the extent of possible touch-points for a company, and in planning an integrated approach to communications the company needs to consider all of these as channels. Again this fits the Interaction Model of Communications (Baines & Fill, 2014: 355) and the need to understand the audience perspective, their multiple touch-points, sources of information and influences, in order to establish the channels, in the broad sense defined above, which will be most effective in influencing each stakeholder. In some instances this may mean building support among, or addressing the concerns of one stakeholder audience in order to influence another audience. For example when Standard Life went through major structural change in 2006, an extensive campaign was undertaken to convince voting policyholders that this was the best direction for the company. An online blog, run by a small group of policyholders with industry experience, was identified as an important influence as *thought leaders* (Baines and Fill, 2014) on policyholders to vote against the proposed change. Significant effort was then invested in understanding the concerns of the group behind the blog and trying to address these concerns both directly and in the press, targeting business and personal finance journalists. This approach was more effective than trying to persuade policyholders directly, when some of them were heavily influenced by the blog run by a group that they could identify with.

Results

The fourth pillar of Kliatchko's model is Results. Businesses need to take an integrated approach to measuring the effectiveness of their communications by looking at their outcomes in terms of behavioural or attitudinal changes among target stakeholders. As IMC is driven by a strategic focus on stakeholder needs, accountability has to be a central feature of its implementation. A number of financial measures can also be used to measure the effectiveness of IMC, including *customer value*, which looks at the value of individual customers, or *return on customer investment* (ROCI), which compares the spend on a specific target customers with their predicted value in terms of sales.

Kliatchko's model is intended to operate both at a higher strategic level and at a more operational level as an integrated approach to communications. In the Standard Life case study we can see how the high-level strategic communications framework applies both at the strategic level and in a more operational level, managing communications exercises around specific events, such as the example given for a business acquisition. In the example of the acquisition, identification of key stakeholders and their communication needs are central to the communications plan which then integrates activity to address these across both content and channels. Finally, the plan has a set of objectives against which results can be measured.

Another example of the IMC approach in action can be seen in the international retailer Marks and Spencer Group plc. The following mini-case sets out how the group's corporate purpose drives communications strategy and then feeds through to tactical campaign activity, which is integrated across several markets and media.

Mini case: Marks and Spencer Campaign – "The Art of"

The company's 2015 Strategic Report defines the group's core purpose as "*Enhancing Lives Every Day*" through the high quality of its own brand food, clothing and home products. The report identifies the quality and provenance of its products as the group's main source of competitive advantage and therefore central to its brand. The brand is supported by four core values: inspiration, innovation, in-touch and integrity.

The report goes on to identify revenue growth as the overarching strategic objective, but building the group brand is seen as an essential part of this growth strategy. The brand and core values are woven in throughout the report contents, supporting strategy in product and channel development, human resource management, and building and managing relationships with customers, shareholders and other stakeholders.

This strategic focus on quality and provenance flows through the organisation from group strategy to marketing strategy and individual campaign level. In September 2015 the group launched a campaign entitled "*The Art of*", described as "*a new campaign across TV, print and digital platforms designed to put a spotlight on the unique quality and style of M&S products. The new campaign uses a stylish and cutting edge format to celebrate the craftsmanship and fashion credentials across M&S.*" Elements of the campaign were used across 50 different global markets.

The following quote from Patrick Bousquet-Chavanne, Executive Director, Marketing and International, highlights the integrated nature of the communications approach. "*To find a distinctive and consistent voice for Marks and Spencer that creates a more joined up journey and ways of talking about the unique qualities of Marks and Spencer.*"

By talking about creating "a more joined up journey", Bousquet-Chavanne focuses on the needs of customers and the importance of making it easy for them to know what the business stands for.

Source: Marks and Spencer (2015a) , Marks and Spencer (2015b)

The Marks and Spencer mini case highlights an important aspect of integrated marketing communications, which is the need to find the right balance between central control and flexibility for different parts of the business, to respond to the needs of their customers and other stakeholders or local market conditions. This campaign can be traced right back to the group's core purpose and strategic business plan, but is also able to be implemented across 50 different markets. Striking the right balance between centrally determined frameworks and flexibility for subsidiary business units or geographically diverse operations is a critical skill in designing and implementing an IMC approach. While some companies have very uniform approaches to positioning, messaging, tone of voice and look and feel others such as Standard Life and Marks and Spencer have greater flexibility, but all operations will follow some centrally determined brand or messaging guidelines. Lack of integration is more prevalent with social media campaigns, where many of the social media channels are used but only one particular channel is used more than most, for example, Twitter. In addition, there is the issue of detractors, as McDonald's found out, and which has proved to be a lesson to all managers in managing corporate social media consultants (Hill, 2012). The agents launched a Twitter campaign but lost control of the overall picture, and did not realise the volume of detractors. The launch was an invitation to share stories and experiences of McDonald's at #McDStories (via Twitter). Unfortunately, control was lost when detractors turned the campaign into a #bashtag to share their #McDHorrerStories. Thus, the degree of control versus flexibility that is best for any company will depend on a number of factors, including the organisation's history and culture and the sectors and markets in which it operates.

Why IMC is important

Having an integrated approach to communications is increasingly important for organisations because:

■ It makes it easy for customers to know what the organisation stands for

■ Consistent positioning and messaging is needed across multiple media

■ Cross media effects and synergies generated by IMC can impact both brand equity and sales.

■ Once established, IMC infrastructure helps to manage and control unplanned communications, such as responding to negative media coverage.

Producing IMC strategies has become increasingly critical for modern organisations for several reasons. In an increasingly global marketplace for most products and services, consumers face greater choice than ever and look for cues to determine which of the available options best meet their needs. In doing so they will consider information from multiple sources including the media, social media and word of mouth. This makes it vital for brands to have a clear positioning, which allows consumers to understand what they stand for, and that this positioning is consistent across multiple touch-points through which a customer might receive information about them. While companies cannot control word-of-mouth and online chat about themselves, they can work to have a consistent messaging which engages with the relevant audiences in the communications that they do control, such as advertising, and thus influence the way the company is portrayed in the media it does not control, such as word of mouth. Finne and Grönroos (2009) found that consumers also develop their views of brands over time, which means that an integrated approach and consistency of core messaging needs to be sustained over time rather than as a quick fix. As marketing has shifted from a transactional focus to that of customer relationship management (CRM), companies need to be consistent in their positioning and proposition to customers and other stakeholders who are less likely to engage with a company that seems to change its values or market positioning from one month to the next or across different media. It is also important for companies to be consistent in their core positioning and values across different audiences, as many individual customers may also experience the company in other capacities, such as shareholders, employees, suppliers or neighbours. Consistency is therefore important at a number of levels.

The proliferation of media and fragmentation of consumer markets also makes integration vital for many companies. Social and technological advances have led to increasingly fragmented consumer markets, making it more challenging to identify and target sizable customer segments through specific media. At the same time the proliferation of television, radio and other channels, as well as digital media, has resulted in significant fragmentation in media channels. This means that campaigns generally have to be executed across multiple channels to reach their target audiences. Furthermore the value of cross media effects in driving campaign results has been shown in studies such as that of Voorweld et al. (2011), who found that cross media campaigns triggered two positive responses in consumers. First, *multiple source perception* was triggered, where respondents built their perception of a brand from multiple media sources. The second response was *forward encoding*, where consumers' interest is raised in an advertisement where they have previously experienced other related communications. This may mean that a deeper level of processing is applied to the second material encountered. Operating in a multi-media environment requires careful management to ensure an integrated approach and avoid sending mixed messages through the multiple media involved.

Furthermore, an integrated approach to communications can be invaluable for organisations in dealing with any adverse circumstances, as it means that the organisation already has established processes in place to manage communications across all of its channels and audiences. As well as being important in managing day-to-day communications and campaigns, this control is invaluable in the event of a crisis or any event that could potentially be damaging to the organisation. For example, VisitScotland's new '*Autumn Gold*' £1.6m campaign was launched to a London audience two days before the death of Diana, Princess of Wales in August, 1997 and was cancelled as it was felt that even having spent up to £250k on media space, the London audience was not in a favourable frame-of-mind to receive promotional messages and appeals of taking an autumn break in Scotland (Bell, 1997). Thus, having integrated processes in place allows an organisation to respond in a more co-ordinated and controlled way to any unforeseen circumstances. For a large company such as Standard Life, having an integrated communications framework in place is essential in being able to respond to any news or developments either from within the company or in the broader market. In planning any communications project, from responding to media criticism or announcing annual results, having an integrated framework in place gives the organisation much better control over messaging across a broad range of stakeholders, channels and geographic areas.

Finally, since the financial crisis of 2008, marketing departments have been under increased scrutiny and pressure to show that they add tangible value to their organisations in delivering measurable returns. A number of studies have shown the value of an integrated approach to communications. Madharavam et al. (2005) show that synergies and efficiencies generated by IMC play an important role in building and maintaining brand equity, while Reid (2005) also shows a positive link between IMC and brand outcomes including awareness and sales. Focussing on specific communications channels, Spotts et al. (2014) find that publicity can affect the impacts of advertising on increasing sales in business to consumer markets.

As well as being important, IMC also has a number of benefits for organisations when it is effectively implemented. Pickton and Broderick (2005: 28) identify 4Es and 4Cs of IMC to stress the benefits an organisation can gain from IMC. The 4Es and 4Cs, illustrated in Table 6.3 below provide a useful way of remembering the benefit of IMC and ensuring that a business is maximising these in its approach.

There are therefore significant benefits for organisations that can effectively implement and manage IMC, in terms of relationships with customers and other stakeholders and more efficient and effective use of resources in achieving communications objectives. These benefits also combine to generate competitive advantage for organisations through having a clear and consistent proposition to consumers across all touch-points, which is delivered through the most efficient use of resources, enabling companies to get more from their marketing spend than their competitors.

Table 6.3: Pickton and Broderick's 4 C's and 4E's of integrated marketing communications. Adapted from Pickton and Broderick (2005, p28)

Enhancing	The different elements in the communication mix work together to augment and intensify each other.
Economical	Synergies generated make best use of financial and other resources.
Efficient	Doing things the best way to get desired results through more detailed planning across media and tools
Effective	Doing the right things to produce the desired outcome by ensuring the right tools and media are used.
Coherence	Communications are logically connected for customers and other stakeholders.
Consistency	Communications don't contradict or undermine each other but are in tune with each other across media, channels and stakeholders.
Continuity	Messages are connected over time for audiences, building and reinforcing positioning.
Complementary	Communications items work together to deliver communications objectives

The challenges of IMC

Attempts to design and implement an integrated approach to communications may face a number of challenges both from within the organisation and beyond.

Key challenges are:

Within the organisation

- Organisational structures and politics
- Organisational culture and internal communications
- Internal processes

Outside the organisation

- International regulations and cultures
- Agencies
- Distributors and other 3rd parties

One of the biggest challenges is organisational structure, which often mean that the ownership of different communications channels or stakeholders sits with different parts of the organisation and controlled by different managers. For example while all marketing communications tools and channels may be controlled by a central marketing management structure, customer service and sales communications may be the responsibility of other parts of business. For instance, see the BA 'Tailfins' debacle where the marketing department launched a £60m global campaign, which included new logos on planes but did not include the 32,000 BA employees in the planning of the campaign. Lack of buy-in by staff and customers resulted in the Union flag being reinstated on the tailfins. (Marston, 2001). This means all parts of the business have to be bought into the need for integration and may require some managers to relinquish some control. Often politics can act as a barriers to this and some functions such public relations may demand more autonomy for their work.

Organisational culture can also be a barrier to IMC, especially where the culture is such that different parts of the organisation are seen as competing with each other, or where internal cultures differ across the organisation. For example, Ots and Nyilasy (2015) report that where there is a tension between head office and branch cultures this can add to structural challenges in implementing IMC. Linked to this, internal processes and communications can either help or hinder IMC. If internal communications do not promote and support the prioritisation of an integrated approach to customers, then it will not be a priority. Similarly if business processes and technology do not facilitate and support integration, then it is too easy for parts of the business to continue to follow their own agendas.

To overcome challenges from internal structures, politics and cultures, IMC needs to be founded on a strategic decision to pursue integration, which is endorsed and led by senior managers as part of corporate strategy and supported across the organisation in its processes, communications and measures of success.

Where an organisation operates internationally, cultural and other market differences can present problems with integration. For example in China, certain colours carry particular significance, and the colour yellow represents a higher social standing and so needs to be used cautiously. This presented a challenge for Standard Life when setting up a joint venture there, as the company's branding at the time involved a bright shade of yellow. Other challenges can come from nuances of particular words or images used in brand slogans or imagery, but which carry particular connotations in some countries. At the same time culture affects how different nationalities respond to marketing messages and the sorts of messaging and advertising that are most successful in different markets. All of this means that companies must consider local cultures and values when developing IMC, and find a suitable balance between centrally driven positioning and messaging and the needs of local markets.

Where a company works with multiple agencies across different media this can present a challenge to integration, as each agency will have its own interpretation of the brief. Furthermore as strong personalities are often involved, strong management is needed to ensure that the integrity of the positioning and messaging is not diluted or undermined by very different interpretations. Managers responsible for commissioning and managing agencies need to have a very clear view of their positioning and messaging and use this to evaluate all proposed materials. Careful diplomacy may be required to bring some agencies in line with the direction being taken.

Standard Life, which features in Case study 4 in Chapter 11, has faced similar challenges with separate business units in the UK and around the world. The approach by Standard Life was to develop a high-level communications strategy and messaging framework, which supported the group's business strategy. This high-level strategy set out communications objectives and key messages that were agreed to by communications teams across the group. This enabled the group to ensure a level of integration and consistency, whilst also allowing individual business units flexibility in their communications activity to take account of local market conditions.

6

The current drivers of IMC

As consumers become increasingly well informed, connected and critical, having an integrated approach that gives a consistent view of what company stands for is more important than ever. Advances in digital media and how consumers interact with media have huge implications for marketing communications, as software such as Google's Adsense enables a more flexible and real time targeting of consumers, with items that are relevant to them there and then and in the right format for whatever device they are using. At the same time consumers themselves have more control over what they see and are able to share or pass judgements on brands through social media. So while digital advances give advertisers the ability to manage their interaction with consumers at a more individual level, they also have to deal with a more vocal and interactive consumers who will comment on, adapt and share their messaging as they see fit, thus reducing control over how their brand and messaging are seen. Mulhearn (2009) identifies a number of ways in which these developments specifically affect the future of IMC.

- First, consumer insight, which drives IMC, is becoming increasingly sophisticated and enables companies to combine data from multiple sources to build detailed pictures of their consumers, allowing more accurate targeting of campaigns.

- Second, digital media are able to provide valuable live data on consumer behaviours and responses to materials online. This creates the opportunity for much more detailed and responsive planning of campaigns, which previously relied on static demographic categories or previous purchases to identify target customers. This also enables much more precise monitoring and measurement of activities, which should feedback into on-going campaign planning to focus resources where there is greatest success or to improve effort where communications are failing to achieve desired responses.

- Third, digital media make it easier for companies to co-ordinate communications with multiple stakeholder groups. At the same time it means that each stakeholder group is able to see the communication directed at other audiences, which raises the importance of consistency. This also presents opportunities for brands to build communities around them, incorporating a variety of stakeholders.

- Finally, as multiple media channels are deployed in marketing and other communications it becomes easier to integrate communications across media and to ensure consistency.

Digital media and an increasingly global marketplace create great opportunities for increasingly sophisticated integrated communications planning. At the same time this leads to higher expectations from consumers who increasingly expect to receive marketing materials relevant to them and their current circumstances. Consumers are also taking more control over which materials reach them and are more likely to share their views on things they don't like. So while the digital era presents opportunities for integrated marketing, it also presents greater risks for those who get it wrong. For companies that are able to exploit the opportunities of IMC in the digital era, this should give them a source of competitive advantage in being able to target more relevant content to more specific groups of clients, thus building stronger relationships and strengthening brand equity.

Further resources and reading

The Institute of Practitioners in Advertising – www.ipa.co.uk

The Institute of Promotional Marketing – www.theipm.org.uk

The Chartered Institute of Marketing (CIM) - www.cim.co.uk

Kliatchko, J. (2008) Revisiting the IMC Construct: a revised definition and four pillars, *International Journal of Advertising*, **27**(1), 133-160

Review questions

1. What should IMC be driven by?

   a) The marketing department
   b) The SWOT analysis
   c) The marketing strategy
   d) Competitor analysis

2. What does the interaction model of communications stress interaction between?

   a) Consumers
   b) Staff
   c) Media
   d) All of these

3. In Kliatchko's model of IMC, what does the content column refer to?

   a) Sales materials developed by the company
   b) Media coverage of the company
   c) All communications by and about the company
   d) The companies key messages

4. What are customer touch-points?

   a) Anything tangible related to the company that customers can touch
   b) All customer service interactions
   c) Any contact the customer has with the company or about it
   d) Anything the company sends to customers

5. What does the financial measure ROCI help companies to understand?

   a) How much return they get from their marketing budget
   b) Their return for spend on particular customer groups
   c) The return for spend on individual customers
   d) The rate of customers expressing interest in the company

6. What is multiple source perception?

   a) Consumer buy products and services from multiple sources
   b) Consumers build their perceptions from multiple media sources
   c) Consumer perceive some sources of information to be better than others
   d) Consumers have mixed perceptions of media sources

7. What are the main considerations that need to be balanced in IMC?

   a) Foreign and local languages
   b) Central control and business unit autonomy
   c) Costs and likely income
   d) The needs of customers and distributors

6

8. Why does tennis player Andy Murray appear in Standard Life's website for Hong Kong but not the Republic of Ireland (ROI)?

   a) Tennis is less popular in the ROI than rugby and golf, but popular in Hong Kong

   b) He offended Irish people in a press interview

   c) As a British sports star he relevant to expat residents in Hong Kong but not to Irish consumers

   d) It is more cost effective for the Hong Kong marketing team to copy content from the group website than to devise its own.

9. The 4 columns in Kliatchko's model are?

   a) Customers, competencies, channels and media

   b) Stakeholders, channels, content, results

   c) Stakeholders, media, tools, touch-points

   d) Clients, channels, content, visuals

10. What does Kiatchko mean when he talks about stakeholders?

   a) Shareholders

   b) Customers and staff

   c) Customers, staff and shareholders

   d) All of the organisation's audiences

Answers

The answers to these questions can be found at the back of this book, or at the Marketing Communications page at Goodfellow Publishers:

https://www.goodfellowpublishers.com

References

Baines, P. & Fill, C. (2014) *Marketing*. 3rd ed. Oxford University Press.

Bell G (1997) Personal communication by email/telecon. Featherbrooksbank Media Agency, Edinburgh. August/September, 1997.

CIM (2015) Available from http://www.cimmarketingexpert.co.uk/wp/?wpp=the%20development%20of%20integrated%20marketing%20communications%20(IMC)&WPID=3277.

Finne, A. & Grönroos, C. (2009) Rethinking marketing communication: From integrated marketing communication to relationship communication'. *Journal of Marketing Communications*, **15**(203) 179-195.

Hill, K. (2012) #McDStories: when a hashtag becomes a bashtag. *Forbes Magazine*. www.forbes.com/sites/kashmirhill/2012/01/24/mcdstories-when-a-hashtag

-becomes-a-bashtag/#1e2d2261193f.

Keller, K.L. (2001) Mastering the marketing communications mix: Micro and macro perspectives on integrated marketing communication programs, *Journal of Marketing Management*, **17**(2), 819-847

Kliatchko, J. (2008) Revisiting the IMC Construct: a revised definition and four pillars, *International Journal of Advertising*, **27**(1), 133-160

Kotler, P. (2000) *Marketing Management*, London, Prentice-Hall.

Madhavaram, S., Badrinarayanan, V., & McDonald, R. E. (2005). Integrated marketing communication (IMC) and brand identity as critical components of brand equity strategy: A conceptual framework and research propositions. *Journal of Advertising*, **34**(4), 69-80.

Marks and Spencer (2015a) Press Release: The Art Of Campaign For Autumn 2015. http://corporate.marksandspencer.com/media/press-releases/2015/the-art-of-campaign-for-autumn-15

Marks and Spencer (2015b) Strategic Report 2015, http://corporate.marksandspencer.com/media/ad70c9716d2041cc89cdd3821f1e53e6

Marks and Spencer (2016) Welcome to Plan A, http://corporate.marksandspencer.com/plan-a

Marston, P. (2001) http://www.telegraph.co.uk/news/uknews/1329843/BA-restores-Union-flag-design-to-all-tailfins.html.

Mulhearn, F. (2009) Integrated Marketing Communications: From media channels to digital connectivity. *Journal of Marketing Communications*, **15**(2-3) 85-101.

Ots, M. & Nyilasy, G. (2015) Integrated Marketing Communications (IMC): Why does it fail?, *Journal of Advertising Research*, **55**(2), 132-45.

Pickton, D. and Broderick, A. (2005). *Integrated Marketing Communications*. Harlow, UK: Pearson Education.

Reid, M. (2005). Performance auditing of Integrated Marketing Communication (IMC) actions and outcomes. *Journal of Advertising*, **34**(4) 41-54.

Spotts, H., Weinberger, M.G. & Weinberger, M.F., (2014) Publicity and advertising:what matter most for sales?, *European Journal of Marketing*, **48**(11/12), 1986-2008

Voorveld, H., Neijens, P. & Smit, E. (2011) Opening the black box: Understanding cross-media effects, *Journal of Marketing Communications*, **17**(2), 69-85

6

7 Creativity in Advertising and Promotion

Babak Taheri

This chapter aims to make sense of creativity within the context of marketing management and marketing communications. Moreover, it specifically addresses the topics of advertising and promotion. In the first instance, it takes creativity to mean the 'big idea' in marketing management, then it tackles creativity in the production and translation of images and other creative materials used in advertising. These two interpretations of creativity make up what is referred to as the 'the creative platform' in advertising and promotion, oftentimes known as 'the creative', or simply as 'the creative treatment', especially amongst agents and practitioners designing, developing and producing creative marketing materials.

Why does creativity in advertising matter?

Advertising matters because, according to a recent report by Deloitte (2013), it Advertising matters because, just look at advertising expenditure in the UK. According to a recent report by UK Advertising Association and (2023), UK Ad Market reached £31.9bn in 2021, supporting creative industries and associated employment.. For example, there are the TV and cinema screens as well as the pages of newspapers and magazines, and the space on billboards and in social media. Alongside which there is also the presence in web searches. Within the digital economy, advertising funds the majority of content and services, supporting online consumer research and boosting e-commerce. However, the impact, arguably, stretches across the economy, because it also enables markets to be more efficient. For instance, advertising is at the core of the cycle of competition, innovation and businesses. An increase in advertising spend elevates competition, improving quality and pricing for consumers. Advertising Association evaluations that UK ad spending of £31.9bn results in a figure of £190 billion contribution to GDP for 2023.

One of the essential points in how well advertising may or may not work, is the notion of creativity, which according to Smith and Yang (2004) is a key factor on how effective your advertising can be. The authors assert that creativity contributes to the above-effectiveness equation. As well as advertising paying, as outlined above, there are several other variables that are known to drive advertising effectiveness. For instance, we know how persuasive a selling message can be, along with the fact that the larger your market share is the more likely your advertising is going to perform. And we also know that the execution and delivery is important, for example, media choices, timing and resources. And so, the question is, what contribution does creativity make to the advertisement and does creative advertising matter?

Dahlen et al. (2008) carried out an experiment where they exposed over 1000 consumers to a variety of different creative treatments of the same advert. The most creative of these adverts were selected and agreed as best practice exemplars by an expert panel of advertising executives. Results showed that the consumers who had been exposed to these creative exemplars perceived the brand to be of a higher quality, the sender (firm) to be smarter and the proposition to be superior, and that the firm was much more likely to develop more interesting products in the future.

Therefore, creativity can be seen as a further driver of advertising effectiveness. It is a multiplier in its effect. Dahlen et al (2010: 319) quotes the American Association of National Advertisers as saying that the *"selling power of a creative idea can exceed that of an ordinary idea by a multiple of 10"*. And they describe people's reactions to ads as a continuum from a "Ha!", to an 'Aha!' to an 'Ah!'.[1] This expression of evaluating creative advertising is summarised below as:

Table 7.1: Dahlen's Response Continuum

Ha!	Aha!	Ah!
That's original	Aha, so that's what it means	Ah, that's clever

Source: Dahlen et al (2010: 319); and see Lehnert et al (2014: 275)

Ad repetition plays a crucial role in advertising, as it helps to familiarize consumers with the message, ultimately increasing brand recognition and effectiveness.

---

1 See Kounios, J. and Beeman, M. (2009). The Aha! moment: the cognitive neuroscience of insight. *Current Directions in Psychological Science.* **18** (4) 210-216. The authors underpin the science of the eureka moment which forms the basis of development of Dahlen's approach to evaluating creative advertising using a response continuum.

Typically, the impact of repeated ad exposures follows an inverted U-shape curve: initial repetitions lead to increased positive responses (wear-in), but after a certain point, further repetitions result in decreased effectiveness and even negative responses (wear-out). Chen et al. (2016) reveal that creativity significantly alters this pattern. Creative ads, characterized by high divergence, referring to how novel or unique an ad is to the consumer, and relevance, referring to how meaningful and valuable the ad, do not only achieve immediate wear-in but also show remarkable resistance to wear-out. This means that creative advertisements remain engaging and effective for a longer period, even with repeated exposures, compared to less creative ones

Defining a creative advertisement

In dictionary terms, to create something implies making something new by way of a form which requires imagination and skill. The ideal is that the onlooker responds to it positively. This is underpinned by two approaches to creativity: one is about newness and imagination and the second is about appropriateness and/or solving an issue. Thus, an effective creative advert is defined as:

> *"A creative ad is perceived by its audience to be novel and different, and whose central message is interpreted meaningfully by, and connects with its audience."* Ang et al. (2007: 232).

7

Characteristics which determines advertising effectiveness

Two dimensions are noted: *divergence* (new, novel, unique) and *relevance* (important, of value and appropriate) as being the two main determinants of creativity in advertising (Smith & Yang, 2004). This is interpreted and summarised in Table 7.2

Table 7.2: Determinants of advertising effectiveness

<u>**Divergent**</u> - Ad contains 5 elements that have:

- **Originality** = novel, unique, surprising
- **Flexibility** = able to switch perspectives/ viewpoints easily and quickly
- **Synthesis** = able to integrate and blend easily with other ideas/platforms
- **Artistic Value** = able to express richness in humour, colour, fantasy and artistic impressions, & aesthetic representations
- **Elaboration** = able to extend above & beyond

Relevance - conveys meaningful info:

- **Ad-to-consumer**: stimulus elements of the advert which create a meaningful link, e.g. music, voice-over, touchstone or situation linking to Generation X for instance.

- **Brand-to-consumer**: stimulus elements and/or useful information attained from the ad which creates & reinforces deeper meaningful links, e.g. Twiggy in M&S ads shows Baby Boomers how to wear the garment/what you would look like, or Apple's iPOD showed audience how to dance and have fun with its new music technology.

In this context, the authors have added a sub-text to the point of relevance, as illustrated in Table 7.2. What they suggest is that connectedness goes beyond relevance as being meaningful. It does this because relevance implies that ad information is relevant to the product and thus meaningful, whereas connectedness is connecting to the target audience, and also where the audience is connecting to the advert by being the ad co-creator (Thompson & Malaviya, 2013), implying that co-ownership deepens the connection. Hence ad creativity has the three notable dimensions which make up an ad creativity cube:

- novel (divergent)
- meaningful (conveying data in relation to product) and
- connectedness (to, and 'co-owned' by, the target audience).

How the three dimensions work together is complex, but Ang et al's (2007) 'ad creativity cube' suggests that in pursuing creativity, managers should not necessarily emphasize novelty at the expense of meaningfulness and connectedness. Whilst novelty allows ads to cut through clutter, ads need to adhere to relevant product meaningfulness and be connected to the audience to be effective. Thus, novelty, combined with meaningfulness and connectedness, takes account of both the advertiser and the audience perspectives. Moreover, the ad creativity cube proposes that creative ads which exemplify all three dimensions would generate better recall, more positive feelings, and more favourable attitudes than less creative adverts (Ang et al., 2014). In other words, the creativity cube is more likely to get us, the consumer, to better attend to advertisements.

This helps us to understand the effort by managers to include consumers in the creation of advertising or even in the evaluation of ad concepts, such as Samsung, Dove, Converse and so on. (See *Converse 'Brand Democracy' campaign wins award*.) Likewise, it also suggests that advertising which has explicit direction, for instance a strategic goal, and which scores well against the dimensions of creativity, is more likely be to be successful, but this is not necessarily the case. A compelling and creative advertisement may miss its strategic goal, and still score highly as being creative, and vice versa. And an advert which falls short against the creative dimensions may of course fulfil its strategic intent (Lehnert et al., 2014:275). An example would be where the source is judged in a positive or negative manner.

Source Credibility Theory (SCT) tells us that consumers view the integrity of products and services based on source. Any form of communications, whether it be face-to-face, written text or by electronic means, has been found to be highly influenced by the perceived credibility of the source of the communications. This being the case means that we can take it that SCT forms the basis for shaping persuasive marketing communications along with building both reputation and brands.

Coca-Cola's "Real Magic" Campaign

Coca-Cola launched its new global brand philosophy and platform called "Real Magic" in 2021. This innovative campaign refreshed the brand's promise to unite and uplift people, drawing from recent global experiences to highlight the magic that happens when people come together in unexpected ways.

The "Real Magic" platform, emphasizing dichotomies like being both humble and iconic, aims to make the world more interesting. Manolo Arroyo, Chief Marketing Officer for The Coca-Cola Company, stated that this philosophy captures Coca-Cola's essence: a real taste that is unique and magical. The campaign introduced a refreshed visual identity and a new "Hug" logo, which frames moments of magic across Coca-Cola's communications.

"Real Magic" includes creative collaborations with artists, photographers, and illustrators to depict moments of everyday magic in inclusive and expressive ways. Notably, Coca-Cola partnered with Wieden+Kennedy London, KnownUnknown, and Kenyon Weston for the visual identity, including photography, animations, and illustrations.

The inaugural campaign, *"One Coke Away From Each Other,"* launched digitally on September 27, 2021. This campaign blends real and virtual worlds to celebrate common humanity, featuring gamers DJ Alan Walker, Team Liquid's Aerial Powers, and Average Jonas.

Coca-Cola's collaboration with the gaming community is a key aspect of the "Real Magic" campaign. Partnering with Twitch's Brand Partnership Studio, Coca-Cola created an interactive code hunt starting on October 11, 2021. Fans could win prizes, including gameplay sessions with celebrity gamers, by finding hidden codes within the campaign's film. Twitch gaming creators unlocked additional codes during their livestreams.

7

By engaging with the gaming community and incorporating real and virtual interactions, Coca-Cola aims to create unique experiences. The "Real Magic" platform seeks to increase the Coca-Cola consumer base through experiences tied to consumption occasions and consumer passion points like music and gaming.

"Real Magic" is a long-term brand philosophy guiding Coca-Cola's marketing and communications. As Arroyo noted, it supports Coca-Cola's purpose to refresh the world and make a difference, serving as the North Star for the brand's next chapter.

Through this campaign, Coca-Cola demonstrates how brands can innovate by blending traditional advertising with digital engagement, particularly within the gaming community. The "Real Magic" campaign represents a modern approach to brand marketing, leveraging diverse creative collaborations and interactive digital experiences to connect with consumers on a deeper level.

For more details on this campaign, visit: https://www.businesswire.com/news/home/20210929005116/en/The-Coca-Cola-Company-Unveils-New-Global-Brand-Platform-for-Coca-Cola-Trademark

Lowry et al. (2008; 2014), for instance, explain how we treat websites as 'surrogates' of the underlying company.

Websites express both visual and nonverbal traits and are an effective exemplar of *surface credibility* (see Table 7.3, based on Fogg, 2003a, as cited in Lowry et al., 2014).

Table 7.3: Type of source credibility

	Meaning	Example
Surface credibility	Our first impressions of external or surface traits; those on the 'face of' something (judging a book by its cover).	Judging someone or something by initial inspection – the way someone looks; what a firm stands for on first sight of its logo/webpage; product packaging – for me, or not for me.
Presumed credibility	We believe something to be more credible because of all the general assumptions we hold	A known brand is better than an unknown brand; a more organised fashion retail environment is better than a disorganised one
Reputed credibility	Credibility that comes from a third party reference point	A recommendation from a friend, family member, colleague to buy/not to buy
Earned credibility	Derived from past experience with this entity – person or object	Colleague has positive past experience so this particular music festival is credible

Credibility can be broken down into three sub-dimensions each with several traits, according to Lowry et al. (2013) and these are:

- ◼ **trustworthiness** – safety, fair, honest and just

- ◼ **expertise** – trained, experienced, skilled and authoritative

- ◼ **dynamism** – energetic, fast, colourful, bold, consistent and interactive.

In advertising contexts, especially online, marketing and sales information is framed using these credibility traits in presenting data. But contemporary communications is challenging the status quo. Take for example crowdsourcing – the making of information for the people by the people – which is becoming increasingly important in an advertiser's toolkit. According to Aquino (2013: 31) crowdsourcing is advertising which is commissioned by companies and supplied by the public. Crowdsourcing hooks into the creativity of the masses as a means of increasing engagement and getting fresh content. Intel, for example, invited Millennials to enter into a contest to design a 60 second TV/viral advert around the question "What does Intel mean to you?" and the result was a large volume of submissions. The key for Intel is to show how vital their feedback is, and they do this by connecting more deeply with their millions of Facebook 'fans'. The advantage for firms is that they are initiating a conversation on the one hand, and accruing much needed branded artwork on the other. Fans of this method of creating advertising say that it is about good storytelling, because the stories have an authenticity about them, whereas critics point out that it is speculative and lowers the value of design services. Whatever your view, curating crowdsourcing does require someone to sift through a pile of submissions and take an impression of the creative treatment and make a judgement.

The creative platform: a framework for understanding creativity in advertising

This discussion centres on the creative product, as per Sasser and Koslow's creativity framework (2008), which specifically defines the creative product as that which relates to creativity within the marketing materials in applied contexts. It does not include either media channels (place) or a focus on addressing how consumers think (process) and consume, and thus respond, to advertising (people). Within the creativity framework, the creative product is taken to mean the creative product/deliverables or creative materials which are subject to content analysis (e.g. pictures, print and billboard ads, video recordings, movies, pictures, radio ads, and so on)

However, it is important to note that what shapes and drives creativity is the both the product and other deliverables; and a good starting point is creating a 'frame of reference' (Kotler et al., 2016; Keller, 2013).

Creative platform: shaped by positioning

A frame of reference is shaped by identifying not only the target market but also the competition. This is where an understanding of consumer behaviour is vital, for example, the factors that consumers consider in making choices. In addition, the likely intentions of other brands needs to be considered. Where the product sits by way of category is important here. Consumers process data to help them compare products and also they seek out the criteria which they will use to like one product over another. A competitive frame of reference draws on consumer behaviour, marketing management and competitive strategy and this is what underscores the positioning, customer-value proposition or promise and the brand associations which are translated into creative executions containing the message and appeal – this is then what drives and shapes creativity in advertising. This includes creativity in the form of a 'big idea', which is used as the creative platform, positioning and anchoring the advertising across all elements of the communications mix, and also enabling the development of an 'image' in the minds of the audience. It does this by using creative devices such as humour, music, fun, art, adventure and so on, which makes the message more compelling and appealing and makes us sit up and attend to the communications. A deeper discussion on the positioning concept can be found in Chapters 1, 4 and 5.

The creative platform: translating the creative idea

Once the strategic and tactical positioning has been agreed, the message design has to be developed and created. The creative treatment, the translation of the creative idea into creative materials, signals an assurance about the brand so creativity needs to be aligned to the promise (customer-focused proposition). This forms the basis of the marketing communications 'creative brief'. The brand positioning has not yet formed in consumer's minds – the actual communications do this, and do it by projecting a coherent, single voice which reflects and reinforces an ongoing storyline to which the target audience can engage and connect and even help to co-create. The clearer the proposition, the easier it is to execute. In summary, the best propositions are the ones that are the most easily understood, because this makes it possible to communicate a brand's position in an original, attention-getting, but easy-to-catch way – and that is fundamentally the essence of the creative idea (De Pelsmacker et al., 2013).

Strategies for making creative advertising generate increased attention

The 'creative' interpretation of marketing communications strategy involves a creative idea which acts as a conduit for orchestrating communications across different types of platforms such as advertising, brand-led communications or participatory interactions (this is discussed in detail in Chapter 4).

We know that creative adverts are those that are viewed as being divergent, containing elements of novelty, aesthetic expression and which are different and new, and that they make a strong connection. That being said, how do you actually make what you want to say more appealing? In other words, what strategies can you draw on to design, develop and produce advertising that is deemed to be highly creative? Creative strategies are the way marketers translate their messages into a specific communication.

Informational and transformational appeals

Creative strategies can be classified into two general strategies: *informational* and *transformational* appeals (Kotler et al., 2016; Fill & Turnbull, 2016). Within the process of designing advertising communication, the two creative motivations – informational and transformational appeals, have several different creative approaches which can be specifically applied to this general categorisation of creative strategy. These creative approaches are discussed and laid out below.

Informational: rational processing

Informational appeals are motivations that appeal to those consumers who have a need for information to help them solve a problem by alleviating negative concerns. A general 'rule of thumb' here is that the market offering tends to be around pricing and quality.

Informational appeals tend to be directed at motivations which are negatively charged, where the feelings of concerns can be reduced by acquiring the relevant information/direction to the product or service.

Table 7.4: Informational: problem-solving through logic and reason

Creative appeal	Typical sponsor	For example
Source of problem	Healthcare and detergents – solves a problem	Nurofen "fast targeted relief from pain" or 'kills 99.9% of household germs'
Clear benefit	Household cleaners	"Cillit Bang and the dirt is gone" or a hand wash that "…kills 99.9% of bacteria.."

Product comparison	Best deals such as comparison websites/best service/quality	"Sky TV offers the best satellite programmes", or "To be the best" in the British Army, or Sony Bravia's "Like no other colour"
Testimonial	Celebrity endorser/ influencer	The celebrity/actress, Joanna Lumley endorses Sky TV, whilst Brian Cox (physicist) is used as an expert (influencer) for UK T&I in "Exporting is Great" Britain.

Transformational: emotional feelings

This is where the proposition or promise, relates to consumer feelings. The appeal is designed to 'transform' behaviour in that the intention is to change the end-user's emotional state in order to effect a change of behaviour.

Table 7.5a: Transformational: negative appeals

Creative appeal	Typical sponsor	Source/example
Fear, anxiety, distress, guilt, shame.	Charities, and government, and also trade associations. For instance, fundraising, social care, animal protection, adult/child social issues	Cancer UK "loss" of a loved-one, Save the Children, RSPCA, Alcohol abuse "Drink Responsibly", and personal care such as 'Brush your teeth'!
Stop (what you're doing) – dread, alarm, worry, surprise	Government – Public Liability/ duty of care to public eg health departments, safe transport,	Stop smoking, Drive safely, Safe sex/sexual disease.

Table 7.5b: Transformational: positive appeals

Creative appeal: Humour, love, pride, joy, happiness, laughter – uses borrowed-interest devices, e.g.	Typical sponsor	Source/example
Babies, children	Family health sector, food/ drink, outdoor activity	Education sector, Nestle, Kraft, Cadbury, Unilever and P&G
Animals/puppies	Low-involvement goods/ services. Animation technique becoming increasingly popular especially in new media.	Andrex toilet paper puppy; Dulux dog; McVitie's biscuits; Meerkats in www.gocompare.com; Cadbury's chocolate
Popular music	Lifestyle -fashion, motor, food/drink, entertainment.	See Insight re: *Paloma Faith*, p. 162

| Provocative sex | As above, especially textiles/ fashion, beauty. | Calvin Klein, and perfume ads, e.g. DVB |
| Surprise/astonishment, awesome/'wow' | As above, especially, drinks, entertainment, sport, leisure | Schweppes' 'sizzle'; Coca Cola's 'Taste' |

Borrowed-interest devices are a means of providing a 'hook' to wrap-up your creative treatment. They attract attention and raise the consumer's involvement in the advertising, which in turn increases persuasion and intention. Most brands capitalise on using this technique as a means of cutting through the 'clutter' of today's modern communications environment. Animation in particular is becoming a short-cut to making advertisements more creative in terms of costs of production, and more appealing in terms of attention.

Forcing and subversion

Whilst the informational and transformational appeals provide a classification as to motivation, Fill and Turbull (2016) cite the methods of forcing and subversion as being the two key creative tactics of note as a means of getting people to sit-up and take note, that is, attend to your advertising.

- **Forcing** is where the advert forces you to attention through surprise, or shock tactics or through being irreverent in 'far-fetched way'. Examples include Apple's famous "1984" advert shown during the Super-Bowl of 1984, but where Apple mocked IBM, leading the George Orwell estate to regard it as an infringement of copyright. This advert was subsequently hailed as a masterpiece in advertising and garnered a lot of 'hype' around Apple in terms of how dare it take on the might of IBM. Other examples might be AIDS[2] 'tombstone' which forced us to talk about sexual health in the 1980s, and Australia's "Where the bloody hell are you?" for cultural offence, and more recently Honda's 'car crash' which negatively correlated with the idea of driving freely and safely.

- **Subversion** on the other hand, is where the advert seduces you into a world which is mellow, comfortable, blissful – almost divine! M&S used this strategy with its ads featuring the seductive voice-over of Irish actress, Dervla Kirwan. These ads have not been shown in the UK for the last 10 years but are still memorable – who can forget the 2005 chocolate pudding advert with a sultry female voice telling us that *"this is not just any chocolate pudding, but a Marks and Spencer chocolate pudding!"* Consequently, sales increased ten-fold around the time it was aired and for some considerable time after. See the case study in Chapter 11, where Marks and Spencer once again tries to seduce us with its food advertising.

2   See www.bbc.co.uk/news/magazine-15886670 for more information on this campaign.

Creative content: framing creative appeals

The content of creative advertising is structured around positive and negative appeals underpinned by sociology and psychology (Tsai, 2002) and are based on the hedonic principles of approach to happiness and our avoidance of pain.

- **Positive framing** is where we pursue a positive outcome – such as psychological or monetary advantage, and is supported by the **approach** principle, which is to maximise our happiness, e.g. subverting you to eat chocolate.

- **Negative framing**, in contrast, centres on negative outcomes (psychological or monetary loss) and is based on the **avoidance** principle to minimise pain/loss, e.g. the forcing you to attend to an anti-smoking advert.

The choice appeal is dependent on whether your advertising has a motivation to inform, or one to transform behaviour through emotional appeal. Either way, both use aesthetic appeals by way of creative techniques such as storytelling, music, animation, fear/shock, fantasy and surrealism and humour. There is room here to explore storytelling, and humour and music in more detail.

Storytelling

Stories and storytelling, because of their ability to influence and persuade us, has long been a tradition in our way of life. We tend to think naturally in a story-like form and this form is organised in such a way that stories help us to make sense of our world – explaining things, making decisions, creating identities and trying to motivate others with our storytelling abilities. Stories, be they scripts, maps, metaphors or models, are narratives that help us organise our experiences in such a way as to give structure. Moreover, they are easily absorbed. Stories are a type of discourse that draws on poetic and literary genres, and which adhere to dramaturgical styles, most of which is delivered with plenty of ceremony in mind (Whittle et al, 2009: 426). The more exciting the story, the more tension is built and disequilibrium is created relative to our balanced state (Söderlund & Dahlén, 2010).

Therefore, it is every advertiser's intent to exploit the mediated environment available, e.g. advert, TV programme, film, novel, package and event, and create a narrative which typically embeds a story in the form of entertainment, emotion and heightened spectacle. While the story is more likely to be fictional, it can still be personally relevant and provoke authentic reactions - who didn't cry when Elsa the lioness died during *Born Free*? Pop a box of cereal in the film-footage and we'll gladly eat "Simba's best breakfast flakes"!). Soderlund and Dahlen note that some authors have tried to explain the paradox whereby we experience *"emotions from stimuli that are obviously not real by stressing that our thoughts (i.e. our imagination) can elicit emotions if we are willing to inactivate our beliefs that the story is not real. We appear to be willing to do so"* (2010: 1815). Once we are immersed, we then cluster our further thoughts which are inferred by the story.

A computer vision technology company in the UK, called GumGum, has developed a b2b marketing campaign by asking creative agencies to 'reimagine' seminal campaigns. The Reimaging Advertising campaign asks industry creative chiefs what they would do, given the new media environment, with seminal television campaigns. One of the campaigns they've had to look at is the seminal Nescafe Gold campaign which ran from 1987 to 1993 (https://www.youtube.com/watch?v=RyLHK77YhGQ). Nescafe, and McCann Erickson, all but invented the art of storytelling with the love story of two opposites (actors Tony Head and Sharon Maughan) who slowly attract over a cup of Gold Blend coffee. The adverts themselves became the focus of PR attention with news of a new advert featuring an update of the love story eagerly awaited. In reimagining the campaign, none of the industry stalwarts wanted to deviate from the story, given the new media environments. Of note is that the story still holds sway and new media is used to enhance and extend the reach across the variety of platforms that are now available. As expected, technology plays a bigger part in the story-lines, e.g. kettles and coffee machines, but so does the end-user in co-creating the next phase of the storyline. One idea is to co-create the storylines into valid scripts in order to increase the depth of tension and excitement in waiting for the next instalment, and then for the client/agency to release the TV commercial and develop competitions to see whose draft story was closest to the paid-scriptwriters. The story has been changed to reflect current lifestyles – still the 'boy-girl' romance but with surprise. Meanwhile, Nescafe Gold Blend is the number one coffee brand in the UK (The Independent, 1998; The Drum, 2016) and stories are underpinning digital media as being a key feature of user generated content (UGC). Fill et al. (2013: 752) organises storytelling around two key points of themes and plot. Within these two points are clustered several elements of storytelling. Themes, for instance, include hardship, reciprocity, anticipation and defining moments, and for plot there are the likely elements of help along the way, crises and goal achievement. Again, this outline applies to digital media and creating short films for viral use. The idea here, in terms of co-creation, is to get the consumer to become part of the story themselves, and for the story to underpin word-of-mouth (WOM) which is a key means of communicating and advertising.

Exercise

Collect a couple of adverts from both online and a magazine collection that are deemed to be revealing, interesting and different. Discuss and evaluate them using Arkwright's strategy for storytelling in creative advertising.

Arkwright (2014) suggests that we follow five key questions in developing strategies for good storytelling for advertising:

Table 7.6: Arkwright's key questions in developing strategies for storytelling

Strategy	Question	Creative idea/example
Ideological connection	What is the connection with the brand's past?	Snickers – 'Diva' or 'Warrior' knows how to satisfy hunger (see Mr Bean below)
Deeper connections – level of purpose & emotion	Why (not what)	Persil (OMO) 'Dirt is Good' where it's OK to be dirty because I'm a kid and it's good for me.
Find the brand's resolution	What is the deep desire the brand realises, or what is the deep problem in resolves	BMWs 'MINI UK' which is a great ride! Apple iPOD gives me music on the move.
Experiential (rituals)	Can the story be told by experience (and not just words)	Exhilaration (MINI UK); Attraction (Nescafe Gold); Heritage (Hovis); Togetherness (Harley Davidson)
Innovate (reimagine the brand in the future)	Can the brand's story (central idea) be extended across multi-platforms? Can you create a new chapter in the story?	Aesthetic (Apple)

Source: www.marketingmagazine.co.uk and see Arkwright (2014) .

Mr Bean sells Snickers

Rowan Atkinson returns to advertising Snickers for Mars Chocolate UK. The British comedian, Rowan Atkinson, has returned to advertising and is reprising his Mr Bean character in a martial arts spoof. He stars as a Kung Fu master who is not quite feeling himself until he eats a Snickers bar with the proposition being "You're not you when you're hungry". The promise is that because you are very hungry, you turn into something else, for example in a previous execution the celebrity actress Joan Collins was featured behaving like a 'diva' whose behaviour was somewhat questionable. You then have a Snickers bar and your behaviour returns to normal. In the current commercial, Rowan Atkinson plays his iconic character Mr Bean – a character who is comically absurd, awkward, foolish, and yet hilariously funny and beloved by us all. The opening depicts a rooftop scene which reminds us of martial art epics such as 'Crouching Tiger, Hidden Dragon' where one of the group of warriors turns into Mr Bean making the group realise that they have a hopeless warrior in their midst and they don't like this because they want someone who can show what he's made of. He eats his Snickers and returns to being an adventurous and courageous warrior with intent. The commercial has been made in Mandarin with English subtitles reflecting the global target audience as well as the heritage of the ad. This humourous episode has translated well into an extended campaign which features TV, cinema, trade, social media, events and sponsorship. Several other executions are in the pipeline and still featuring Mr Bean in his typically calamitous scenarios.

Sources: Campaign (2014) and Adweek (2014)

Humour

No discussion on creating appeals in advertising would be complete without mention of the use of humour. Humour crosses all boundaries – both country, culture and peoples. Mr Bean was successful in every country not only because of humour (he is depicted in funny, wacky, haphazard situations) and British irony, but because of the technique of mime where the character Mr Bean expresses himself visually through storytelling in an entertaining and humorous way – there is no text – no voice-over to reinforce meaning and support the content. Critics often refer to Mr Bean as being the ultimate situation comedy. In the case of Mr Bean, visual rhetoric predominates where the consideration is in how images work alone or in partnership with other elements (such as humour and music) to create a line of reasoning to connect to an audience to get them to attend to it and provoke a reaction – drama, entertainment, advertising (Borghini et al., 2010). Rhetorical communication includes both verbal and visual, for example in animation and storytelling, and can also be used in isolation, such as the visual rhetoric in Mr Bean, which has been reconfigured creatively in pastiche and parody, or the verbal rhetoric in an advert with just large text such as the The Economist's "Trump Donald" or "To Be" posters. All of which are humourist depictions of advertising reflecting popular culture and art. In fact, on occasion, the advertising does become art (e.g. Nescafe Gold Blend, product placement in James Bond's Skyfall, and Guinness 'surfer') whereby the advert becomes the focus of the media itself.

Rhetorical convention in advertising uses both visual and verbal creative codes captured from material culture such as irony, playfulness, exaggeration, paradox, metaphor, pastiche (imitation) and parody (satire) and as such are used in-the-moment to reflect current cultural contexts. These codes drive persuasion and are therefore part of the rhetoric and creativity in advertising.

Music

A popular means of connecting your brand with consumers is through music. Brands increasingly recognise the value of music in dramatizing their adverts to enhance engagement and boost brand awareness and appeal. There is no doubt that the 1985 Levi commercial called 'launderette' which featured a rendition of the classic Motown track *I Heard It Through the Grapevine* awakened both the advertising and pop music industry to the potential of working together. Fast forward to 2015, and the two sectors are 'locked in an ever more mutually-reliant relationship' (Burgoyne, 2015) so much so, that the music embedded in the John Lewis seasonal advertisement adds to its 'sonic identity', meaning that music may not just be a short term tactical measure but a more strategic long term asset.

According to the British Phonographic Industry (BPI, 2016), the top three industries making the most of music in adverts in 2015 were motoring (Ford, Honda and Volkswagen), food (Sainsbury's, Waitrose and Tesco) and fashion (H&M, JD Williams and House of Fraser), while the brands that turned to music most often for their ads were Apple, who topped the chart with 23 tracks synched to adverts, followed by Tesco with 17 and MacDonald's with 10. It also reveals that pop music which is 5 years old or less, is the number one choice for brands reaching out to younger consumers accounting for nearly a quarter (24.%) of music used in ads, as opposed to heritage recordings that are 20 years or older. BRIT awards CEO, Geoff Taylor, strongly supports an increased collaboration between the advertising and music industry by reinforcing that music plays a vital role in strengthening the appeal of the narrative, making the broadcast, be it a TV drama or an advert, more memorable and giving it stand-out, thus forging a deeper emotional engagement between the viewer and the content.

Insight: Having Faith on your side could guarantee a hit product!

The British Phonographic Industry (BPI) has recently published research (June, 2016) which confirms advertisements as being a key channel for British popular tunes. Music recordings or 'syncs' (synchronisation – the use of music in an ad, film or video game) from British acts accounted for 41% of the tracks used by brands and creative agencies to promote products and services to the public. Leading the way was premier British female artist Paloma Faith, whose music was synced by four major brands (Calvin Klein, Dixons, Simply Be and Eastern Western) in 2015. Faith's hit song *Ready for the Good Life* also lays claim to being the 'most synced' song of 2015 which she shares with Motown classic *Sunny*. Relative newcomers Jess Glynne, Ella Eyre, Charlie XCX and Foxes also led the way with their sounds accompanying adverts for well-known brands such as Emporio Armani, Coca-Cola, O2 and H&M as well as campaigns by Oxfam, National Citizen Service and the United Nations.

Ian Neil of Sony Music UK pays testament to Faith's appeal saying that her principal draw to advertisers is that of a talented artist. *Upside Down* has been a popular track for several years but her breakthrough came with her "astonishing" take on the INXS classic *Never Tear Us Apart* for John Lewis, which has also been licensed by Calvin Klein. And of course, *Ready for the Good Life* conveys the "perfect message for advertisers".

Historically, artists have always been reluctant to allow their music to be used in advertising writes Fildes in *The Times* (10.06.2016), mainly because of artistic control, but the downturn in record sales and smaller deals from record labels have made synchronisation much more appealing to artists to generate more income.

In fact, sync remains an important revenue stream for the whole of the UK music business. Income from music synchronisation to adverts, video games, TV programmes, films and trailers totalled £22.68 million in 2015, up 13.5% on the previous year. TV advertising does best, followed by video games. However, at a global level, the sector is dominated by the USA with 57% of all synch revenues generated – out of a total global revenue estimated to be valued at $335m - with the UK capturing only 9% of worldwide income.

Adapted by G Bell from *The Times* 10/06/2016, UK Trade & Investment and see BPI, https://www.bpi.co.uk/media for more details.

An area that is becoming more important is in the trade of *synchronisation* or sync. (See the *Insight* into Paloma Faith's success.) This is an industry term where the holder to the rights to a piece of music licenses a song or piece of music to a third party who will place the music into audio visual content such as advertisements, trailers, video games, films and TV programmes (BPI, 2016; Burgoyne, 2015). This collaboration requires all partners to work together, for example, the artist, the artist's management, the music publisher, the record label and the creative agency syncing the new production. The British government agency, United Kingdom Trade and Investment (UKTI) supports an annual trade mission to the USA which enables networking amongst the UK delegation of creative industries in an effort to expand and build future relationships in this sector. This just shows how important this sector is in terms of export of services especially within the area of TV drama.

There is no doubt then, that for brands, a popular and successful music track (and even artist) can be a short cut to the emotional connection that is agreed to be so important in contemporary marketing communications. John Lewis has built a musical world around its brand. It does this by treating music as a core element in its mix, linking the music into its tone of voice (slow and measured) which further illustrates what John Lewis stands for – its values, beliefs, trust. Arguably, it is using music not only to achieve short term objectives, but to also tap into the consumer's deep subconscious, thus creating emotive reactions around its brand values in order to achieve long lasting equity. Sonic branding, as a dimension in both marketing management and marketing communications adds to creative strategy by creating brand expression in sound and providing consistency across all touch points. A brand's armoury would be weakened if it did not have sonic branding to express emotion – as long as it is part of a coherent approach and not bolted-on as an afterthought.

Summary

Advertising is often referred to as the *"last remaining unfair competitive advantage"* (IPA, 2007) and this is because it is one of the key variables that can make *"all other things unequal"*. Thus it is key, because advertising has considerable power and influence in conveying a good idea. This influence is underpinned by the view that creative advertising is perceived as being *"more favourable, more likeable and more able to bestow value on brands"* (West et al., 2008: 35). Creativity in advertising allows brands to stand out and to influence customer decision making.

This chapter acknowledges that marketing communications draws on consumption, but its emphasis here is on how marketers and 'creatives' develop, design and produce creative advertisements and other marketing materials – hence it takes an organisational point of view in the managing and supply of creative advertising.

Recommended reading

Ang, S.H., Lee, Y.H. & Leong, S.M. (2007) The Ad Creativity Cube: conceptualisation and initial validation. *Journal of the Academy of Marketing Science.* **35**, 220-232.

This paper explains the ad creativity cube in more detail.

Bernardin, T., Kemp-Robertson, P., Stewart, D.W., Cheng, Y., Wan, H., Rossiter, J.R., et al. (2008) Envisioning the future of advertising creativity research: Alternative perspectives, *Journal of Advertising*, **37** (4), 139-144).

This will be useful to those looking to carry out further research into this topic.

Darley, W. K., & Lim, J.-S. (2023). Advertising creativity and its effects: A meta-analysis of the moderating role of modality. *Marketing Letters*, **34**(1), 99–111.

This paper uses a meta-analysis of 48 studies to explore how traditional and non-traditional media moderate the effects of ad creativity on cognition, attitudes, and behavioral intentions.

Reinartz, W. & Saffert, P. (2013) Creativity in advertising: when it works and when it doesn't. *Harvard Business Review.* June. 107-112.

The authors carry out research into the dimensions of creativity. They then divide the dimensions into 'pairings' to assess the least and most likely pairings to affect creativity in advertising.

Rosengren, S., Eisend, M., Koslow, S., & Dahlen, M. (2020). A meta-analysis of when and how advertising creativity works. *Journal of Marketing*, **84**(6), 39–56.

Despite its recognized importance, the marketing literature lacks a comprehensive empirical understanding of how and when advertising creativity is effective. This paper employs a meta-analysis to consolidate findings from 93 data sets, revealing the significant impact of creativity on advertising while emphasizing the roles of originality and appropriateness.

7

Review questions

1. A creative ad is perceived by its audience to be

   a) Novel, different and meaningful to its audience
   b) Novel, meaningful and connects with audiences
   c) Novel, meaningful and excites the audience
   d) Novel, new and appropriate for the audience

2. Which five key elements best describe an advert which is considered to be divergent (novel)

   a) Originality, flexibility, synthesis, management value and elaboration
   b) Originality, flexibility, synthesis, organisational value and elaboration
   c) Originality, flexibility, synthesis, artistic value and elaboration
   d) Originality, flexibility, synthesis, monetary value and elaboration

3. Surface credibility is a type of credibility which is a component part of what type of theory

   a) Source Credibility Theory
   b) Presumed Credibility Theory
   c) Reputed Credibility Theory
   d) Earned Credibility Theory

4. Sasser & Koslow's 2008 creativity framework includes

   a) People who create advertising and people who consume advertising
   b) Process whereby the creator and the consumer follow stages of thinking and understanding
   c) Place where advertising is created and the environment where it is consumed
   d) Product creation which are the creative materials subject to content analysis
   e) All of the above

5. A customer-focused value proposition includes

   a) Functional, emotional and societal benefits of the offering
   b) Functional, environmental and societal benefits of the offering
   c) Functional, equality and societal benefits of the offering
   d) Functional, ecological and societal benefits of the offering

6. Borrowed interest devices are a means of

   a) Looking at you through a lens
   b) Hooking you into the artwork
   c) Booking you for aesthetic damage
   d) Cooking for you with recipes

7. Transformation appeals are motivations where the creative approach is both positive and negative.

   a) True
   b) False

8. Advertising has creative appeals designed to

   a) Covert you thereby forcing attention
   b) Overt and force you to attend to it
   c) Assert force on you to attend to it
   d) Force and subvert you to attention

9. The more exciting the story (in the advert) the more

   a) Tension is built up and disequilibrium is created
   b) Apprehension is built up and disequilibrium is created
   c) Stimulation is built up and disequilibrium is created
   d) All of the above

10. In advertising, good story-telling has to be

   a) Innovative, connected, deep, resolute and experiential
   b) Innovative, shallow, connected, resolute and experiential
   c) Innovative, connected, dissolving, deep and experiential
   d) Innovative, experiential, disengaging, resolute and deep

7

Answers

The answers to these questions can be found at the back of this book, or at the Marketing Communications page at Goodfellow Publishers:

https://www.goodfellowpublishers.com

References

Adweek (2014) Mr Bean is a hopeless Kung Fu warrior. www.adweek.com/adfreak/mr-bean

Arkwright, D. (2014) Dirt is good: how storytelling gave Persil a boost. *Marketing*. www.marketingmagazine.co.uk

Ang, S.H., Lee, Y.H. & Leong, S.M. (2007) The ad creativity cube: conceptualisation and initial validation. *Journal of the Academy of Marketing Science*, **35**, 220-232.

Ang, S.H., Leong, S.M., Lee, Y.H. & Lou, S.L. (2014) Necessary but not sufficient: Beyond novelty in advertising creativity. *Journal of Marketing Communications*, **20**(3) 214-230.

Aquino, J. (2013) The pros and cons of crowdsourcing. *Customer Relationship Management*. **17**(2) 31-34.

Borghini, S., Visconti, L., Anderson, L. and Sherry, J.F. Jnr (2010) Symbiotic postures of commercial advertising and street art. *Journal of Advertising*, **39**(3) 113-126.

British Phonographic Industry (BPI) (2016) British Female Artists are spot on for music 'synch' TV ads. www.bpi.co.uk/media-centre/British_female_artists_spot_on_for-music_sync.aspx.

Burgoyne, P (2015) The Creative Review Report: Music. *The Creative Review*. **35** (1). Centaur Communications.

Campaign (2014) Rowan Atkinson returns to ads after an 18 year break. www.campaignlive.co.uk/article/

Chen, J., Yang, X., & Smith, R. E. (2016). The effects of creativity on advertising wear-in and wear-out. *Journal of the Academy of Marketing Science*, **44** (3), 334–349.

Dahlen, M., Lange, F. & Smith, T. (2010) *Marketing Communications: a brand narrative approach*. UK: J. Wiley & Sons.

Dahlen, M., Rosengren, S. & Torn, F. (2008) The waste in advertising creativity is the part that matters. *Journal of Advertising Research*, **48** (3) 392-403

Deloitte LLP (2013) *Advertising Pays: How advertising fuels the UK economy*. An AA/WARC Report.

De Pelsmacker, P., Geuens, M. & Van Den Bergh, J. (2013) *Marketing Communications: a European Perspective*, UK: Pearson

Drum (2016) Nescafe's Golden Blend couple: how would today's marketers reimagine this classic ad campaign www.thedrum.com.

Fill, C. & Turnbull, S. (2016) *Marketing Communications*. 7th ed. Pearson.

Fill, C., Hughes, G. & de Francesco, S. (2013) *Advertising: Strategy, creativity and media*. Pearson.

Independent (1998) TV Ad: Gold Blend – Another saga in the ultimate coffee break. http://www.independent.co.uk/life-style/tv-ad-gold-blend--another-saga-in-the-ultimate-coffee-break-1145610.html# (accessed 19/02/1998)

IPA (2007) *Judging Creative Ideas*. Institute of Practitioners in Advertising.

Keller, K.L. 2013. *Strategic Brand Management: Building, measuring and managing brand equity*. 4th ed. Pearson.

Kotler, P., Keller, K.L., Brady, M., Goodman, M. & Hansen, T. (2016) *Marketing Management*, 3rd ed. Pearson.

Koslow, S. (2015) I love creative advertising: what it is, when to call for it, and how to achieve it. *Journal of Advertising Research*. **55**(1) 5-8.

Lehnert, K., Till, B. D. & Ospina, J. M. (2014) Advertising creativity: the role of divergence versus meaningfulness. *Journal of Advertising*, **43**, (3), 274-285.

Lowry, P.B., Vance, A., Moody, G., Beckman, B. & Read, A. (2008). Explaining and predicting the impact of branding alliances and web site quality on initial consumer trust of e-commerce web sites. *Journal of Management Information Systems*, **24**, 199-224.

Lowry, P.B., Wilson, D.W. & Haig, W.L. (2014) A picture is worth a thousand words: Source Credibility Theory applied to logo & website design for heightened credibility and consumer trust. *International Journal of Human-Computer Interaction*, **30**, 63-93.

Rosengren, S., Eisend, M., Koslow, S., & Dahlen, M. (2020). A meta-analysis of when and how advertising creativity works. *Journal of Marketing*, **84**(6), 39–56.

Sasser, S.L. & Koslow, S. (2008) Desperately seeking advertising creativity. *Journal of Advertising*. **37** (4) 5-19.

Söderlund, M. & Dahlén, M. (2010) The "killer" ad: an assessment of advertising violence. *European Journal of Marketing*, **44**(11/12) 1811 - 1838

Smith, R. & Yang,. X (2004). Toward a general theory of creativity in advertising: Examining the role of divergence. *Marketing Theory*, **4**(1/2), 31-58.

Thompson, D. V. & Malaviya, P. (2013) Consumer-generated ads: Does awareness of advertising co-creation help or hurt persuasion. *Journal of Marketing*, **44**, 33-47.

Tsai, S. (2002) Message framing strategy for brand communications, *Journal of Advertising Research,* **47**(3), 364-380

West, D. C., Kover, A. J. & Caruana, A. (2008) Practitioner and customer views of advertising creativity: same concept, different meaning? *Journal of Advertising*, **37**(4), 35-45.

Whittle, A., Mueller, F. & Mangan, A. (2009) 'Storytelling and 'Character': Victims, villains and heroes in a case of technological change. *Organization*, **16**(3) 425-442.

7

8 Digital Media and Marketing Interactivity

Kathryn Waite and Rodrigo Perez-Vega

Do you receive marketing communications using digital technology such as a smart phone, a tablet, a computer? Then you are a consumer of digital media. Digital media is an example of a *disruptive technology* (Bower & Christensen, 1995). A disruptive technology transforms the way that business is conducted within a sector, and digital media have transformed communication industries such as television broadcasting, film, journalism, publishing and music. For example, the digitisation of music has reduced the demand for records, cassettes and CDs, and has resulted in music sales taking place online rather than through physical stores. More recently, technologies like generative AI are disrupting how media is created, and it brings new challenges and opportunities for marketing practice. One of the most urgent questions that organisations are asking themselves today is: "How do we make sure that we are using digital media to the best effect within our marketing communications?" What follows is an overview of the core knowledge areas that will help you navigate this exciting new communications landscape.

Defining digital media

Digital media can be audio, video, written or image-based material that has been digitally compressed (encoded), transmitted and then decoded (activated) upon a digital device. Analogue or 'traditional' media such as print and broadcast media differs from digital media in terms the ease and the degree to which it can be accessed, shared, modified and stored. Analogue media is 'push media', where communications are broadcast to a passive audience of viewers, readers or listeners (Jørgensen & Knudsen, 2022). Digital media is 'pull media', or a form of 'inbound marketing', where the individual actively seeks information and interacts with brands (Haldbork and Hongsmark 2022). 'Push media' places an advertising message within a marketplace; in contrast pull-media facilitates and stimulates interactions (Mollen & Wilson, 2010).

A key factor determining the choice of digital channel within integrated campaigns is the degree of interactivity.

Interactivity

An interaction occurs when an object has an intended effect upon the other, for example during the process of communication. The addition of "ivity" signifies that interact*ivity* refers to the quality and process of interaction taking place. Consumers like interactivity and this leads to a positive attitude towards the digital communication (Lou et al., 2015). According to Liu and Shrum (2002) there are three dimensions of interactivity: active control, two-way communication and synchronicity (Table 8.1).

Table 8.1: Three dimensions of interactivity. Adapted from Liu and Shrum, 2002

Dimension of interactivity	Definition	Digital communications example
Active control	Voluntary and instrumental action that directly influences the controller's experience	Banner advertisements that allow you to click through.
Two-way communication	Implicit or explicit reciprocal communication	Changing the ads that you see based on previous search tracking (implicit) Online chat with a organisation representative (explicit)
Synchronicity	The delay between sending a message and receiving a reply. Digital media provide an almost instant response.	Entering a search term and getting an immediate response. Customisation of page content

A communications strategy of maximum interactivity would be challenging and expensive. Consumers differ in terms of how much interactivity they want, and some do not value interactivity as highly as others, which means that an increase of interactivity might result in a reduction of message effectiveness (Kim et al., 2011). For example, *digital immigrants* (consumers born before 1980) do not value two-way communication as much as *digital natives* (consumers born after 1980) (Prensky, 2001; Kirk et al., 2015). This means that managers should critically evaluate the degree of each dimension of interactivity for the characteristics of their target audience.

Exercise

Select three digital marketing communications that you saw today, one from e-mail, one from social media and one from a webpage. For each digital marketing communication identify the extent to which you had active control, two-way communication and the degree of synchronicity. Assess whether an increase in interactivity would have increased or reduced the effectiveness of the advertisement for you.

Evolution of communication models

In response to digital disruption, marketing communication models have evolved to account for one-to-many to a many-to-many interactivity (Table 8.2). The one-to-many model represents a one-way communication process where a message is formulated, sent, received and decoded. This does not account for the interactivity that characterises digital media. The one-to-one model reflects developments in digital communications that enable consumers to engage not only in communication with a brand but also with each other in a dialogue. A many-to-many model is where customers can interact with other customers and with the brand (Hoffman & Novak, 1996). This is called a "trialogue" (Chaffey & Ellis-Chadwick, 2022).

8

Table 8.2: Differences between communications models

Communication model	Description	Example
One-to-many model	One source contacts many receivers with one message, the medium does not allow the customers to respond to the brand	Television advert
One-to-one model	One source contacts each recipient with a different personalised message and the customers can each respond to the source through the same medium	E-mail advertisement
Many-to-many model	One source sends a different message to each participant , customers can each send a message to each other, response to each sender- receiver can be made through the same medium	Social media post

Selecting digital platforms

Digital media provides choice in where, how and when communications are accessed, and this causes two types of fragmentation: *audience* and *digital*.

- **Audience** fragmentation refers to a situation whereby individuals make significantly different communication choices that result in a loss of a common understanding and a reduction in social cohesion (Sunstein, 2009). Audience fragmentation means a reduction in the effectiveness of mass communications strategies that are associated with analogue media, for example booking advertising slots at peak viewing times or placing advertisements on the back page of a popular magazine (Chafee & Metzger, 2000). Hence audience fragmentation means that the "reach" (or viewing figures) of analogue communication is reduced.

- **Digital** fragmentation refers to the proliferation in the number and form of devices and platforms upon which the individual accesses digital content. Consumers are moving from device to device and even use devices and platforms simultaneously. This activity means consumer decision-making involves overlapping and multiple sources of information (Powers et al., 2012). Digital fragmentation increases the need for integrated campaign strategies that work together across a range of digital channels and which avoid wasted expenditure and audience attention fatigue, whilst being sensitive to the needs of different consumer groups. Selecting the appropriate platforms for a marketing communication campaign is key to achieving strategic objectives.

Digital channels are selected according to *reach*, *impact* and *control*.

- **Reach** is measured as the number of times content is accessed, the number of page visits and the time spent on a particular page. A visit, or session, is a "single set of continuous activity attributable to a cookied browser or user which results in one or more pulled text and/or graphics downloads from a site" (Capacity Grid, 2015). Cookies, which are a small data packets placed on the browser, distinguish individual browsers (Google, 2015). However, a cookie does not measure the use of more than one browser (PC + table + smartphone) or the sharing of a browser (two or more people sharing the same computer).

- Digital channel impact is measured using online customer engagement (OCE). OCE can be active or passive and is a key digital communication success measure (Morgan-Thomas & Veloutsou, 2013). Active OCE includes: message creation, content sharing and commenting on the content provided by others, whilst passive OCE includes liking a fan page and viewing content

(Mollen & Wilson, 2010). OCE can be evaluated using either quantity or quality measures. Quantity measures count the actions of consumers in response to a digital campaign such as the likes given to a brand, the number of brand followers and the number of times a piece of digital content is shared. Quality measures categorise the nature of the action taken, such as whether a positive or negative comment is made about a brand, satisfaction ratings, whether comments were made on shared content and the length of posts given and whether these are made over a period of time.

- Digital channels differ in the level of marketer **control** (Fill, 2009). Social media facilitates communication among consumers and empowers consumers to actively seek and share information (Rezabakhsh et al., 2006; Harrison & Waite, 2015). It is usual to classify digital media into owned, paid and earned media (Table 8.3).

Table 8.3: Media types and digital platforms. Adapted from: Corcoran, 2009

Media type	Definition	Examples
Owned media	Digital platforms owned by or managed by the organisation	Organisation website Organisation blog Facebook Fan page Organisation's Twitter account
Paid media	Where the organisation is paying for content to be placed on a digital platform	Display ads (banners) in third party websites Sponsored posts in third party blogs
Earned media	Where the organisation "earns" mentions on digital media	Non-paid mentions in third party websites Mentions in social media (Facebook, Twitter, blogs) User reviews

Each media type has strengths and weaknesses.

- **Owned** media gives the maximum level of organisational control but can be considered as less credible as it can be biased towards the organisation (Chu and Kim, 2011). The reach and frequency of owned media is many times lower than with other types, unless the owned media has a high volume of organic traffic already visiting the sites. In addition, owned media in Web 2.0 platforms such as blogs or Facebook fan pages are susceptible to the effects of highly engaged consumers who can express their views and affect both positively and negatively the organisation's image.

- **Paid** media allows for very specific segmentation of viewers in terms of geographic and psychographic variables. In paid media the organisation has control over what is being said, as well as the frequency of message display.

However, consumers can have "advertising blindness" which means they ignore paid media on digital platforms (Margarida Barreto, 2013).

- **Earned** media is a form of word-of-mouth (see next section). Earned media is perceived as being the most credible and unbiased. However, organisations have limited control over message content, which can be not only positive but also negative. There is also no organisational control over reach. Positive messages on earned media can have a lesser reach if not complemented by other paid marketing efforts (such as paid posts), however negative messages can become viral and out of control.

The concept of eWOM

Marketing messages that use the opinion of other consumers are very powerful. Word-of-mouth (WOM) influences consumer choice, consumer expectations and attitudes, before and after purchase (De Bruyn & Lilien, 2008; Bone, 1995). Electronic word of mouth or eWOM is "any positive and negative statements made by potential, actual, or former customers about a product or organisation, which is made available to a multitude of people and institutions via the Internet"(Hennig-Thurau et al., 2003: 39). The difference between WOM and eWOM is that eWOM is accessible online. eWOM is considered to be commercially unbiased, and is usually supported by the degree of trustworthiness that the source has, whether that source is a friend or someone who is respected such as an expert or a celebrity.

Exercise

Organisations are trying to promote the generation of positive eWOM from their customers. Identify three organisations from different industries and list the activities that they are doing in order to achieve this goal.

eWOM characteristics

There are five main characteristics of eWOM communication according to literature (Table 8.4): valence, focus, timing, solicitation and intervention (Christodoulides et al., 2012; Yang et al., 2012).

Table 8.4: Five eWOM Characteristics

Characteristic	Definition
Valence	How positive or negative the message transmitted by the sender is.
Timing	When the message is received, i.e. pre- or post-purchase
Focus	The audience(s) of the communication and the outcome desired from that audience
Solicitation	Whether the message was sought by the users, of if the user had access to that experience without asking for it.
Intervention	The efforts that organisations make to promote the interaction between consumers within their own controlled platform

- **Valence** can be complex. Positive messages help to sell a product, but negative valence can also positively affect awareness of certain products and increase purchase likelihood if the receiver does not identify with the sender, i.e. you might like restaurants your parents do not like.

- The **timing** of eWOM can have a significant effect on product evaluation (Arndt, 1967; Herr et al., 1991; De Bruyn and Lilien, 2008; Bone, 1995; Lim & Chung, 2011). eWOM from other consumers prior, during and after their purchase can influence not only purchase but also post-purchase satisfaction.

- **Focus** means not only targeting prospective customers of a product but also a wider audience who might be linked to the brand, for example employees, suppliers, job-seekers for recruitment, as well as decision influencers and referrers. For example, recruitment eWOM is found on websites such as Glassdoor, where current employees share their work satisfaction rankings, their salary and the questions they were asked at interview.

- **Solicited** eWOM is more influential than unsolicited; since the receiver is actively seeking information. However, unsolicited eWOM is most common and passes as informal conversation between friends. As Table 8.5 shows consumers might share eWOM for reasons such as self-involvement or to find relief for the tensions that the purchase originated. Certain social media websites (e.g. Facebook Check-ins, Linked-In Sponsored Stories, Instagram picture postings) push unsolicited eWOM messages to their users. Indeed, additional exposure to brand names and logos increases the probability of product purchase through creating familiarity and awareness (Mitchell & Valenzuela, 2005).

- Organisations might promote and reward eWOM. This is called **intervention**. For example, organisations might allow their consumers to review their products or send direct emails in order to entice customers to generate reviews based on their experience.

Motivations behind eWOM communication

Understanding the motives that consumers have to generate eWOM is important as it can help organisations develop activities to harness this type of marketing communication. One of the most prominent studies in this subject is Dichter's work (1966) that identifies four main motivations: product-involvement, self-involvement, other-involvement, and message-involvement. However, the study only considered traditional WOM and did not account for the possibility of positive and negative valence of this type of communication. A later study by Sundaram et al. (1998) takes into consideration the valence of WOM communication and identifies four motivations for positive WOM and four for negative WOM (Table 8.5).

Table 8.5: Motivations for the generation of positive and negative eWOM. Adapted from: Sundaram et al. (1998)

eWOM valence	Motivation	Description
Positive eWOM	Altruism	Consumers want to help other consumers to make satisfying purchase decisions.
	Product-involvement	Consumers' use of the product/service is highly important that speaking about it helps vent those positive feelings.
	Self-enhancement	Consumers share their experiences to enhance their image among other by projecting themselves as intelligent shoppers.
	Helping the organisation	Similar to altruism, only that in this case the consumer wants to help the organisation because of the positive experience that they had with it.
Negative eWOM	Altruism	Consumers want to help other consumers by preventing other consumers experiencing the same problems that they had encountered.
	Anxiety reduction	Consumers want to share their negative experience with others in order to reduce their own anger, anxiety and frustration.
	Vengeance	Consumers express their negative experiences publicly to retaliate against the organisation associated to that experience.
	Advice seeking	Consumers share their negative experience with the intention to get advice on how to resolve their problems.

Organisations looking to generate positive eWOM among consumers should take into account the different motivations behind the generation of it. Organisations taking a passive approach to eWOM would not try to facilitate the generation of this valuable type of marketing communication, and would let consumers express themselves in online media without enticing and monitoring the generation of this type of messages. An organisation taking an active approach would generate the platforms where consumers can express themselves, and set in place mechanisms that would entice consumers to express their views. For example, several mobile applications introduced pop-up messages for their users to share their views on the app via online reviews. These pop-up messages appear a few days after the consumers has been using the app (Figure 8.1). Consumers agreeing to share their views of the app may do so from a desire to be altruistic for other prospective users and spare them the bad experience of downloading the app if it crashes and has many bugs, or to download it if its performance is considered beneficial or enjoyable.

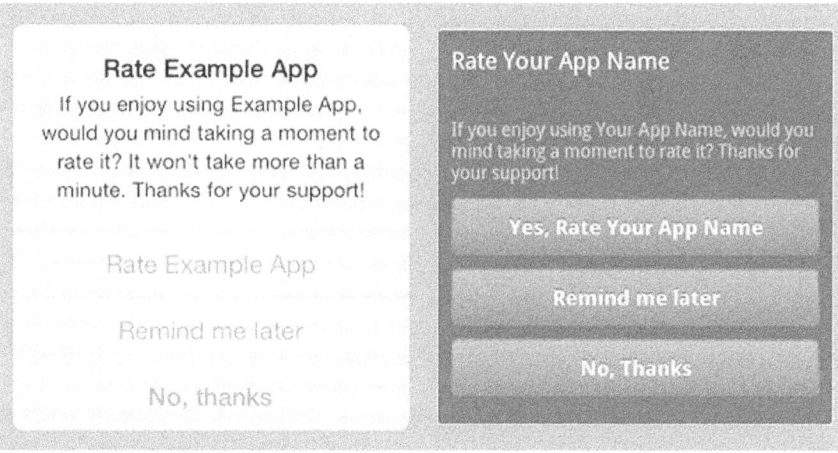

Figure 8.1: Example of online mechanisms to encourage eWOM in mobile applications. Source: Kissmetrics, N.D.

Viral marketing

Viral marketing is when consumers mutually share and spread marketing information, initially sent out by marketers to stimulate and capitalise on word of mouth (WOM) behaviours (Hinz et al., 2011). There are several advantages to viral campaigns. The content is a form of e-WOM which gives the message credibility (Dobele et al., 2007: 292). Viral campaigns can be cost-effective and able to reach niche consumer groups, which solves the problem of audience fragmentation (Dobele et al., 2005). However, viral campaigns offer limited control over the message reach, the speed of spread and message content. Viral campaigns can be a stimulus for user generated content or UGC and the original message can be reformulated either positively or negatively.

Planning a viral campaign

The key elements of planning a viral marketing campaign are shown in Figure 8.2.

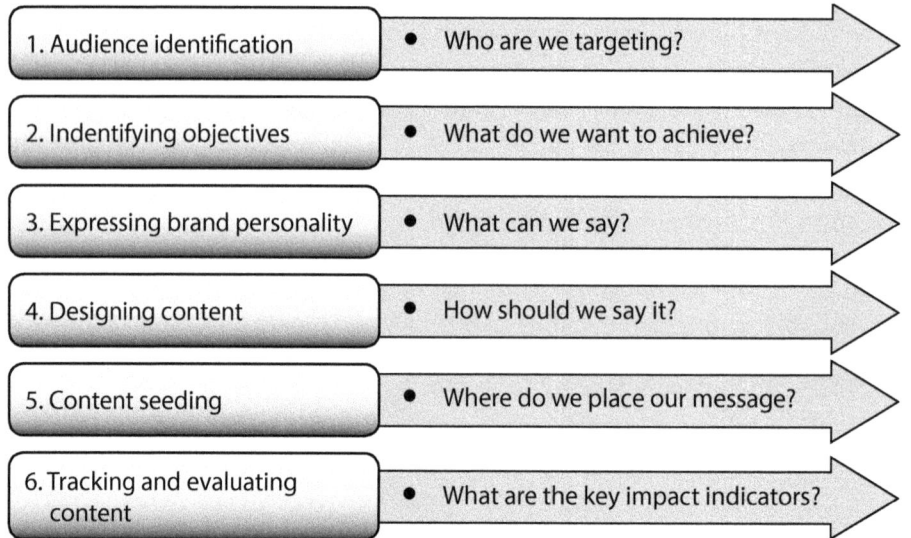

Figure 8.2: Planning a viral campaign

Viral audience identification? Who are we targeting?

Consumers generally dismiss digital mass messaging, which is often called 'spam'. This means it is important to use segmentation to define the target audience and fine tune the message in terms of content and placement. In addition to using behavioural, psychological and demographic profile variables, we can also use digital technology to define the target audience. For example, a leisure organisation found that the majority of the women between the ages of 18-34 years within its target audience used Facebook and tended to access this platform through smart phones when commuting. It is important not confuse the terms *target audience* and *target market*.

- A **target market** comprises the people we wish to buy and use the product or service.

- A **target audience** includes not only potential consumers but also influencers, who shape the opinions and behaviours of the target market (Pickton & Broderick, 2005). Influencers might be the consumer's social circle, celebrities or experts, such as bloggers, tweeters or vloggers (video bloggers).

Organisations can use a range of online monitoring tools to identify influencers such as: Hootsuite, Synthesio, Radian6, Brandwatch, Lithium and Socialradar.

For example, Facebook uses an algorithm called EdgeRank to decide who will see a Facebook Fan page post depending on the type of message, how the user has interacted before with that message and the temporal immediacy of the message itself (Edgerank, 2015). In choosing which tool to use, it is important to check that it meets the criteria listed in Table 8.6.

Table 8.6: Criteria for selecting an online monitoring tool

Criteria	Key criteria	Key questions
Platform coverage	Does the tool pull data from platforms that are of importance for the brand?	Is there coverage of both social and mainstream media? Can this tool be used for a range of languages and countries? How long does an enquiry take?
Data presentation	Is the data presented in a way that is informative, engaging and interactive?	Are real-time dashboards available? Can the dashboard be customised? Can data be exported and stored?
Data analysis	Can we apply the appropriate filters to group data in a way that is meaningful for our brand?	Can we analyse responses but age, gender, country, interests, influence etc? Is trend analysis available?
Data drill down	Is it possible to move from headline results to finer levels of detail?	Can we see how the follower base breaks down across social networks? Can we measure positive and negative sentiment?

Exercise

Visit the website of one or more organisations that provide online monitoring tools to learn about what the range of services they offer; focus if you can on the client case studies. Use Table 8.6 to differentiate the organisations.

Viral campaign objectives: What do we want to achieve?

Viral campaign objectives will link to the overall marketing communications objectives and strategic plan (see Chapter 4). Table 8.7 summarises objectives for a viral campaign. I is common to have several objectives but all viral campaigns need the message to be shared (a conative marketing objective). For example, a car manufacturer combined multiple objectives to gain insight into the barriers to adoption of one of its brands. A viral campaign used a short video clip of a car being parked into a particularly tight parking space. An analysis of shares and likes showed that female drivers tended to forward the clip with supportive and positive comments, whilst male drivers tended to forward the clip with negative comments. Based on this insight the organisation designed a follow-up marketing campaign using the positive sentiments and targeted female drivers.

Table 8.7: Viral communication objectives

Objective	Definition	Example
Conative	Aiming to result in a particular form of behaviour	Purchase or product through accessing voucher
		User engagement such sharing content
Affective	Seeking to change or reinforce attitudes	Liking a particular post
		Communicating humour
Cognitive	Aiming to create knowledge and awareness	Communicating a particular idea about an issue

Brand personality: What can we say?

A brand personality is "the set of human characteristics associated with a brand" (Aaker, 1997: 347). Brand personalities differ along key dimensions such as sincerity, excitement, competence and sophistication (Ivens & Valta, 2012). Brand personality can be expressed in social media through the brand's "tone of voice", which covers vocabulary, grammar and register (mood). Several organisations issue tone of voice documents, which outline whether the brand would write posts that were, for example, formal or chatty, detached or warm, professional or wacky, serious or humorous, relaxed or lively. The brand personality guidelines may cover not only how the brand communicates proactively but also how it responds to customers.

Viral content design: How should we say it?

Viral content should make a connection with the consumer (Dobele et al., 2007). In Chapter 7 you read how advertising appeals can be divided into rational and emotional appeals. Viral campaigns are successful if they make an emotional connection (Eckler & Bolls, 2011). Surprise, joy, sadness, anger, fear and disgust all result in message forwarding behaviour, and messages that combine humour and surprise are more likely to be shared (Dobele et al., 2007). In addition, campaigns which are high in uniqueness create a 'buzz' which results in more sharing (Dobele et al., 2007: 292).

Viral content seeding: Where do we place our message?

Content seeding is the planned release of content within digital channels and involves not only channel selection but the order of use. Simple seeding is where the content is initiated within owned media, and advanced seeding is where content is placed within earned or paid media. Advance seeding involves more effort, cost and planning, however if the appropriate influencers are selected then the campaign may spread faster and further than only using owned media. The aim of content seeding is to get content read, noticed and spread, and it is possible to use advertising consultants who specialise in content seeding.

Evaluating viral campaign impact: What are the key performance indicators?

Each person who shares a viral campaign validates its content and increases its reach. Barker et al. (2012) identify three forms of sharing:

- **Primary** sharing, when the creator posts content online,
- **Secondary** sharing, when fans, friends and customers spread the video within their social circles and
- **Tertiary** sharing, when content is shared by individuals who have no connection with the original video's creator i.e. non-customers.

Other forms of OCE are adapting and mimicking of the original content as discussed in *Old Spice* Case study in Chapter 11. A very successful viral campaign might become an internet meme, which is when a message stimulates UGC that spreads rapidly. An example meme is the 'Ice bucket challenge' (IBC), which involved each person being filmed having a bucket of water with ice cubes in it poured over their head, and sharing this on social media to raise money for the charity, Amyotrophic Lateral Sclerosis association (Motor Neurone Disease Association in the UK). As of 2014, there had been 2.4 million videos placed on Facebook and 28 million people had made IBC related posts.

Digital media in the era of generative AI

Generative AI refers to a subset of artificial intelligence (AI) that focuses on creating new data or content. It involves algorithms that can generate new content, such as images, text, or even music, based on patterns and examples in the data they have been trained on (Kshetri et al., 2023). Some example of commercially available GenAI tools include Chat GPT, Gemini and Midjourney. Generative AI poses several new opportunities to marketers, including the ability to create new content in different formats in a rapid manner, which can allow for hyper-personalisation of campaigns through the use of digital channels (Wu & Wen, 2021). Another benefit can be the possibility to brainstorm ideas or improve copy based on parameters that are prompted to the technology. All these potential benefits are thought to improve performance for brands and marketing practitioners. Some early studies in relation to the use of Gen AI in marketing have found that use of Chat GPT among marketing practitioners improved their performance by 40% (TED, 2023).

Despite its potential benefits, there are also concerns around the biases that these algorithms could bring, since they have been trained using datasets that contain them (Davenport et al., 2020). This also poses important challenges to creativity, as wider adoption of these technologies could easily lead to less differentiation (Cambell et al., 2022). There are also concerns about the potential harm that deepfakes could cause, particularly since images could be used to spread misinformation. Therefore, while generative AI offers a wealth of potential benefits for marketers, including personalised campaigns and enhanced performance, it also raises significant ethical concerns regarding biases, originality, and the potential for misuse, which marketers should consider carefully as they implement these technologies in their daily practice.

Summary

Digital marketing communication channels offer a distinct combination of performance attributes that are not always fully captured within analogue communication models. It is important to recognise the interactive and pull characteristics of digital media and also the reduction in the degree of control that an organisation has over message content and reach. Digital channels enable an organisation to leverage the benefits of positive electronic word of mouth. This chapter has provided a range of motives that consumers have to generate eWOM, which can help organisations develop activities to harness this type of marketing communication. It also introduces the concept of viral marketing and provides a six-stage process by which marketers might stimulate and capitalise on word of mouth (WOM) behaviours.

Further reading

Davenport, T., Guha, A., Grewal, D., & Bressgott, T. (2020). How artificial intelligence will change the future of marketing. *Journal of the Academy of Marketing Science*, **48**, 24-42.

Kietzmann, J. H., Hermkens, K., McCarthy, I. P. & Silvestre, B. S. (2011). Social media? Get serious! Understanding the functional building blocks of social media. *Business Horizons*, **54**(3), 241-251.

Beverland, M., Dobele, A. & Farrelly, F. (2015). The viral marketing metaphor explored through vegemite. *Marketing Intelligence & Planning*, **33**(5).

Exemplar paper

Perez-Vega, R., Waite, K. and O'Gorman, K. (2016). Social Impact Theory: an examination of how immediacy operates as an influence upon social media interaction in Facebook Fan pages. *The Marketing Review*, **16**, 4.

> A conceptual paper that reviews the literature on social influence and presents Social Impact Theory as an appropriate theory to explain consumer engagement behaviour on Facebook fan pages. The paper looks at the types of interactions that occur with Facebook fan pages and the associated meaning of these interactions. The paper argues for a need to develop the concept of immediacy in online contexts and proposes that physical, social and temporal immediacy can have different effect on engagement behaviours in social media settings. The paper presents a framework to be tested empirically.

Review questions

1. Digital media can be defined as

   a) Communications content which is shared
   b) Communications content which is viewed on a screen
   c) Communications content which has been digitally encoded
   d) Communications content which is interactive

2. An important characteristic of digital media is interactivity which has three dimensions these are:

   a) Passive control, three-way communication, empowerment
   b) Active control, two-way communication, synchronicity
   c) Consumer control, brand communication, reactivity
   d) Touch-screen control, dialogue, fragmentation

3. Digital developments have resulted in the one-to-many communications model evolving to become a many-to-many communications model, which is defined as:

   a) One source sends each recipient with a different personalised message and the customers can each respond to the source through the same medium
   b) One source contacts many receivers with one message, the medium does not allow the customers to respond to the brand
   c) One source sends a different message to each participant, customers can each send a message to each other, response to each sender-receiver can be made through the same medium
   d) One sources sends each recipient many different messages and the customers respond through many different channels

8

4. A conative marketing objective is one that aims to generate:

    a) Attitude change
    b) Behavioural change
    c) Knowledge change
    d) Awareness change

5. Simple seeding is a technique where

    a) Content is initiated within paid media
    b) Content is initiated within owned media
    c) Content is initiated within earned media
    d) Content is initiated within all media

6. According to Corcoran (2009), digital media can be classified into:

    a) Paid and free media
    b) Paid, earned and owned media
    c) Online and offline media
    d) One-to-one, one-to-many and many-to-many media

7. What are the negative aspects of owned media?

    a) Low credibility and limited reach
    b) Low credibility and limited market intelligence information
    c) Low control and limited reach
    d) Low control and limited market intelligence information

8. Which of the following is NOT an example of electronic word-of-mouth:

    a) A book review on Amazon
    b) A tweet about a negative experience at a restaurant
    c) An email recommending a restaurant to a friend
    d) A YouTube video added to the user's private library

9. Which of the following is NOT a characteristic of electronic word-of-mouth:

    a) Platform
    b) Valence
    c) Focus
    d) Solicitation

10. Which of the following is NOT a motivation for consumers to engage in eWOM?

    a) To reduce anxiety
    b) To fill in spare time
    c) To help other customers
    d) To help the organisation

Answers

The answers to these questions can be found at the back of this book, or at the Marketing Communications page at Goodfellow Publishers:

https://www.goodfellowpublishers.com

References

Aaker, J. L. (1997). Dimensions of brand personality. *Journal of Marketing Research*, **34**, 347-356.

Arndt, J. (1967). Role of product-related conversations in the diffusion of a new product. *Journal of Marketing Research*, **4**, 291-295.

Barker, M., Barker, D. I., Bormann, N. & Neher, K. (2012). *Social Media Marketing: A Strategic Approach*. Cengage Learning.

Bone, P. F. (1995). Word-of-mouth effects on short-term and long-term product judgments. *Journal of Business Research*, **32**(3), 213-223.

Bower, J. & Christenson, C. (1995). Disruptive technologies: Catching the wave *Harvard Business Review*, **73**(1), 43-53

Campbell, C., Plangger, K., Sands, S., Kietzmann, J., & Bates, K. (2022). How deepfakes and artificial intelligence could reshape the advertising industry: The coming reality of AI fakes and their potential impact on consumer behavior. *Journal of Advertising Research*, **62**(3), 241-251.

Capacity Grid (2015), Internet Advertising Glossary, http://www.capacitygrid.com/wp-content/uploads/2015/03/Advertising-Glossary1.pdf

Chaffee, S.H. & Metzger, M.J. (2001), The end of mass communication?, *Mass Communications and Society*, **4**(4), 365-379

Chaffey, D., & Ellis-Chadwick, F. (2022). *Digital Marketing*. Pearson Higher Ed.

Christodoulides, G., Michaelidou, N. & Argyriou, E. (2012). Cross-national differences in e-WOM influence. *European Journal of Marketing*, **46**(11/12), 1689-1707.

Chu, S. C., & Kim, Y. (2011). Determinants of consumer engagement in electronic word-of-mouth (eWOM) in social networking sites. *International Journal of Advertising*, **30**(1), 47-75.

Corcoran, S. (2009). Defining earned, owned and paid media. Available from: http://blogs.forrester.com/interactive_marketing/2009/12/defining-earned-owned-and-paid-media.html (Accessed 12-07-2015).

De Bruyn, A. & Lilien, G.L. (2008). A multi-stage model of word-of-mouth influence through viral marketing. *International Journal of Research in Marketing*, **25**, 151–163.

Dichter, E., (1966). How word-of-mouth advertising works. *Harvard business review*, 44(6), pp.147-160.

Dobele, A., Lindgreen, A., Beverland, M., Vanhamme, J. & Van Wijk, R. (2007). Why pass on viral messages? Because they connect emotionally. *Business Horizons*, **50**(4), 291-304.

Dobele, A., Toleman, D. & Beverland, M. (2005). Controlled infection! Spreading the brand message through viral marketing. *Business Horizons*, **48**(2), 143-149.

Eckler, P. & Bolls, P. (2011). Spreading the virus: Emotional tone of viral advertising and its effect on forwarding intentions and attitudes. *Journal of Interactive Advertising*, **11**(2), 1-11.

Edgerank (2015). What is edgerank? http://edgerank.net/ (Accessed 12-07-2015).

Fill, C. (2009). *Marketing Communications: Interactivity, communities and content.* Pearson Education

Google (2015). Measuring reach and frequency. https://support.google.com/adwords/answer/2472714?hl=en.

Harrison, T., & Waite, K. (2015). Impact of co-production on consumer perception of empowerment. *The Service Industries Journal*, 1-19.

Hennig-Thurau, T., Walsh, G. & Walsh, G. (2003). Electronic word-of-mouth: Motives for and consequences of reading customer articulations on the Internet. *International Journal of Electronic Commerce*, **8**(2), 51-74.

Herr, P. M., Kardes, F. R., & Kim, J. (1991). Effects of word-of-mouth and product-attribute information on persuasion: An accessibility-diagnosticity perspective. *Journal of Consumer Research*, **17**, 454-462.

Hinz, O., Skiera, B., Barrot, C., & Becker, J. U. (2011). Seeding strategies for viral marketing: An empirical comparison. *Journal of Marketing*, **75**(6), 55-71.

Hoffman, D. L., & Novak, T. P. (1996). Marketing in hypermedia computer-mediated environments: conceptual foundations. *The Journal of Marketing*, **60**, 50-68.

Ivens, B., & Valta, K. S. (2012). Customer brand personality perception: A taxonomic analysis. *Journal of Marketing Management*, **28**(9-10), 1062-1093.

Jørgensen, H. R. & Knudsen, H. G., (2022). Media context: a literature review and research agenda. *Journal of Marketing Management*, 38(17-18), 1937-1957.

Kim, J., Spielmann, N. & McMillan. S. J. (2012) Experience effects on interactivity: functions,processes, and perceptions. *Journal of Business Research* **65**, 1543-1550.

Kirk, C. P., Chiagouris, L., Lala, V. & Thomas, J. D. (2015). How do digital natives and digital immigrants respond differently to interactivity online? a model for predicting consumer attitudes and intentions to use digital information products. *Journal of Advertising Research*, **55**(1), 81-94.

Kissmetrics (N.D.). 5 clever ways to increase mobile apps reviews. Available from: https://blog.kissmetrics.com/increase-mobile-app-reviews/.

Kshetri, N., Dwivedi, Y. K., Davenport, T. H., & Panteli, N. (2023). Generative artificial intelligence in marketing: Applications, opportunities, challenges, and research agenda. *International Journal of Information Management*, 102716.

Lim, B. C. & Chung, C. M. (2011). The impact of word-of-mouth communication on attribute evaluation. *Journal of Business Research*, **64**(1), 18-23.

Liu, Y. & Shrum, L. J. (2002). What is interactivity and is it always such a good thing? Implications of definition, person, and situation for the influence of interactivity on advertising effectiveness. *Journal of Advertising*, **31**(4), 53-64.

Lou, C., Kang, H. & Tse, C.H., (2022). Bots vs. humans: how schema congruity, contingency-based interactivity, and sympathy influence consumer perceptions and patronage intentions. *International Journal of Advertising*, **41**(4), 655-684.

Margarida Barreto, A. (2013). Do users look at banner ads on Facebook? *Journal of Research in Interactive Marketing*, **7**(2), 119-139.

Mitchell, A. & Valenzuela, A. (2005). How banner ads affect brand choice without click-through. In Haugtvedt, C.P., Machleit, K.A. & Yalch, R. (eds.) *Online Consumer Psychology: Understanding and influencing consumer behavior in the virtual world*, pp 125-142, Mahwah, N.J. : Lawrence Erlbaum Associates.

Mollen, A. & Wilson, H. (2010). Engagement, telepresence and interactivity in online consumer experience: Reconciling scholastic and managerial perspectives. *Journal of Business Research*, **63**(9), 919-925.

Morgan-Thomas, A. & Veloutsou, C. (2013). Beyond technology acceptance: Brand relationships and online brand experience. *Journal of Business Research*, **66**(1), 21-27.

Pickton, D. & Broderick, A. (2005). *Integrated Marketing Communications*. Financial Times Prentice Hall.

Powers, T., Advincula, D., Austin, M. S., Graiko, S. & Snyder, J. (2012). Digital and social media in the purchase decision process: a special report from the Advertising Research Foundation. *Journal of Advertising Research*, **52**(4), 479-489.

Prensky, M. (2001). Digital natives, digital immigrants, 1. *On the Horizon*, **9**(5), 1-6.

Rezabakhsh, B., Bornemann, D., Hansen, U. & Schrader, U. (2006). Consumer power: a comparison of the old economy and the Internet economy. *Journal of Consumer Policy*, **29**(1), 3-36.

Sundaram, D. S., Mitra, K., & Webster, C. (1998). Word-of-mouth communications: A motivational analysis. *Advances in Consumer Research*, **25**(1), 527-531.

8

Sunstein, C. R. (2009). *Republic.com 2.0*. Princeton University Press.

TED (2023). *What Will Happen to Marketing in the Age of AI?*, Jessica Apotheker, TED [video]. Available at: https://youtu.be/3MwMII8n1qM?si=2QVtqeJsQuka PId1.

Wu, L., & Wen, T. J. (2021). Understanding AI advertising from the consumer perspective: What factors determine consumer appreciation of AI-created advertisements?. *Journal of Advertising Research*, 61(2), 133-146.

Yang, J., Kim, W., Amblee, N., & Jeong, J. (2012). The heterogeneous effect of WOM on product sales: why the effect of WOM valence is mixed? *European Journal of Marketing*, **46**(11/12), 1523-1538.

9 Digital Transformation and Marketing Communications

Hamid Shaker and Mostafa Purmehdi

In the rapidly evolving marketing landscape, new disruptive technologies such as Artificial Intelligence (AI) and Extended Reality (XR) are revolutionising how brands connect with consumers, ushering in an era beyond digital and social media marketing. Companies like Nike are leveraging AI for personalised customer experiences, while brands such as Gucci are creating virtual stores in the Metaverse. Welcome to the new frontier of marketing communication, where artificial intelligence and immersive virtual worlds are the cornerstones of brand innovation and consumer interaction.

Understanding Artificial Intelligence

What is Artificial Intelligence?

Artificial Intelligence (AI) refers to the capability of a machine to imitate intelligent human behaviour (Huang & Rust, 2018). Unlike traditional computer programs that explicitly require instructions for every step, AI systems are designed to use algorithms to parse data, learn from it, and make decisions or predictions based on their learning. **Narrow** AI excels in specific tasks like language translation or facial recognition, while **General** AI can perform any intellectual task a human can (De Bruyn et al., 2020). Later in this chapter, we will introduce some of the marketing tools built from artificial intelligence that enable machines to perform tasks that typically require human intelligence from the marketing team.

Levels of AI: Mechanical, Thinking, Feeling AI

Marketing researchers Huang and Rust (2018) explore AI adoption in the marketing field and introduce a framework that categorises AI into three distinct levels based on the type of intelligence. These levels indicate the complexity of tasks that AI can undertake and how closely they mimic human capacities:

1   **Mechanical AI**: This is the most basic level of AI, involving the automation of routine and repetitive tasks. Mechanical AI operates under predefined rules and procedures with limited learning and adaptation. For example, Roomba vacuum cleaners sensing and interacting within a house, or robotic arms used in manufacturing lines for assembling cars demonstrate Mechanical AI by performing predefined, repetitive tasks efficiently. Businesses also use various forms of mechanical AI to help with packaging, automated inventory management, and self-service robots to deliver services, just to name a few (Mende et al., 2019; van Doorn et al., 2017).

2   **Thinking AI**: At the next level, AI systems can perform tasks that require data analysis, learning by pattern recognition, and predictive decision-making. These AI models can process and analyse large datasets (big data) to learn and generate personalised outputs. An example is IBM's chess player, Deep Blue, which is capable of rational decision-making, or IBM's Watson, which can analyse vast amounts of data to provide insights or diagnostics, supporting healthcare professionals in identifying personalised treatment options (to learn more watch: youtube.com/watch?v=yXcDir9Y9CI).

3   **Feeling AI**: The most advanced form of AI, Feeling AI, analyses human emotional data to understand and replicate human emotions and sensitivities, making it capable of more personal interactions. While current AI technology does not possess true biological human feelings or emotional intelligence, AI models can analyse large amounts of emotional data and adapt their responses to the user's detected emotional state, making interactions more empathic and human-like (Huang & Rust, 2022). An example of Feeling AI is a customer service chatbot designed to detect and adapt to the emotional state of customers, such as those used by airlines to handle booking inquiries and complaints sensitively.

AI business capabilities

The progression of AI technology in marketing has enabled the development of increasingly sophisticated applications across various domains. The different levels of AI have opened up new opportunities for marketers to leverage intelligent systems to enhance customer experiences, optimise campaigns, and drive business growth. Davenport and Ronanki (2018) classify AI applications broadly into three categories, each serving different business needs:

1 **Process Automation**: This type of AI is closely aligned with Mechanical AI and involves automating digital and physical marketing tasks typically performed by marketing people, such as updating records, data entry, and handling simple customer queries. For example, *Salesforce Marketing Cloud* can analyse customer data to segment audiences for targeted marketing campaigns. Robotic Process Automation (RPA) tools like *UiPath*, *Appian* or *Pegasystems* automate data entry and process standard transactions, freeing up human marketer for more complex duties.

2 **Cognitive Insight**: Cognitive insight applications use algorithms to predict, optimise, and discover new trends, aligning with Thinking AI. In marketing, cognitive insight algorithms can do specialised tasks such as collecting customer data, online behaviour, purchase data, and social media engagement. Google Analytics 4, launched in April 2024, can analyse large amounts of consumer usage data to detect patterns and provide insights. By analysing data, such models can detect patterns or predict trends that can be used in decisions of segmentation, targeting, *personalised* positioning, *dynamic* pricing, customer behaviour forecasting, and marketing campaign optimisation. Cognitive AI also has crucial applications for functions like fraud detection, risk management, and personalised marketing.

3 **Cognitive Engagement**: AI systems in this category engage customers and employees using natural language processing (NLP), recommendations, and personalised communication. These systems are often employed in customer service chatbots, employee advisors, and personalised recommendation systems. A notable example is the virtual assistant *ChatGPT* from *OpenAI*, which uses AI to understand and respond to user queries in a conversational manner, providing personalised information. Businesses can use AI tools such as *ManyChat* to integrate a virtual customer service agent over various platforms such as their website, social media, or text message services.

9

Are humans expendable? Augmenting vs. replacing human intelligence

Researchers (e.g., Huang and Rust, 2022; Raisch & Krakowski, 2021) believe the relationship between artificial intelligence and human intelligence can result in either of two primary scenarios: Augmentation or Replacement.

- **Augmenting human intelligence**: In this scenario, AI supports and enhances human capabilities by handling data-intensive tasks, allowing humans to focus on higher-level strategic activities. This collaboration can improve decision-making, increase productivity, and enhance creativity. For example, in the medical field, AI-driven diagnostic tools like those developed by *DeepMind* can analyse medical images to detect diseases such as cancer earlier and more accurately than human doctors, aiding rather than replacing medical professionals.

- **Replacing human intelligence**: AI also holds the potential to replace human roles, especially in tasks that are hazardous, extremely repetitive, or require high precision and speed. While this raises concerns about job displacement, it also offers opportunities for humans to engage in more meaningful and creative tasks. Autonomous vehicles, like those developed by *Tesla* and *Waymo*, aim to replace human drivers, potentially reducing accidents caused by human error and leading to safer roads. However, they also raise concerns about job displacement in driving professions.

Types of AI Models

AI can be seen not just as a single technology but as a broad field of study, overarching any technique that enables computers to mimic human intelligence, including Machine Learning (ML), rule-based systems, expert systems, robotics, Natural Language Processing (NLP), computer vision, and more. **Machine learning** is a subset of AI that focuses on the development of algorithms and models that enable computers to learn from and make predictions or decisions based on data. Instead of being explicitly programmed to perform a task, machine learning models improve their performance over time as they are exposed to more data. While our focus is on understanding the applications of AI in marketing rather than AI technologies, Table 9.1 provides a brief overview of key types of AI models.

Table 9.1: Categories of AI Models

Description	Examples of marketing application
Deep Learning	
A subset of ML that focuses on neural networks with many layers (hence "deep") to model complex patterns in data and perform complex tasks like image recognition, natural language processing, and autonomous decision-making.	Customer Segmentation: Grouping based on behaviour or demographics. Predictive Analytics: Forecasting future customer actions or sales. Recommendation Systems: Personalizing product or content recommendations.
Supervised Learning	
A type of ML where models are trained on labelled data, meaning the input comes with corresponding output.	Churn Prediction: Identifying customers likely to leave. Customer Lifetime Value (CLV) Prediction: Estimating the value of a customer over their lifetime. Targeted Advertising: Optimising ad placements based on historical data.
Unsupervised Learning	
A type of ML that deals with unlabelled data, identifying patterns or groupings without predefined labels.	Market Basket Analysis: Discovering item purchase patterns. Anomaly Detection: Identifying unusual behaviour or fraud. Customer Segmentation: Grouping based on similarities in behaviour.
Natural Language Processing (NLP)	
A branch of AI that focuses on the interaction between computers and human language. NLP models understand and generate human language. Language models like GPT-4 are a form of GenAI that uses NLP techniques to generate coherent and contextually appropriate text based on input prompts.	Chatbots: Automating customer service and interactions. Sentiment Analysis: Assessing customer opinions from social media or reviews. Content Generation: Creating personalised marketing copy or blog posts.
Computer Vision	
AI models that interpret and make decisions based on visual inputs, such as images and videos.	Visual Search: Allowing customers to search for products using images. Ad Analysis: Evaluating how customers interact with visual ads. Product Recognition: Identifying products in images or videos for targeted marketing.

9

Generative AI	
Models that create new data by learning from existing datasets. This includes Generative Adversarial Networks (GANs). GANs consist of two neural networks, a generator and a discriminator, that are trained together in a way that improves the quality of the generated content. Used primarily for generating realistic images, videos, and audio.	Content Creation: Generating custom ads or marketing materials. Synthetic Data Generation: Creating data for training or testing. Personalised Experiences: Crafting unique user experiences or product designs.

Reinforcement Learning	
A type of ML where an agent learns to make decisions by interacting with an environment (e.g., website). The agent (e.g., a marketing algorithm) receives feedback in the form of rewards or penalties (e.g., a click on an ad) based on the actions (e.g., displaying an ad) it takes, and the goal is to maximize the cumulative reward over time.	Dynamic Pricing: Adjusting prices in real-time based on demand and competition. Campaign Optimization: Fine-tuning marketing campaigns based on performance metrics. Ad Bidding Strategies: Automating bid adjustments for ads.

Case study: Stitch Fix, a data-driven fashion service

Stitch Fix (https://www.stitchfix.com) is a personalised online styling service that leverages AI to enhance customer experiences, optimise operations, and drive business growth. By integrating both human expertise and advanced AI models, Stitch Fix provides tailored clothing recommendations, efficient product descriptions, and innovative outfit combinations. Stitch Fix's business model revolves around understanding individual client preferences and providing curated selections of clothing and accessories.

Personal styling and recommendations. One of the core strengths of Stitch Fix is its ability to provide personalised styling advice. When clients sign up for the service, they fill out a detailed style profile that includes their size, style preferences, and price range. This information is then processed by AI algorithms that analyse the data and generate a curated selection of clothing items tailored to the client's unique tastes.

Stitch Fix employs deep learning and natural language processing (NLP) models to interpret the vast amounts of textual data clients provide. For instance, when clients leave feedback about their Fixes or provide specific style notes, the AI models use embeddings from large language models to understand and summarise this input, allowing the algorithms to provide highly relevant recommendations. These recommendations are shared with a human stylist, who will then curate the final pieces for the individual client.

Efficient Product Descriptions. Managing an extensive inventory of clothing items requires detailed and accurate product descriptions. To streamline this process, Stitch Fix uses GenerativeAI to generate informative and engaging product descriptions. The AI is trained on a dataset of existing descriptions and client feedback, enabling it to produce high-quality content that is both accurate and appealing. This automated approach allows Stitch Fix to quickly generate thousands of product descriptions, with human copywriters reviewing and approving the content for final use. This not only speeds up the process but also ensures consistency and accuracy across the inventory.

Dynamic Outfit Combinations. Stitch Fix goes beyond individual item recommendations by helping clients visualise complete outfits. The Outfit Creation Model (OCM) is an AI-driven system that generates millions of outfit combinations daily. This model considers real-time inventory, client preferences, and past purchases to suggest outfits that align with current trends and personal styles. Clients can see these outfit suggestions in their personalised shopping feeds, emails, and advertisements. This feature enhances the shopping experience by providing inspiration and helps clients make more informed purchasing decisions.

Conclusion. Stitch Fix continues to explore new ways to integrate generative AI and other advanced technologies into its operations. The company is experimenting with AI to predict future fashion trends, deepen the personal connection between stylists and clients, and further personalise the shopping experience. By staying at the forefront of AI innovation, Stitch Fix can maintain its competitive edge and continue delivering value to its clients.

Activity

1. Visit their website at www.stitchfix.com and identify the status of their service.

2. Read the case study and identify examples of AI applications Stitch Fix uses. Can you create a table categorising these applications based on their AI level and the type of AI applications discussed in this chapter?

3. Assess the impact of AI on marketing communications and customer experience.

4. Apply your understanding of AI to propose a new feature for Stitch Fix. Develop a presentation (5-7 slides) outlining your proposed AI feature, including its purpose, how it works, and its anticipated impact on Stitch Fix's marketing communications and customer satisfaction.

9

AI transformation of branding and marketing communications

As we delve deeper into the applications of AI in various industries, it is critical to understand how AI is transforming branding and marketing communications. Table 9.2 links back to the categories of AI business capabilities discussed earlier—Process Automation, Cognitive Insight, and Cognitive Engagement—by showcasing the application of AI in major marketing functions.

Table 9.2: AI transformation across marketing functions

Marketing Functions	Process Automation	Cognitive Insight	Cognitive Engagement
Consumer Insight and Market Research	Inventory management Streamline supply chain Always-on testing and optimization	Trend prediction Real-time targeting Predictive analysis	Customised offer (Spotify, Nike, Coca-Cola)
Service Automation	Service Automation (McDonald's smart displays)	Marketing strategy: consistency and integration Cross-Channel Optimization	AI-first solutions (OpenAI's Dall-E) Transforming touchpoints (chatbots, service bots)
Data-driven Personalization	Product customisation Product opportunities	Dynamic Pricing	AI-powered Recommendation Agents (AIRS) Responsive Consumer Journey
Integrated Marketing Communication	Proofreading and editing Ad creation Advertising Email marketing	Public relation AI-Driven Content Creation Advertising consistency and integration	Consumer-generated ad Customer Service Chatbots (post and pre-purchase)

Consumer insight and market research

AI provides unprecedented opportunities for market research and eliciting consumer insights. Huang and Rust (2022) developed a three-stage framework for strategic marketing planning, incorporating multiple artificial intelligence (AI) benefits, as shown in Figure 9.1. In marketing research, mechanical AI is fit for automating repetitive marketing research functions and activities, whereas thinking AI specialises in processing data to arrive at decisions. Finally, Feeling AI enables companies to analyse interactions and human emotions.

Figure 9.1: AI for Marketing Strategy. Source: Adapted from Huang and Rust, (2021).

Let's go over a few examples of AI tools used for consumer insights and market research:

- **Social Media Marketing**: Using AI, *Brandwatch* aggregates relevant consumers' comments, brand mentions, and conversations across social media platforms, then segments the feedback into specific topics or opinions.
- **Automated lead nurturing and email drip campaign:** Leads can go cold without timely nurturing, which means missed brand opportunities. *HubSpot* automates email campaigns to move prospects further down the funnel. AI builds beautiful emails without coding and sets up triggers, conditions, and actions to send the right emails to the right leads at the right time.
- **AI-generated customer review highlights:** To make it easier for customers to understand the common themes across reviews, Amazon uses generative AI and provides a short, summarised paragraph right on

the product detail page, highlighting the product features and customer sentiment frequently mentioned across written reviews to help customers determine at a glance whether a product is right for them.

Service automation

Service automation has emerged as a transformative force in the business and marketing landscape, facilitating efficiencies and enhancing customer experiences across various industries. Consider the multifaceted aspects of service automation at McDonald's as an example. McDonald's is testing automation powered by AI in its drive-throughs, smart displays and order prediction. The fast-food giant has implemented self-service kiosks powered by generative AI across its drive-through outlets, allowing customers to place orders more efficiently (Gerken, 2024). McDonald's integration of machine learning and cloud technology provides the opportunity to offer digital displays that suggest menu items based on factors such as time of day, current order selections, what other consumers ordered, or even weather conditions. These technological advancements result in better order prediction, providing seamless customer experience from digital to physical touchpoints.

The service industry increasingly relies on service robots to assist in customer-firm interactions, speed up response times, and free up human resources for more complex issues (Sarang, 2023). *Connie*, a Watson-enabled robot concierge at Hilton hotels, is generally advantageous to human service providers. Robots work without sick leave, are not affected by pandemic virus outbreaks, will not get burned out from harassment or need holidays, guaranteeing that the hotel guests can always get the answers they are looking for.

Chatbots and service bots have also become integral components of digital marketing strategies, significantly enhancing customer engagement and personalising user experiences in various marketing functions, including lead generation, feedback collection, and tailored marketing communications. They also play a pivotal role in optimising conversion rates of integrated marketing communications by automating interactions across multiple channels, from initial contact to guiding potential customers along the sales funnel.

Data-driven personalization

In today's digital marketplace, personalisation powered by AI is not just a luxury; it is more accessible than ever. For example, companies analyse large datasets to predict customers' desired products. Such product customisation allows businesses to offer unique products that meet the specific needs of their customers, enhancing the customer experience (Tsekouras et al., 2022). Coca-Cola has effectively integrated AI into its vending operations by using AI algorithms that allow it to promote the drinks and flavours that are more popular overall and make suggestions to users depending on the location of the drinks dispenser machines. Additionally, Coca-Cola's Freestyle machines use AI to offer customisable drinks and gather consumer insights via a connected mobile app, enhancing customer experience and engagement (Farrell, 2019).

The use of AI in personalisation is data-driven. Using dynamic learning algorithms, companies make real-time pricing decisions based on insights from customers (and competitors and a wide range of strategic factors), including channels. For instance, grocery stores utilising this technology can adjust prices multiple times daily to optimise revenue and reduce food waste by aligning prices with consumers' willingness to pay (Adams, 2017). Similarly, *JPMorgan Chase* is leveraging AI to provide scalable, customised portfolio management services. Their new IndexGPT software analyses and selects financial securities that align with customer profiles (Daniel, 2023).

AI-powered Recommendation Agents (AIRS) transform how consumers find and engage with products. These systems analyse data to recommend products or services tailored to an individual. For example, streaming services like Netflix use recommendation algorithms to suggest movies and TV shows based on a user's viewing history, enhancing user engagement and satisfaction.

Zhang et al. (2021) reviews different categories of AIRS based on the contextual and behavioural awareness level AIRS uses to make recommendations:

- **Content-based recommender systems** suggest items by analysing the attributes of items a user has previously engaged with, recommending similar items based on content-like themes or genres. For example, platforms like Spotify recommend songs and artists by analysing the genres and artists a user frequently listens to. They effectively manage new items and provide transparent recommendations using item features, but they face challenges with new users and often need more diversity in their recommendations.

- **Collaborative filtering systems** generate recommendations based on the preferences of a user community, either by finding similar users (user-based) or similar items (item-based). Amazon recommends products by showing, *"Customers who bought this item also bought..."* Collaborating filtering systems excel in personalisation but struggle with the cold-start problem for new users and items, scalability, and data sparsity.

- **Knowledge-based Systems** recommend items based on understanding how item features align with user needs, which is helpful for complex products like financial services. They can address new user issues and enhance user trust through transparent recommendations but require extensive, accurate domain knowledge to function effectively.

Integrated marketing communications

Cross-channel marketing optimisation is another critical area where AI plays a pivotal role. By leveraging automated AI-based content, businesses can ensure that their marketing messages are consistent across all channels (e.g. social media, email, or traditional advertising platforms). This consistency allows for higher brand recognition and helps build trust with consumers. Automation tools can also analyse customer data across these channels to contribute to the integration and optimisation of marketing communications, thereby increasing the effectiveness of marketing campaigns. The general applications of AI in integrated marketing communication encompass a variety of functions that enhance efficiency and effectiveness across marketing strategies:

- **Proofreading and editing**: AI tools are utilised to ensure that all marketing materials are error-free and maintain a high standard of professionalism, supporting the brand's quality assurance in communications.

- **AI-driven content creation**: AI facilitates the generation of personalised and brand-consistent content across various channels, improving engagement and communication coherence. *Copy.ai* can automate content workflow using generative AI to generate, refresh, and repurpose content.

- **Ad analysis and optimization**: AI algorithms optimise ad placements and content on various online platforms, analyse performance data to optimise in real-time, allocate budgets more effectively and increase return on investment (ROI) while targeting users more likely to engage based on their behaviour and preferences.

- **Email marketing**: AI enhances email marketing by personalising emails based on user behaviour and optimising key elements of campaigns to improve engagement rates.

- **Brand monitoring and sentiment analysis**: AI tools continuously scan the internet and social media to gauge public sentiment and reputation, allowing companies to address potential issues or leverage positive publicity swiftly. Through sentiment analysis, AI helps integrate positive consumer-generated content into marketing strategies, enhancing authenticity and trust in the brand.

The dark side of AI: *"DaDa DaDaaa!"*

Exploring the dark side of using technology for marketing requires acknowledging the potential threats and unintended consequences that arise with the advancements of AI. For example, offering personalised experiences with precision targeting is enchanting, but at what cost to our privacy? Chatbots may offer conversation, but can they lead us into a labyrinth of manipulation? Augmented and virtual realities captivate our senses, yet they raise the odds of addiction and manipulate our sense of what's real. The arrival of 5G technology accelerates our interconnectedness but amplifies the shadow of surveillance marketing. Voice search and smart speakers offer ease, but they might also eavesdrop on our most private moments for the sake of a sale.

Bias in AI

One of the critical concerns of AI adoption is bias in AI. For example, Lambrecht and Tucker (2019) found that in online targeted ads, because young women are a prized demographics, leading to stronger competition in real-time ad auctions, they are less likely to see less profitable ads, like job postings in IT. This creates gender bias in how professional opportunities are advertised. While AI applications have the ability to address highly complex and multi-faceted problems, often beyond the analyst's full understanding of causal relationships, they are more prone than traditional models to produce biased outcomes, often disregarding the designer's intended goals (De Bruyn et al., 2020). According to Norori et al. (2021), bias can happen due to several factors:

Data-driven bias occurs when the data used to train AI models does not represent the real-world scenario or target population. This bias can lead to skewed outcomes in AI predictions and decisions, which are critical in marketing applications. For instance, if an AI system is trained predominantly on data from middle-aged consumers, it may not effectively engage younger or older demographics, leading to missed opportunities and potential brand alienation. Examples of data-driven bias:

- *Sampling bias:* If an AI model is trained primarily on data from urban populations but is expected to serve both urban and rural areas, the model may perform poorly in rural settings due to underrepresentation in the training data.
- *Historical bias:* Using historical sales data to predict future trends may inadvertently perpetuate past marketing strategies that favoured certain demographics, thus ignoring potential new markets or changing consumer behaviours.

- *Label bias:* In a sentiment analysis tool used for understanding consumer sentiments about a product, if a biassed individual categorises the data labels, the AI's interpretation could lean towards that individual's subjective perspective.

Algorithmic bias occurs when the algorithms themselves are biassed due to how they are designed or the objectives set to optimise. For example, an algorithm that maximises click-through rates in digital advertisements might inadvertently favour sensational or misleading content, compromising ethical standards and brand integrity. Examples of algorithmic bias:

- *Model overfitting:* An AI model might be overfitted to the peculiarities of the training data, leading to excellent performance on training data but poor generalisation to new, unseen data.

- *Feedback loops:* In a recommendation system, if initial biases cause certain items to be recommended more frequently, those items become more popular, reinforcing the bias in the system.

- *Algorithmic simplification:* Some AI models may oversimplify complex behaviours to achieve computational efficiency, leading to biased outcomes in predictions or classifications.

Human bias in AI stems from the prejudices, preferences, and subjective interpretations of those involved in the AI development process, from data labelling to model training and deployment. This type of bias is introduced by the individuals who design, develop, and deploy AI systems. Human biases can creep into AI solutions through subjective decisions in various stages of the AI development process, such as feature selection or the interpretation of results. For example, a marketing team might prefer data from certain sources over others in the data selection phase, which can skew the AI model's training process (selection bias). Developers might design or tune algorithms that inadvertently confirm their own beliefs or hypotheses about consumer behaviour (confirmation bias). (To learn more, watch: youtube.com/watch?v=BRRNeBKwvNM)

Privacy concerns

The widespread adoption of AI in marketing has also raised significant concerns about consumer privacy. Many AI-powered applications, such as personalised product recommendations and targeted advertising, rely on collecting and analysing vast amounts of consumer data. This creates a 'privacy paradox' as consumers often express strong concerns about the privacy implications of these technologies. Yet, they continue willingly sharing their personal information to benefit from

AI-driven services' conveniences and customised experiences (Willems et al., 2023). Regulators are working to update privacy laws to keep pace with technological changes, though there are challenges in crafting rules that don't overly restrict beneficial AI applications. In May 2024, the European Union passed the EU AI Act as Western countries' first major AI regulation (Chee et al., 2024). Ultimately, navigating the privacy paradox will require ongoing dialogue between industry, policymakers, and the public to find the right balance and ensure AI development aligns with ethical principles around data rights and individual privacy. Moreover, in order to help restore a sense of autonomy in users and to navigate the privacy concerns that are presented by their AI technologies, AI developers are encouraged to employ strategies such as: (1) being transparent about data use; (2) offering granular controls over their data sharing preferences, including the ability to opt out of certain data-driven features; and (3) embedding privacy-preserving techniques into the AI models (Sher & Benchlouch., 2023).

Sustainability

Advocates of environments and sustainability raise concerns about major challenge such as immense energy consumption and carbon emissions associated with rapid adoption of AI. Training large language models, for instance, can generate substantial greenhouse gas emissions comparable to the lifetime emissions of several cars (Nishant et al., 2020). According to an estimate, generative AI systems potentially consume about 33 times more energy to perform a task compared to specialized software (Luccioni et al., 2024). Another critical challenge is the potential for AI-driven marketing to exacerbate social and economic sustainability issues. AI-powered targeted advertising and recommendation systems can perpetuate biases and lead to the exploitation of vulnerable consumer segments, as explained in the Bias in AI section above. Addressing the sustainability of AI in marketing will require a concerted effort to optimise energy efficiency, leverage renewable energy sources, and develop more sustainable data management practices.

Moreover, the automation of specific marketing tasks through AI may disrupt traditional job roles, potentially widening socioeconomic inequalities. Sustainable AI in marketing must grapple with these equity concerns, ensuring that the benefits of AI are distributed equitably, and that the technology does not adversely impact marginalised communities. Developing ethical frameworks, promoting algorithmic transparency, and involving diverse stakeholders will be crucial in shaping a sustainable future for AI in marketing (Nishant et al., 2020).

Transparency and explainability

As marketers increasingly use AI, the ability to explain and justify the logic of these systems will be crucial for realising their full potential while maintaining accountability. More complex models, particularly those based on deep learning, are opaque 'black boxes' and their decision-making processes are not transparent to human users, posing a challenge to understanding the reasoning behind their recommendations and predictions. This lack of transparency can make it difficult for marketing teams to trust the outputs of AI systems and effectively communicate their value to clients or customers (Rai, 2020). There is a call for developing Explainable AI (XAI) techniques that provide insight into the inner workings of models (Rai, 2020). XAI approaches like feature importance analysis and example-based explanations can help users understand how AI arrives at its conclusions, increasing trust and enabling more informed decision-making.

Pitfalls in AI applications

Bias in AI, privacy concerns, and some of the major concerns (e.g., negative impact on the environment) are already being the topic of discussion among sustainability scholars and practitioners. Overall, the pitfalls in AI applications can be seen through four lenses: the data collection step, applications of data, the network effect, and specific technology features. Table 9.3 summarises the existing pitfalls in these four lenses, partitioned by relevance to various stakeholders: consumers, organisations, or society. Note that many of these pitfalls may overlap across several lenses and affect more than one stakeholder.

Table 9.3: Significant AI challenges and impacted stakeholders

Consumers	Company	Society
Lens 1: collection of data		
Erosion of privacy	Mishandling data	Surveillance society Behavioural tracking & profiling
Lens 2: Using data		
Information overload Misinformation & manipulation Loss of consumer autonomy Lack of transparency of explainability	Compliance and legal risks Security threats Algorithmic complexity	Economic disparities Social and digital division Ethical implications

Lens 3: Network effect		
	Brand reputation risks Brand dilution	Cultural homogenisation Increased consumerism Unsustainable consumption patterns
Lens 4: Technology effect (AI, social media, blockchain, AR/VR)		
Vulnerability to addiction (psychological impact)	Technological dependence & obsolescence Over-reliance on algorithmic decision-making	Job displacement

Lens 1: Collection of data

This lens is about the ethical and societal implications of data collection practices in AI-driven marketing. The mishandling of data poses severe risks, including breaches that can lead to significant privacy violations, affecting consumer trust and relationship with the brand (Labrecque et al., 2021). The erosion of privacy is not merely a byproduct but a fundamental issue as AI models increasingly rely on detailed consumer data to model consumer behaviour for marketing purposes such as personalisation and targeting. This lens also tackles the creation of a surveillance society—an environment where consumers are constantly monitored through their digital footprints (Perez-Des Rosiers, 2021). Behavioural tracking and profiling raise profound ethical questions about the importance of consent, as individuals may be unaware of the extent and purpose of the data gathered. These practices, if unchecked, could lead to a dystopian scenario where consumer behaviour is predicted and manipulated, stripping individuals of their privacy and agency. Companies must ensure they comply with data collection regulations, a challenging task given the current lack of clarity in these rules. Governments and policymakers are still developing regulations in this area.

Lens 2: Using data

This lens delves into the consequences of deploying consumer data in marketing strategies. It covers a broad array of challenges, including information overload, which can confuse consumers rather than aid them (Ferguson et al., 2022). The use of data in marketing can exacerbate economic disparities by creating a divide between those who can afford to access and utilise big data and those who cannot. This lens also draws attention to how AI-driven marketing widens social and digital divisions, segregating consumers into echo chambers that reinforce biases and reduce diverse exposure. Misinformation and manipulation through sophisticated data-driven techniques can distort consumer reality and influence behaviours in unethical ways (Dabbous & Barakat, 2020; Favaretto et al., 2019).

The loss of consumer autonomy is evident as algorithms make decisions that previously would have involved human judgment. Moreover, the need for more transparency and explainability in AI systems makes it difficult for both consumers and regulators to understand and trust these technologies. Security threats to consumer data and addressing the ethical implications of its use are paramount to maintaining consumer rights and trust in an increasingly digital market landscape.

Lens 3: Network effect

In this lens, the focus shifts to the broader impacts of network effects due to the mobilisation of a vast number of consumer data points and influencing many customer decisions – eventually creating a ripple effect. Brand reputation risks are significant; a single algorithmic failure can lead to widespread negative publicity and damage consumer trust irreparably. This lens also highlights brand dilution risks when AI-driven marketing indiscriminately saturates markets with messages that may not align with core brand values (Dawar, 2018). Increased consumerism is another concern, as AI models are mostly trained based on the interests of its developers, and they fail to consider how AI models affect all stakeholders including the society, potentially leading to unsustainable consumption pattern (Nishant et al., 2020).

Lens 4: Technology effect

The fourth lens looks at the direct impact of specific technologies, such as AI, social media, blockchain, and AR/VR, on marketing practices. The psychological impact of these technologies, particularly the vulnerability to addiction, is a growing concern (cf. Marriott & Pitardi, 2024). Technologies that encourage constant engagement can lead to behaviour that adversely affects mental health (Puntoni et al., 2021). Technological dependence and the obsolescence of traditional marketing skills pose risks to the workforce, as reliance on advanced technologies can marginalise those without the skills to adapt. Job displacement due to automation is a critical issue, with AI potentially replacing human roles in marketing, leading to economic and social challenges (Gruetzemacher et al., 2020). Over-reliance on algorithmic decision-making can result in a lack of creative and ethical judgement (Zhai et al., 2024).

Mitigating the dark side: A Checklist

Understanding and mitigating the dark side of AI is crucial for developing effective and equitable AI-driven marketing strategies. On the basis of the discussions above, we think marketers must:

- ☑ Ensure diverse and representative data sets for training AI models.
- ☑ Regularly audit and update AI systems to identify and correct biases.
- ☑ Foster a culture of ethical AI use that promotes fairness and inclusivity
- ☑ When designing the algorithms, consider all stakeholders, vulnerable groups, and sustainability objectives (founded upon UN SDG 2023)
- ☑ Adoption of explainable AI techniques (XAI): Developing and integrating explainable AI methodologies that are inherently more interpretable can make it easier to trace and understand the behaviour of AI systems.
- ☑ Data minimization: Collect and process only the data that is necessary for the AI system to function effectively. Avoid storing unnecessary personal information to reduce privacy risks.
- ☑ User consent and control: Implement mechanisms for obtaining explicit consent from users before collecting their data. Provide users with control over their data, including options to access, modify, or delete their information.
- ☑ Privacy-by-design: Incorporate privacy considerations into the design and development of AI systems from the outset. This approach ensures that privacy protection is integral to the system architecture.

9

The Metaverse: A new digital frontier in branding and marketing communications

McKinsey, the acclaimed consulting company, defines the metaverse as *"the emerging 3-D-enabled digital space that uses virtual reality, augmented reality, and other advanced internet and semiconductor technology to allow people to have lifelike personal and business experiences online."* (McKinsey, 2022).

With a mainstream omnichannel commerce ecosystem already in place, the metaverse's potential for virtual transactions is vast, supported by the increasing comfort of younger, digitally-native consumers of Gen-Z and Gen-alpha with virtual worlds and goods. The metaverse is revolutionising marketing by leveraging ongoing technological advances to create expansive and immersive virtual worlds. Major tech companies like Meta and NVIDIA are pouring billions into metaverse development, while the falling cost of augmented- and virtual-reality hardware further fuels this growth (Bambysheva, 2023). The metaverse offers diverse use cases beyond gaming, including immersive retail, spatial entertainment, and even governmental applications, thus broadening its appeal (Porter & Heppelmann, 2017). Additionally, the rise of individual content creators and influencer marketing on various platforms creates potential for consumer-led brand engagement to thrive in the metaverse, providing innovative and engaging marketing opportunities.

Core elements of the Metaverse

Hadi and colleagues (2024) identify five key elements that collectively define the Metaverse (Figure 9.2):

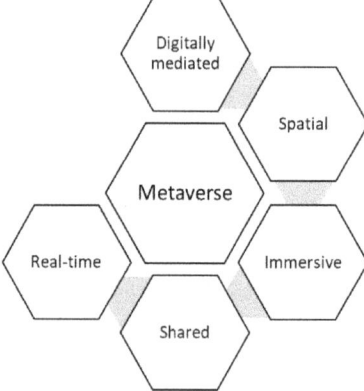

Figure 9.2: Metaverse core elements. Source: Adapted from Hadi et al. (2023)

- **Digitally Mediated:** The Metaverse exists primarily through digital interfaces and platforms such as VRChat or Second Life, where users can interact with each other through their digital devices.

- **Spatial:** Major metaverse platforms, such as Roblox, Decentraland, and Fortnite, offer a sense of space that allows users to navigate and explore the metaverse as they would in the physical world.

- **Immersive:** The environments within the Metaverse engage users in a manner that feels real and engaging, often using virtual reality (VR) devices such as Meta's Oculus headset or augmented reality (AR) using mobile devices.

- **Shared:** These spaces are inhabited by multiple users simultaneously, facilitating social interactions and communal experiences. Users can attend a virtual concert or a fashion show in the metaverse. In 2022, more than 100,000 attended Metaverse Fashion Week on Decentraland, one of the major metaverse platforms, where brands such as Selfridges, Tommy Hilfiger, Guo Pei, Dolce & Gabbana were represented (Schulz & McDowell, 2022).

- **Real-Time:** Interactions and changes within the Metaverse occur instantly, mirroring real-life dynamics. Users can attend live auctions in Metaverse or interact with brands in real time.

The convergence of these core elements signifies a shift in how consumers perceive identity, interact socially, and understand ownership in digital spaces.

- **Consumer identity:** How avatars and virtual representations in the Metaverse allow for new forms of self-expression and identity exploration. For example, avatars in Metaverse can represent the user with changed appearance, attire, and even species, based on user choice.

- **Social influence:** Social interactions in the Metaverse can influence consumer decisions and behaviours. Influencer marketing in the Metaverse can bring popular figures' endorsements to virtual goods or services.

- **Ownership:** The re-definition of ownership through digital assets like non-fungible tokens (NFTs) provides exclusive control over unique digital items. For example, art galleries can use the Metaverse NFTs to own digital art exclusively.

Case study: NikeLand – Using the Metaverse for branding and marketing communications

The Metaverse creates novel opportunities for brands to engage with consumers in more dynamic and interactive ways compared to traditional digital settings. To take advantage of this space, brands need to develop a strategy that fosters communities and social interactions, reinforcing brand identity. Virtual goods and avatar customisations can become new avenues for expressing consumer loyalty and preference. The critical challenge is ensuring that brand managers can translate their brand's values and aesthetics into the Metaverse, ensuring consistency and recognizability in a virtual setting.

NikeLand in *Decentraland* is a prime example of how brands can successfully transition from simply conveying brand messages to creating a compelling, immersive environment for users that fosters ongoing engagement. Nike has leveraged the metaverse to not only tell their brand story but also to immerse visitors in it. By allowing developers to create Nike-themed games, NikeLand transforms passive consumers into active participants in value creation. Visitors can explore the virtual space, participate in interactive games, and engage with the brand in novel and memorable ways. This interactive approach keeps users returning, fostering a deeper connection with the brand.

9

Moreover, Nike bridges the gap between its physical stores and the virtual world. Patrons of brick-and-mortar Nike stores can use in-store devices to access Nike-Land, instantly transporting them into the metaverse to play games and explore virtual environments. This integration enhances the in-store experience, creating a unique blend of physical and digital engagement. By doing so, Nike enhances customer experience and reinforces its innovative brand image. For marketers, NikeLand illustrates the power of the metaverse in creating immersive, interactive brand environments that captivate and engage audiences on an ongoing basis.

Source: Marr (2022)

Activity

- Reflect on core elements of Metaverse and describe how NikeLand is different from a social media platform. What are the main interactive elements used in NikeLand?

- Analyse NikeLand's strategy in the metaverse and evaluate how NikeLand translated Nike's brand identity and aesthetics into the virtual space.

- Evaluate the effectiveness of NikeLand in fostering consumer loyalty and engagement.

Summary

In this chapter, we delved into the transformative role of Artificial Intelligence (AI) and the Metaverse in modern marketing. We began by defining AI and categorizing its levels—Mechanical, Thinking, and Feeling AI—highlighting their applications in automating processes, generating cognitive insights, and enhancing customer engagement. The chapter explored AI's transformation of branding and marketing communications, emphasizing its impact on consumer insights, service automation, and personalized marketing strategies. It also addressed the dark sides of AI, such as bias, privacy concerns, and sustainability issues. The chapter concluded with a discussion on the Metaverse, outlining its potential as a new frontier in branding and marketing, with immersive virtual experiences reshaping consumer behaviour and brand interaction.

Further reading

Davenport, T., Guha, A., Grewal, D., & Bressgott, T. (2020). How artificial intelligence will change the future of marketing. *Journal of the Academy of Marketing Science*, **48** (1), 24–42.

This conceptual paper provides an overview on AI research in marketing strategies and consumer behaviour. The authors propose a framework that describes both where AI stands today and how it is likely to evolve as well as an agenda for future research.

Dwivedi, Y. K., Kshetri, N., Hughes, L., Rana, N. P., Baabdullah, A. M., Kar, A. K., Koohang, A., Ribeiro-Navarrete, S., Belei, N., Balakrishnan, J., … Yan, M. (2023). Exploring the Darkverse: A multi-perspective analysis of the negative societal impacts of the Metaverse. *Information Systems Frontiers*, **25** (5), 2071–2114.

While the Metaverse's benefits are widely discussed, the negative outcomes are less explored. This study addresses these negative aspects including issues like technological and consumer vulnerability, privacy concerns, diminished reality, identity theft, invasive advertising, phishing, financial crimes, abuse, social inclusion issues, mental health impacts, sexual harassment, and unintended consequences, by presenting diverse perspectives from leading academics and experts.

Luo, X., Tong, S., Fang, Z., & Qu, Z. (2019). Frontiers: machines vs. humans: the impact of artificial intelligence chatbot disclosure on customer purchases. *Marketing Science*, **38** (6), 937–947.

Using field experiment data, this research paper examines the consumers' behaviour when they are interacting with chatbots. The findings suggest that while undisclosed chatbots are as effective as proficient workers and four times more effective than inexperienced workers in engendering customer purchases, a disclosure of chatbot identity reduces purchase rates consumers due to negative human perception against machine.

Pantano, E., & Scarpi, D. (2022). I, Robot, You, Consumer: Measuring Artificial Intelligence Types and their Effect on Consumers Emotions in Service. *Journal of Service Research*, **25** (4), 583–600.

This research paper examines the impact of AI on consumers' emotions. The authors build and evaluate a scale for measuring different AI intelligence types and evaluates consumers' emotional responses to the different AI intelligences

Wedel, M., Bigné, E., & Zhang, J. (2020). Virtual and augmented reality: Advancing research in consumer marketing. *International Journal of Research in Marketing*, **37**(3), 443–465.

9

This conceptual paper provides a conceptual framework for VR/AR research in consumer marketing that centers around consumer experiences provided by VR/AR applications along the customer journey and the effectiveness of such applications. The authors also adopt the BASIS (Hoffman & Novak, 2018) terminology to synthesize the assessment of VR effectiveness.

Review questions

1. What does Artificial Intelligence (AI) refer to?
   a) The use of machines to perform tasks without human intervention
   b) The capability of a machine to imitate intelligent human behavior
   c) A system that automates manual tasks
   d) A type of software that processes data

2. Which level of AI is primarily associated with the automation of routine tasks?
   a) Mechanical AI
   b) Thinking AI
   c) Feeling AI
   d) General AI

3. Feeling AI is characterized by its ability to:
   a) Automate repetitive tasks
   b) Analyse and replicate human emotions
   c) Make data-driven decisions
   d) Perform logical operations

4. Which of the following is a concern associated with AI in marketing?
   a) Increased sales
   b) Bias in AI models
   c) Enhanced customer experience
   d) Faster data processing

5. Which of the following is NOT considered a benefit of AI in marketing?
   a) Enhanced personalization
   b) Data-driven decision making
   c) Complete elimination of human oversight
   d) Automated service delivery

6. The Metaverse is described as:
   a) A traditional online shopping platform
   b) A 3D-enabled digital space for immersive experiences
   c) A virtual assistant platform
   d) A social media network

7. Service automation in AI is primarily used to:
   a) Enhance creativity in marketing
   b) Automate customer service interactions
   c) Generate emotional responses
   d) Design marketing campaigns

8. AI-driven personalization in marketing typically involves:
   a) Creating generic marketing content
   b) Developing products with mass appeal
   c) Tailoring offers based on individual consumer data
   d) Reducing the cost of production

9. What are the core elements of the Metaverse?
   a) Digitally mediated, immersive, and real-time
   b) Static, isolated, and asynchronous
   c) Physical, limited, and offline
   d) Generic, broad, and non-interactive

10. Which of the following is a strategy to mitigate the dark side of AI?
    a) Increase data collection without regulation
    b) Reduce transparency in AI algorithms
    c) Ensure diverse and representative datasets
    d) Focus solely on short-term profits

Answers

The answers to these questions can be found at the back of this book, or at the Marketing Communications page at Goodfellow Publishers:

https://www.goodfellowpublishers.com

9

References

Adams, T. (2017). Surge pricing comes to the supermarket. *The Observer*, June 4. https://www.theguardian.com/technology/2017/jun/04/surge-pricing-comes-to-the-supermarket-dynamic-personal-data

Bambysheva, N. (2023) 'Nvidia's AI, metaverse investments keep business humming after crypto mining demand withers', *Forbes*, 23 May. https://www.forbes.com/sites/digital-assets/2023/05/23/nvidias-ai-metaverse-investments-keep-business-humming-after-crypto-mining-demand-withers/

Chee, F. Y., Hummel, T., Chee, F. Y., & Hummel, T. (2024). Europe sets benchmark for rest of the world with landmark AI laws. *Reuters*. https://www.reuters.com/world/europe/eu-countries-back-landmark-artificial-intelligence-rules-2024-05-21/

Dabbous, A., & Barakat, K. A. (2020). Bridging the online offline gap: Assessing the impact of brands' social network content quality on brand awareness and purchase intention. *Journal of Retailing and Consumer Services*, **53**, 101966. https://doi.org/10.1016/j.jretconser.2019.101966

Daniel, W. (2023). *Meet 'IndexGPT,' the A.I. stock picker JPMorgan is developing that may put your 'financial advisor out of business'*. Yahoo Finance. https://finance.yahoo.com/news/meet-index-gpt-stock-picker-170517570.html

Davenport, T. H., & Ronanki, R. (2018). Artificial intelligence for the real world. *Harvard Business Review*, **96**(1), 108–116.

Dawar, N. (2018). Marketing in the age of Alexa. *Harvard Business Review*. https://hbr.org/2018/05/marketing-in-the-age-of-alexa

De Bruyn, A., Viswanathan, V., Beh, Y. S., Brock, J. K.-U., & Von Wangenheim, F. (2020). Artificial Intelligence and Marketing: Pitfalls and Opportunities. *Journal of Interactive Marketing*, **51**(1), 91–105. https://doi.org/10.1016/j.intmar.2020.04.007

Farrell, G. (2019). *Smartsheet BrandVoice: 3 Things Coca-Cola, AWS And Smartsheet Taught Me About Innovation*. Forbes. https://www.forbes.com/sites/smartsheet/2019/02/21/3-things-coca-cola-aws-and-smartsheet-taught-me-about-innovation/

Favaretto, M., De Clercq, E., & Elger, B. S. (2019). Big Data and discrimination: Perils, promises and solutions. A systematic review. *Journal of Big Data*, **6**(1), 12. https://doi.org/10.1186/s40537-019-0177-4

Ferguson, A. N., Franklin, M., & Lagnado, D. (2022). Explanations that backfire: Explainable artificial intelligence can cause information overload. *Proceedings of the Annual Meeting of the Cognitive Science Society*, **44**(44). https://escholarship.org/uc/item/3d97g0n3

Gerken, T. (2024). *McDonalds removes AI drive-throughs after order errors*. BBC News. https://www.bbc.com/news/articles/c722gne7qngo

Gruetzemacher, R., Paradice, D., & Lee, K. B. (2020). Forecasting extreme labor displacement: A survey of AI practitioners. *Technological Forecasting and Social Change*, **161**, 120323. https://doi.org/10.1016/j.techfore.2020.120323

Hadi, R., Melumad, S., & Park, E. S. (2024). The Metaverse: A new digital frontier for consumer behavior. *Journal of Consumer Psychology*, **34**(1), 142–166. https://doi.org/10.1002/jcpy.1356

Huang, M.-H., & Rust, R. T. (2018). Artificial Intelligence in Service. *Journal of Service Research*, **21**(2), 155–172. https://doi.org/10.1177/1094670517752459

Please add this reference: Huang, M.-H., & Rust, R. T. (2021). A strategic framework for artificial intelligence in marketing. *Journal of the Academy of Marketing Science*, **49**(1), 30–50. https://doi.org/10.1007/s11747-020-00749-9

Huang, M.-H., & Rust, R. T. (2022). A Framework for Collaborative Artificial Intelligence in Marketing. *Journal of Retailing*, **98**(2), 209–223. https://doi.org/10.1016/j.jretai.2021.03.001

Labrecque, L. I., Markos, E., Swani, K., & Peña, P. (2021). When data security goes wrong: Examining the impact of stress, social contract violation, and data type on consumer coping responses following a data breach. *Journal of Business Research*, **135**, 559–571. https://doi.org/10.1016/j.jbusres.2021.06.054

Luccioni, A. S., Jernite, Y., & Strubell, E. (2024). Power hungry processing: watts driving the cost of AI deployment? *The 2024 ACM Conference on Fairness, Accountability, and Transparency*, 85–99. https://doi.org/10.1145/3630106.3658542

McKinsey & Company. (2022) *What is the metaverse and where will it lead next?*, McKinsey Explainers. https://www.mckinsey.com/featured-insights/mckinsey-explainers/what-is-the-metaverse.

Marr, B. (2022). *The Amazing Ways Nike Is Using The Metaverse, Web3 and NFTs*. Forbes. https://www.forbes.com/sites/bernardmarr/2022/06/01/the-amazing-ways-nike-is -using-the-metaverse-web3-and-nfts/

Marriott, H. R., & Pitardi, V. (2024). One is the loneliest number… Two can be as bad as one. The influence of AI Friendship Apps on users' well-being and addiction. *Psychology & Marketing*, **41**(1), 86-101.

Mende, M., Scott, M. L., van Doorn, J., Grewal, D., & Shanks, I. (2019). Service robots rising: How humanoid robots influence service experiences and elicit compensatory consumer responses. *Journal of Marketing Research*, **56**(4), 535–556. https://doi.org/10.1177/0022243718822827

Nishant, R., Kennedy, M., & Corbett, J. (2020). Artificial intelligence for sustainability: Challenges, opportunities, and a research agenda. *International Journal of Information Management*, **53**, 102104. https://doi.org/10.1016/j.ijinfomgt.2020.102104

Norori, N., Hu, Q., Aellen, F. M., Faraci, F. D., & Tzovara, A. (2021). Addressing bias in big data and AI for health care: A call for open science. *Patterns (New York, N.Y.)*, **2**(10), 100347. https://doi.org/10.1016/j.patter.2021.100347

Perez-Des Rosiers, D. (2021). AI application in surveillance for public safety: adverse risks for contemporary societies. In T. Keskin & R. D. Kiggins (Eds.), *Towards an International Political Economy of Artificial Intelligence* (pp. 113–143). Springer International Publishing. https://doi.org/10.1007/978-3-030-74420-5_6

Porter, M. E., & Heppelmann, J. E. (2017). Why every organization needs an augmented reality strategy. *Harvard Business Review*, **95**(6), 46–57.

Puntoni, S., Reczek, R. W., Giesler, M., & Botti, S. (2021). Consumers and artificial intelligence: an experiential perspective. *Journal of Marketing*, **85**(1), 131–151. https://doi.org/10.1177/0022242920953847

9

Rai, A. (2020). Explainable AI: From black box to glass box. *Journal of the Academy of Marketing Science, 48*(1), 137–141. https://doi.org/10.1007/s11747-019-00710-5

Raisch, S., & Krakowski, S. (2021). Artificial Intelligence and Management: The automation–augmentation paradox. *Academy of Management Review, 46*(1), 192–210. https://doi.org/10.5465/amr.2018.0072

Sarang, A. (2023). *The Dawn Of Humanoid Robotics: A Glimpse Into The Future.* Forbes. https://www.forbes.com/councils/forbestechcouncil/2023/08/14/the-dawn-of-humanoid-robotics-a-glimpse-into-the-future/

Schulz, M., & McDowell, M. (2022). *Metaverse Fashion Week to return next year.* Vogue Business. https://www.voguebusiness.com/technology/metaverse-fashion-week -to-return-next-year

Sher, G., Benchlouch, A., Sher, G., & Benchlouch, A. (2023). The privacy paradox with AI. *Reuters.* https://www.reuters.com/legal/legalindustry/privacy-paradox-with-ai-2023-10-31/

Tsekouras, D., Li, T., & Benbasat, I. (2022). Scratch my back and I'll scratch yours: The impact of user effort and recommendation agent effort on perceived recommendation agent quality. *Information & Management, 59*(1), 103571. https://doi.org/10.1016/j.im.2021.103571

van Doorn, J., Mende, M., Noble, S. M., Hulland, J., Ostrom, A. L., Grewal, D., & Petersen, J. A. (2017). Domo Arigato Mr. Roboto: Emergence of automated social presence in organizational frontlines and customers' service experiences. *Journal of Service Research, 20*(1), 43–58. https://doi.org/10.1177/1094670516679272

Willems, J., Schmid, M. J., Vanderelst, D., Vogel, D., & Ebinger, F. (2023). AI-driven public services and the privacy paradox: Do citizens really care about their privacy? *Public Management Review, 25*(11), 2116–2134. https://doi.org/10.1080/14719037.2022.2063934

Zhai, C., Wibowo, S., & Li, L. D. (2024). The effects of over-reliance on AI dialogue systems on students' cognitive abilities: A systematic review. *Smart Learning Environments, 11*(1), 28. https://doi.org/10.1186/s40561-024-00316-7

Zhang, Q., Lu, J., & Jin, Y. (2021). Artificial intelligence in recommender systems. *Complex & Intelligent Systems, 7*(1), 439–457. https://doi.org/10.1007/s40747-020-00212-w

10 International Advertising and Communications

Babak Taheri and Sean Lochrie

The internationalisation of marketing communications

International advertising can be defined as a *"phenomenon that involves the transfer of advertising appeals, messages, art, copy, photographs, stores, and video and film segments (or spots) from one country to another"* (American Marketing Association, 2015). International advertising encompasses areas such as planning, budgeting, resource allocation issues, message strategy, media decisions, local regulations, advertising agency selection, coordination of multi-country communication efforts, and regional and global campaigns (Percy & Rosenbaum-Elliott, 2012; Solomon, 2013).

It is suggested that advances in communication technologies have led to consumers around the world increasingly desiring the same products (Levitt, 1983). As Levitt (1983: 93) highlights, *"the world's needs and desires have been irrevocably homogenised. This makes the multinational corporation obsolete and the global corporation absolute"*. Therefore, Levitt (1983) argues that international firms should stop acting like 'multinationals' which tailor their products to fit local markets, instead, they should become global through standardising the manufacturing, distribution and advertising of their goods across all nations. In other words, organisations should follow an internationalisation strategy, which can be described as an approach to designing, producing, distributing and advertising products and services that are easily adaptable to different countries, cultures and languages

(Turnbull & Doherty-Wilson, 1990). Despite this focus on standardization, the need for organisations to embrace local needs and tastes is of great significance (Kanso & Kitchen, 2004; Melewar & Saunders, 1999). For example, American fast food restaurant KFC, originally branded Kentucky Fried Chicken, successfully penetrated the Chinese market by balancing the fundamental core of their brand, fried chicken and fast service, with offering China-specific food to supplement its standard Western cuisine. This exemplifies the argument made by Quelch and Hoff (1986, p. 59) that the pertinent question in international marketing *"is not whether to go global but how to tailor the global marketing concept to fit each business"*.

Internationalisation in advertising can be traced back to the start of the early twentieth century, but the importance of this phenomena was given credence when in 1899 American marketing communications agency, J. Walter Thompson, opened its first office in London. The internationalisation of advertising has been studied from several perspectives. For example, Levitt (1983) argues that a common advertising campaign with some minor adjustments can help to promote the same service or product across borders. However, it requires separate messages for consumers in different markets, as there are some incompatible differences (e.g., cultural, economic and media elements) between countries or even between regions in the same country. Additionally, Pappavassilliou and Stathakopoulos (1997) argue that adaptation of advertising decisions is not a dichotomous one and such decisions can be viewed on the continuum, as there normally exist degrees of international advertising adaptation. Moreover, geographers and economists examine a variety of issues with regards to the international evaluation of ad agencies and the international regulatory implications on the companies as a result of liberalisation of advertising services (Roberts, 1998). Turnbull and Doherty-Wilson (1990: 12) note that *"the internationalisation of the advertising agency business has made it necessary for multinational as well as national agencies to direct more attention to corporate strategy and policy decisions. While agencies generally see internationalisation as a natural business progression, whether they choose to exist as a multinational or a national agency, they must position the agency properly within that environment to ensure their survival and prosperity"*. They also argue that ad agencies sometimes utilise employee-related and non-related diversification strategies in both domestic and international levels.

International marketing communications is a challenging phenomenon. According to Monye (2000: 4) an important element in the planning of marketing communications is how different organisations can communicate with *"a range of messages about value, quality, reliability and brand image to a whole variety of global audiences"*. Pivotal to successful marking communications is the organisation's ability to develop a brand that means something to its target audience. In today's world, geographic and cultural borders are *permeable* because of the internet, cable and satellite television. Globalisation and increased geographical mobility mean that even regional advertising has to attend to the different cultural frames of reference of non-indigenous populations. This in return can create potential foreign markets for domestic producers and increases competition in the market (Hackley, 2012; Percy & Rosenbaum-Elliott, 2012). For instance, in Europe there are stereotypical beliefs that the best policemen are British, the best chefs French, the best mechanics German, the best lovers Italian and the best organisers the Swiss. As the old joke goes, "*Hell is where the police are German, the chefs are British, the mechanics are French, the lovers Swiss and it is all organised by the Italians*" (Hackley, 2010: 196).

As another example, popular Scottish clothing brands such as Harris Tweed and Pringle have been able to penetrate global markets, taking once domestic and local brands to the world stage. If a fashion brand A is successful and active in the foreign market, then fashion brand B also would like to play active role in this particular foreign market and remain competitive in the domestic market. However, international and cross-cultural communication remains an area of tension between local cultural norms of meaning systems and global (often Western) brand ideologies. For example, even within one country a given advert can be exposed to heterogeneous consumers whose interpretive frame of reference is informed by specific cultural norms which reflect ethnic, religion, family, sub-culture, peer-group and other values and presuppositions and advertising regulation (Hackley, 2012; Percy & Rosenbaum-Elliott, 2012). Furthermore, the differences in international advertising regulation and the different interpretation of frame of references in dissimilar cultures can influence the standardisation and advertising campaigns. Therefore, a particular advertising campaign might be acceptable in a country (e.g., portraying nudity) but not be acceptable in another country.

10

Exercise

Consider a popular brand – for example, a sports clothing brand, a car manufacturer, or a restaurant chain. Can you identify elements of their marketing communications which are distinguishable and can be seen to exemplify an internationalisation approach to advertising? You may want to consider things such as logo, colours, and slogans.

Standardisation and localisation of international marketing communications

Grein and Gould (1996: 143) define the globally integrated marketing communications as *"a system of active promotional management which strategically coordinates global communications in all of its component parts both horizontally in terms of countries and organizations and vertically in terms of promotion disciplines. It contingently takes into account the full range of standardized versus adaptive market options, synergies, variations among target populations and other market-place and business conditions"*. Here, globalisation is a process leading to greater interdependence and mutual awareness among economic, political and social units in the world, and among actors in general (Kitchen and Schultz, 1999). Ultimately, when operating in different countries managers must determine how to market and communicate their products and services in each country (Solomon et al., 2009). Therefore, in international marketing, managers must consider a number of key questions. For example:

1 To what degree will the organisation have to adjust their marketing communications to the tastes and needs of the local market?

2 Will the same products and services be attractive to the local market?

3 Will the price of the offering need to be altered?

Much of this debate concerns itself with the different perspectives related to standardisation and localisation of international marketing communications (Terpstra et al., 2012). Standardisation is the process of extending and effectively applying domestic target-market-dictated product standards, tangible and/or intangible attributes, to markets in a foreign environment (Szymanski et al., 1993). For example, in 2013, NIVEA launched a global campaign using the slogan 'It starts with you' to promote the launch of its new men's Active Age Range. Running across various communicative channels, the campaign was first launched in the UK and Germany, before being rolling out globally. The global template used by NIVEA highlights the approach of a company using the same marketing mix to penetrate multiple markets – in other words, standardisation.

The standardise-or-localise question arose partly because communications infrastructure has evolved to make standardised global advertising possible (e.g., DVD technology, satellite TV, the internet and international travel). Creating standardised ads that translate to differing cultures requires a common denominator of meaning for the brand, product or service which allows them to 'travel well' worldwide. In some cases, standardisation is possible because the commodity being promoted has the same meaning to consumers in different cultures.

Localisation can facilitate global marketing strategy by placing global brands in a local cultural context (Ramarapu et al., 1999). This can also facilitate localised positioning and segmentation approaches. For example, local agencies often employ a culturally-specific interpretation of the brand values, which may not always be the interpretation that the organisation conceived in its strategic planning. Interestingly, some international brands have found that neither localisation nor standardisation serves their purpose. In response the term 'glocalisation' has been coined and refers to the local adaptation of globally oriented marketing themes and products (Koekemoer & Bird, 2004). Global brand organisations seek to control the presentation of their brand at a certain level, allowing local ad agencies some licence to portray the brand in ways that will correspond with local cultural meaning systems (Hackley, 2012; Lee & Carter, 2012).

There are also differences between the standardised and adapted marketing mix. The standardised marketing mix involves selling the same products and using the same marketing approaches worldwide, whereas the adapted marketing mix involves adjusting its elements in each target market, which incurs more costs but holds the hope of a larger market share (Egan, 2015; Lee & Carter, 2012). Table 10.1 shows three main questions (when? why? and how?) with regards to standardisation.

Table 10.1: The three questions of standardisation

Question	Explanation
When?	Commonalities in customers' needs across countries
	"Made in" image is important to a product's perceived value - for example, France for perfumes, Sheffield for stainless steel, Scottish salmon, and Aberdeen Angus beef.
	Homogeneity of markets, i. e. markets available without adaptation - e.g., denim jeans, NIVEA for Men, David Beckham aftershave, and Beats by Dr. Dre headphones.
	Cultural insensitivity – e.g., this would be of little problem to products such as Apple iPhones, but is important to fast food providers such as McDonalds and Pizza Hut who operate in Muslim countries where Halal products are a necessity.
Why?	Economies of scale in production, marketing/communications, research & development
	Minimizing costs
	Easier management and control
How?	Usually considered in the context of product, pricing, marketing communications; particularly advertising, branding, packaging

10

However, sometimes marketers don't understand foreign culture, and thus they fail to adapt properly. There are factors that force marketers to focus outside globally consistent marketing communications (Vrontis et al., 2009). Lee & Carter (2012) highlight two main factors preventing standardisation of marketing communications, both are exhibited in Figure 10.1.

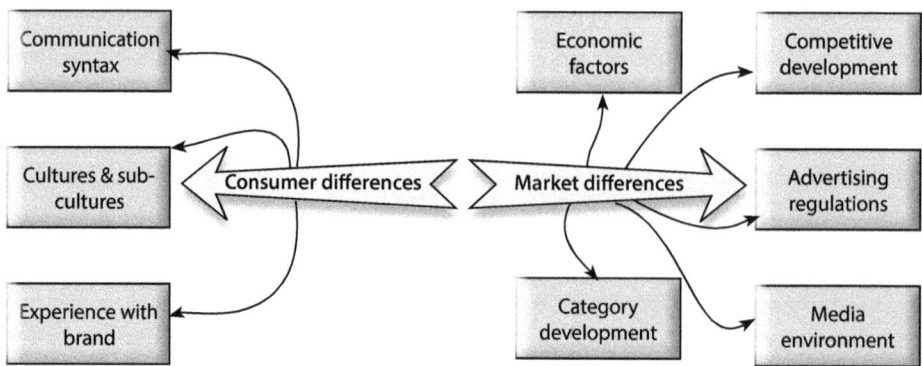

Figure 10.1: Factors preventing standardisation of marketing communications. Adapted from Lee & Carter (2012)

As Figure 10.1 highlights, Lee & Carter (2012) indicate that market and consumer difference are the two main factors which prevent the standardisation of marketing communications.

- First, **market differences** can vary depending on the brand, sector and country. This includes: economic factors (e.g., consumers level of affordability across different countries); media environment (e.g., consumers consume media differently); advertising regulations (e.g., restriction in advertising with regards to certain age groups or vulnerable people); category development (e.g., segmenting markets into different groups or sub-groups); and competitive development (e.g., how to enter into the particular competitive market) (Busch et al., 2006; Martenson, 1987).

- On the other hand, **consumer differences** play an important role, and refer to the disparities between individuals which have the ability to influence the way in which marketing communications are understood and processed. This includes issues relating to: cultural differences (e.g., attitude towards the consumption of particular product in a specific culture); communication syntax (e.g., understanding social habits and values of different countries); and experience with the brand (e.g., understanding how consumers use or engage with a brand).

Advantages and disadvantages of global marketing

Keller (2011) explains the advantages (Figure 10.2) and disadvantages (Figure 10.3) of global marketing with regards to branding and marketing communications.

Figure 10.2: Advantages of global marketing programmes (Keller, 2011)

- **Uniformity of marketing practices** occurs by keeping the core of the marketing program constant, allowing marketers to pay greater attention to making refinements across markets and to improve effectiveness over time.

- **Economies of scale in production and distribution** can be seen as manufacturing efficiencies and lower costs that derive from higher volumes in production and distribution.

- **Lower marketing costs** can arise from uniformity in packaging, advertising, promotion, and other marketing communication activities.

- **Power and scope** refers to the ability of a global brand's profile to communicate credibility. For example, the American car rental company, Avis assures its customers that they can receive the same high-quality car rental service anywhere in the world, further reinforcing a key benefit promise embodied in its slogan 'We Try Harder'.

- **Consistency in brand image** is about an organisation maintaining a common marketing platform all over the world with the intention of nurturing a consistent brand and company image. For example, American Express communicates the prestige and utility of its credit card worldwide.

- The **ability to leverage good ideas quickly and efficiently** takes place when marketers can leverage effective ideas across markets as long as the right knowledge transfer systems are put into place. For instance, IBM has a web-

10

based communications tool that provides instant multimedia interaction to connect marketers. (Keller, 2011).

Despite these benefits, there are disadvantages of global marketing programs.

Disadvantages of global marketing programs

| Differences in consumer needs, wants and usage patterns for products | Differences in consumer response to branding elements | Differences in consumer responses to marketing mix elements |

| Differences in brand and product development and the competitive environment | Differences in the legal environment | Differences in marketing instutions |

| Differences in administrative procedures |

Figure 10.3: Advantages of global marketing programmes (Keller, 2011)

- **Differences in consumer needs, wants, and usage patterns for products** lead customers to behave very differently. Therefore, product strategies that work in one country may not work in another. For example, in France, more expensive cookware products sell much better than in the USA, where customers buy more plastic containers.

- **Differences in consumer response to branding elements** is problematic and normally occurs when linguistic differences across countries can change the meaning of a brand name.

- **Differences in consumer responses to marketing mix elements** relate to the differences in price sensitivity, promotion responsiveness, sponsorship support, and other activities that can occur across countries.

- **Differences in brand and product development and the competitive environment** arise because products may be at different stages of their life cycle in different countries. The nature of competition also differs.

- **Differences in the legal environment** can also be challenging, for example, Venezuela, Canada, and Australia stipulated that commercials had to be physically produced in the native country.

■ **Differences in marketing institutions** is an issue that makes implementation of the same marketing strategy difficult. For example, the penetration of cable television, cell phones, supermarkets, may vary considerably, especially in developing countries.

■ **Differences in administrative procedures** is a problem and aries when it may be difficult to achieve the control necessary to implement a standardised global marketing program. (Keller, 2011)

Exercise

Consider the advantages of a global marketing strategy. Search a popular brand of your choice and identify how they have benefited from such an approach. Don't only consider what they have done well, but reflect on what they haven't. What recommendations would you give them?

Country of origin effects

Country of origin effects can bestow a halo of prestige on brands emanating from particular countries (Pappu et al., 2006). For example, UK and German motor-car design and engineering, Japanese technology, Swiss watches, French food and wine, Italian fashion, Colombian coffee, Indian tea, Belgian beer, and Thai food (Hackley, 2012; Yoo et al., 2000). Country of origin is also a powerful image variable that could be used to achieve competitive advantage in international marketing (Chao, 1993). That images have the power to stimulate and thus affect a consumers' choice process is widely documented. Normally, during the development of a company's marketing communication mix, the marketing or advertising manager is often vigorously involved in creating, adapting, monitoring, maintaining and managing images (Bertoli, 2013).). Recent studies by Chiang and Young (2023) have further emphasized the significance of country-of-origin (COO) as a key determinant in shaping consumer perceptions and behaviors. The concept of COO brand personality suggests that consumers often associate specific personality traits with products from certain countries, such as French sophistication or Japanese serenity. These associations can serve as powerful marketing tools, enhancing brand differentiation and loyalty.

Additionally, brand equity may not be wholly understood without examining its sources, which are the contributing elements to the formation of brand equity in the consumer's mind. The majority of brand equity studies concentrate on the marketing mix variables such as advertising, distribution, price and product quality as the contributing drivers (Yoo et al., 2000). In the buying process, consumers

10

are not just concerned about the quality and price of a product, but also other factors such as the brand's country of origin. One of the most effective conceptual frameworks of brand equity is presented by Yoo et al. (2000) who incorporated country of origin image as an antecedent of brand equity. In this framework, individual dimensions of brand equity are linked to the outcome, and the antecedent of brand equity is linked to the dimensions of brand equity. Thus, to manage brand equity, the relationships between the antecedents and brand equity dimensions and between the dimensions of brand equity and brand equity outcome, should be determined. Integrating COO into the brand's marketing strategy can provide a unique path for emotional connection and self-expression for consumers, ultimately influencing their purchasing decisions and enhancing brand equity (Chiang and Young, 2023).

Recent research by Mandler et al. (2023) investigates the impact of brand origin misclassification on brand evaluation. Their study reveals that when consumers learn about the true origin of a previously misclassified brand, it influences their purchase intentions through cognitive and affective brand re-evaluations. These effects vary depending on whether the misclassification is favourable or unfavourable. For instance, affective brand evaluations are adjusted only if the true origin has a worse country image than the assumed origin. This underscores the importance of accurate brand origin knowledge and its impact on brand perception and consumer behavior in international marketing.

Exercise

Identify a number of the brands which you think have gained a competitive advantage in international marketing through the country of origin effect. What did these brands specifically do which contributed to their success? Can you think of any brands which have been damaged through their association with their country of origin? Can you think of alternative strategies which these brands could have employed?

Advertising translation

The reason why this chapter centres its attention on standardisation and international marketing is because its effectiveness has been questioned in cross-cultural communications. Research in translation studies suggests that layout does not normally carry any cultural meaning, which implies that text and images are utterly independent. Here, it is important to highlight the implications of the terms 'translator' and 'translation'. There is a general belief that translators go beyond their traditional role as experts on linguistic transfer (i.e., cultural mediation, adaptation and creativeness), and therefore these two terms seem to be insufficient to express the multiple dimensions in global communications. Some of the names suggested to replace the term 'translator' include: 'transcreator', 'copywriter' and 'adaptor'. In advertising, the terms 'translation' is normally avoided and replaced by terms such as 'copy adaptation' and 'localisation'. In recent years, there has been a growing amount of literature on global marketing communications with regards to advertising translation. For example, some studies discussed assisting translators with concepts within the decision-making process; some explored the role of translation from a multidisciplinary view; and others researched the effect of globalisation on the media, which is a common channel of distribution for commercial advertising. The main concern here is the fact that globalisation can lead to homogenisation as well as the dominance of the Anglo-Saxon culture and language from world power countries resulting in irregularities and an 'unequal cultural exchange' (Hackley, 2012; Keller, 2011).

As a result, researchers should pay attention to whether the powerful stand-ard commercial messages distributed through global media convey the same meaning to consumers from different cultural backgrounds. Marketing scholars can use cultural-dimension frameworks. For example, Edward Said's Orientalism focuses on the interplay between the 'Occident' and the 'Orient'. The Occident is his term for the West (e.g., Britain, France, and the United States), and the Orient is the term for the romantic and misunderstood Middle East and Far East. Michel Foucault concentrates on social power, cultural imperialism and feminism. Greet Hofstede's six dimensions of national cultures including *power distance, individualism, uncertainty avoidance, masculinity, long term orientation*, and *indulgence vs. restraint*. However, one should give extra attention to selecting the most suitable framework in different research settings in global marketing communications and advertising studies.

Conclusions

Today's marketplace is truly global in nature and offers organisations the opportunity to enter various countries and target different consumer groups across the world. However, for organisations and their brands to flourish successfully, marketing managers must learn to tackle the intricacies of the global marketplace. This chapter has highlighted that there are advantages for an organisation that can successfully standardise the marketing communication process and find a common denominator of meaning that transcends cultures. Despite this, the attractions of international markets and the appeal of brands that cross national boundaries have to be understood in terms of local cultural meaning systems. All communications are very sensitive to local culture and conditions and, without due attention, can be problematic for marketers. This chapter has also emphasised the importance for marketing managers to consider the advantages and disadvantages of global marketing programs, as well as the issues surrounding country of origin effects. All forms of international marketing communications have a central purpose: to ensure that the intended messages are communicated accurately between the transmitter and the recipient. However, as this chapter has highlighted, the choices which encompass international advertising and marketing are complex and require carefully planning and strategic thinking.

Recommended reading

Holt, D. B., Quelch, J. A., & Taylor, E. L. (2004). How global brands compete. *Harvard Business Review*, **82**(9), 68-75.

This article is essential reading for understanding the dynamics of global brand competition. It delves into strategies that global brands employ to navigate cultural differences and local market challenges. The authors discuss how successful global brands create a balance between global consistency and local relevance. This article provides valuable insights into brand management and marketing strategies in an increasingly globalized economy.

Katsikeas, C., Leonidou, L., & Zeriti, A. (2019). Revisiting international marketing strategy in a digital era: Opportunities, challenges, and research directions. *International Marketing Review*, **37**(3), 405–424.

This paper presents the opportunities and challenges facing firms in this new digital era concerning their international marketing strategy and examine how international marketing practices can be revisited in the light of these developments.

Levitt, T. (1983). The Globalisation of Markets. *Harvard Business Review*, **61**, 92-102.

This is one of the classic articles published more than four decades ago in which the Theodore Levit declared that a global market has emerged in which brands should sell standardized products in international markets using the "economics of simplicity".

Makrides, A., Kvasova, O., Thrassou, A., Hadjielias, E., & Ferraris, A. (2021). Consumer cosmopolitanism in international marketing research: A systematic review and future research agenda. *International Marketing Review*, **39**(5), 1151–1181.

The paper provides a systematic literature review of consumer cosmopolitanism (CCOS) from an international marketing perspective and to provide a foundation for future research on the subject matter to proliferate and prosper.

Pappavassilliou, N., & Stathakopoulos, V. (1997). Standardisation versus adaptation of international advertising strategies: towards a framework. *European Journal of Marketing*, **31**, 504-527.

This article addresses the debate between standardization and adaptation of international advertising strategies. It presents a comprehensive framework for determining appropriate strategies, considering local, firm, and intrinsic factors. The article argues that standardization and adaptation are not dichotomous but exist on a continuum, providing a nuanced understanding of international marketing. This makes it essential for comprehending how to tailor advertising strategies to different global markets effectively.

Review Questions

1) Which of the following areas can be associated with international advertising?

a) Local regulations.

b) Coordination of multi-country communication efforts.

c) Budgeting.

d) All of the above.

2) According to Levitt (1983) what has made multinational corporations obsolete and the global corporation absolute?

a) Advancements in communication technologies.

b) Global needs becoming more differentiated.

c) The worlds needs and desires becoming irreversibly homogenised.

d) Increasing levels of deregulation.

3) Considering people and different economic, political and social units in the world, what has the process has globalisation resulted in?

a) Greater interdependence and mutual awareness.

b) Fractured relations between nations.

c) A reduction in interdependence.

d) Mutual awareness of different cultures becoming less significant.

4) In relation to international marketing, what does standardisation refer to?

a) A marketing approach which requires limited focus on its ethical implications.

b) A marketing approach which is only relevant to a specific market segment.

c) A marketing approach which is homogeneous and can be used internationally.

d) A marketing approach which requires limited investment.

10

5) Which of the following is not a possible advantage of a global marking program?

   a) Economies of scale
   b) Lower marketing costs
   c) Differences in consumer responses to marketing mix elements
   d) Power and scope

6) What is one of the disadvantages of global marketing programs, as discussed by Keller (2011)?

   a) Consistency in brand image.
   b) Economies of scale in production.
   c) Differences in consumer needs and usage patterns.
   d) Leveraging good ideas quickly across markets.

7) During the development of a company's marketing communications mix, which of the following is not a task that the marketing or advertising manager is often vigorously involved in?

   a) Monitoring
   b) Maintaining
   c) Adapting
   d) Vamoosing

8) What does the term 'glocalisation' refer to in international marketing?

   a) Standardizing all aspects of the marketing mix across global markets.
   b) Adapting global marketing themes to fit local cultural contexts.
   c) Creating entirely new products for each market.
   d) Ignoring local cultures to promote a global brand image.

9) According to Hackley (2012), which issue arises from the dominance of Anglo-Saxon culture and language in global media?

   a) Increased costs of global advertising.
   b) Unequal cultural exchange and potential homogenization.
   c) Greater consistency in global brand messaging.
   d) Simplified communication with global audiences.

10) Which of the following is NOT a potential disadvantage of a brand being closely associated with its country of origin?

   a) Negative country reputation affecting brand perception
   b) Inconsistent brand image across markets
   c) Decreased production costs
   d) Misalignment with local cultural expectations

Answers

The answers to these questions can be found at the back of this book, or at the Marketing Communications page at Goodfellow Publishers:

https://www.goodfellowpublishers.com

References

American Marketing Association (2015) American Marketing Association Dictionary, available at: https://www.ama.org/resources/Pages/Dictionary.aspx

Bertoli, G. (2013). *International Marketing and the Country of Origin Effect: the global impact of 'made in Italy'*. Cheltenham: Edward Elgar Publishing.

Busch, R., Seidenspinner, M. & Unger, F. (2006). *Marketing Communication Policies*. Berlin: Springer Science & Business Media.

Chao, P. (1993). Partitioning country of origin effects: consumer evaluations of a hybrid product. *Journal of International Business Studies*, **24**(2), 291-306.

Chiang, L.-L. (Luke), & Yang, C.-S. (2018). Does country-of-origin brand personality generate retail customer lifetime value? A Big Data analytics approach. *Technological Forecasting and Social Change*, **130**, 177–187.

Egan, J. (2015). *Marketing Communications*. London: Sage Publications Limited.

Grein, A. F. & Gould, S. J. (1996). Globally integrated marketing communications. *Journal of Marketing Communications, 2*, 141-158.

Hackley, C. (2012). *Advertising and Promotion: An Integrated Marketing Communications Approach,* 2nd ed. London.

Kanso, A. & Kitchen, P. J. (2004). Marketing consumer services internationally: Localisation and standardisation revisited. *Marketing Intelligence & Planning*, **22**(2), 201-215.

Keller, K. L. (2011). *Strategic Brand Management: Building, measuring, and managing brand equity,* 4th ed. UK: Pearson.

Kitchen, P. J. & Schultz, D. E. (1999). A multi-country comparison of the drive for IMC. *Journal of Advertising Research*, **39**(1), 21-21.

Koekemoer, L. & Bird, S. (2004). *Marketing Communications*. South Africa: Juta and Company Limited.

Lee, K. & Carter, S. (2012). *Global Marketing Management,* 3rd ed. London: Oxford University Press.

Levitt, T. (1983). The globalisation of markets. *Harvard Business Review, 61*, 92-102.

Mandler, T., Bartsch, F., & Zeugner-Roth, K. P. (2023). Are brands re-evaluated when consumers learn about brand origin misperceptions? Outcomes,

10

processes, and contingent effects. *Journal of Business Research,* **164**, 113941.

Martenson, R. (1987). Is standardisation of marketing feasible in culture-bound industries? A European case study. *International Marketing Review,* **4**(3), 7-17.

Melewar, T. C. & Saunders, J. (1999). International corporate visual identity: standardization or localization? *Journal of International Business Studies,* **30**(3), 583-598.

Monye, S. O. (2000). *The Handbook of International Marketing* Oxford: Blackwell

Pappavassilliou, N. & Stathakopoulos, V. (1997). Standardisation versus adaptation of international advertising strategies: Towards a framework. *European Journal of Marketing,* **31**, 504-527.

Pappu, R., Quester, P. G. & Cooksey, R. W. (2006). Consumer-based brand equity and country-of-origin relationships: Some empirical evidence. *European Journal of marketing,* **40**(5/6), 696-717.

Percy, L. & Rosenbaum-Elliott, R. (2012). *Strategic Advertising Management,* 4th ed. London: Oxford.

Quelch, J. A., & Hoff, E. J. (1986) Customizing global marketing. *Harvard Business Review,* **64**(3), 59-68

Ramarapu, S., Timmerman, J. E. & Ramarapu, N. (1999). Choosing between globalization and localization as a strategic thrust for your international marketing effort. *Journal of Marketing Theory and Practice,* **7**(2), 97-105.

Roberts, J. (1998). *Multinational Business Service Firms: The development of multinational organisation structures in UK business services sector,* Aldershot: Ashgate Publishing.

Solomon, M. R., Marshall, G. W., & Stuart, E. W. (2009). *Marketing: Real people, real decisions.* Harlow: Pearson Education.

Solomon, M. (2013). *Consumer Behavior: Buying, having and being.* Harlow: Pearson.

Szymanski, D. M., Bharadwaj, S. G., & Varadarajan, P. R. (1993). Standardization versus adaptation of international marketing strategy: an empirical investigation. *The Journal of Marketing,* **57**(4) 1-17.

Terpstra, V., Foley, J. & Sarathy, R. (2012). *International Marketing.* US: Naper Press.

Turnbull, P. W. & Doherty-Wilson, L. (1990). The internationalisation of the advertising industry. *European Journal of Marketing,* **24**, 7-16.

Vrontis, D., Thrassou, A. & Lamprianou, I. (2009). International marketing adaptation versus standardisation of multinational companies. *International Marketing Review,* **26**(4/5), 477-500.

Yoo, B., Donthu, N., & Lee, S. (2000). An examination of selected marketing mix elements and brand equity. *Journal of the Academy of Marketing Science,* **28**(2), 195-211.

11 Case Studies

Geraldine Bell, Kitty Shaw, Elaine Collinson and Kathryn Waite

There are six case studies in this chapter. The case studies have been designed so that deeper insight is gained and developed, and to give an opportunity to evidence critical application of theory. These are mini-cases which give an overview of a marketing management and marketing communication(s) problem which has either been resolved or is being evaluated with several options open to marketing managers. In some cases, it may be that the scenario is a review of a campaign which requires you to evaluate it. You should tackle the case by underpinning the scenario with the theoretical concepts drawn from the relevant chapters in this book, and by answering the questions relative to both theory and the practice illustrated in the scenario, and also critically question the case by looking at alternative exemplars to enrich your answer. Note that most of these cases relate to more than one chapter in this book and therefore the chapter references are for guidance only.

Outline answers are available online at:
www.goodfellowpublishers.com/marcomms

1: 'Dirt is good' – Planning for marketing communications

Persil's new research says Dirt is good!

"Who would've thought that dirt could be so good", said the researcher on reading the results from the recent consumer feedback. Unilever, which manages Persil/Omo, had just created one of the most noted modern-day brand stories ever developed. The brief had been to not just understand that the brand had a strong connection with the human side of consumers and their relationship with laundry, but to be more meaningful in the space within which the brand existed. Thus, the backbone of being 'humanist and connected' was formed. The value link was between mothers, children and dirt. The creative agency however, made it more value-creating when they pitched it as being not just between mothers, kids and dirt, but also between adventures and experience. This spark of ingenuity came about through research into exploring the link between true emotion and the everyday chore of cleaning laundry. This deep insight was translated from "if you are not free to get dirty, you cannot experience life and grow". The meaning here was that a parent's desire for a 'free' child was relative to the constraints of being clean and not messy. Growing up can be a dirty business indeed! Persil were now able to develop a narrative arc based around the promise that "dirt is good" because without it there would be no experience. On the Persil website they outline the basis of this assurance with the premise that:

"Dirt is the mark of adventure. It's a sign that we're getting stuck in and learning from life. Children don't only learn by being taught. They learn by doing. Hands on experience, discovery, and trial and error are vital to every child's healthy happy development. Laundry might not be fun, but don't worry – Persil will take care of even the toughest of stains, so you can concentrate on the important stuff. Dirt is essential experience of life".

As David Arkwright, the former global brand director for Unilever's laundry business says this is the story "that would shift the banal to the truly meaningful" and live on for a long time. Industry experts view "Dirt is Good" as a best practice illustration in creative development within brand communications, because it resonates by addressing parent's inherent tension between controlling instincts relative to getting too dirty and their desire for a child to grow up through play and being free to do so. Prior to this dirt was seen as the enemy. The big idea here is a game-changer and is disruptive in that it was fairly provocative and generated buzz around the brand. The creative treatment can now be fully developed across multiple media platforms.

Source: Adapted from Hernandez R (2012) www.millwardbrown.co.uk , Arkwright (2014) in www.marketingmagzine.co.uk and www.persil.co.uk.

Review questions

To help you develop and gain insight, you can draw on Chapters 5 *Planning for Marketing Communications*; 6 *Brands and Brand Communications*; 8 *Creativity in Advertising and Promotion* and 11 *Evaluating Marketing Communications*.

Discuss what is meant by a creative treatment which is developed to be used across multiple media platforms. What kind of a creative platform is "Dirt is good"?

What exactly is a brand's promise and identify the underlining meaning of Persil's promise that "Dirt is good"?

How important is the customer value proposition in terms of

Integrated Marketing Communications (managerial perspective)
Consumer (the consumer/end-user perspective)

3   a) Explain how you would use research in developing brand communications? And,

b) How would you expect to use research in evaluating the outcome?

11

2: 'Cadbury's Taste' – Translating creativity in advertising and promotions

It's all in the words when two global players collide over 'taste'!

Cadbury has replaced its 'Free the joy' tagline with 'Tastes like this feels' and commentators in the trade press have been quick to point out that this proposition is very similar to the mighty Coca Cola's 'Taste the feeling' – in fact, so similar, that they are predicting a 'war on words'!

Cadbury has rolled out a new global brand campaign for its Dairy Milk brand. The tagline 'Taste like this feels' is a departure from the previous one which was all about wanting us to feel free to make more of those 'joyful' moments. (Remember comic actor James Cordon in Cadbury's 2014 'free the joy' campaign which features him lip-synching to an Estelle track. See more at http://www.campaign-live.co.uk/article/james-corden-frees-joy-cadbury-campaign/1281269). The new advertising is centred on the premise of the 'consumption experience', hence the word 'taste' in 'Taste like this feels'. This is translated into executions which focus on the unique taste sensations that each chocolate bar in the range delivers, leading to that ultimate 'moment of joy'. Cadbury's say that they are moving on now but the aim is still to remind people that joy is never too far away. Taste is a sub-branch of the 'free the joy' idea, according to Cadbury's global brand equity director, Nikhil Rao when questioned recently in marketing week, reinforcing that in going forward "the spotlight was now on taste".

And so for now, Cadbury is saying that this focus is a point of difference from Coke's. Whilst its focus is on the consumption experience, Coke's 'Taste the feeling' is focused on the consequence of when a customer consumes its products. In other words, Cadbury is saying that *taste* comes before *feeling*, that is, the sensation of taste predetermines the way that taste makes you feel, hence, the consequence. In asking several chocoholics and committed coke drinkers for their views, it turns out that the consumption experience includes both taste and the consequence, so the end-user just thinks it's all a bit of a war on words. The point of difference may well be in the execution and the medium, for example, the storyline and social media platform. Cadbury's creative treatment includes animals enjoying a delightful moment set to popular music tracks – Cadbury's Dairy Milk Medley features a cat and a dog relaxing and having an indulgent moment, Cadbury's Dairy Milk Big Taste features a dog having an adventurous experience enjoying a free-ride as a motorbike sidecar passenger, and Cadbury's Dairy Milk classic features a bear getting intense satisfaction by satisfying its itch up against a tree. (You can see the bear enjoy a good scratch to the music of KC & the Sunshine Band's 'That's the Way (I Like it)' at https://www.youtube.com/watch?v=Dd_GSSQQGNY.)

All three creative treatments are using a metaphor to elicit that 'wonderful feeling' which Cadbury's Dairy Milk product variants can give you. The first TV spot was aired during a commercial break in the UK during Saturday night's Ant and Dec show (2 April, 2016). However it is a multi-platform push and will extend to social, experiential, digital and PR. Following its prime spot airing on STV, there was an experiential event at Westfield, one of London's large shopping malls. Shoppers were invited to take their weight off their feet by slipping off their shoes and stepping onto the some bubble wrap and indulge in a chocolate treat having a blissful few moments of fun during their hectic shopping day. (You can see more of this at https://www.youtube.com/watch?v=JFGbizQShPI.)

Meanwhile, Coke's advertising "dramatizes everyday moments in life and how Coke makes you feel as a result of consumption", says Rao of Cadburys. Sound familiar? In this case, forget about the battle of words – what about the visual? The battle here is in the *pencil* as well as the pen.

Adapted from: www.marketingweek.com [accessed 05/04/2016]; www.thedrum.com/news 01/04/2016 [accessed 05/04/2016]; www.campaignlive.co.uk [accessed on04/04/2016] and www.adnews.com [accessed 05/04/2016].

Review questions

To help you develop and gain insight, you can draw on Chapters 5 *Planning for Marketing Communications*; 6 *Branding and Brand Communications* and 8 *Creativity in Advertising and Promotion*.

Discuss the rationale for a brand proposition.

Evaluate the creative strategies that a marketing manager and/or creative agent can draw on, and discuss the tactics applied in this case.

11

3: Creativity in advertising and promotion: 'Seduction'

Marks and Spencer tries to seduce us yet again!

It is almost 10 years since M&S's iconic food advertising put the food department of the lifestyle retail store on the specialist 'foody' map with its "this isn't just…" strapline. In 2010, M&S finally ditched this strapline and moved towards a new proposition "just because …" it's Marks and Spencer. Today, in 2016, it has tinkered with the positioning and now its advertising features "adventures of…" see for example, *Adventures in Fiesta*, summer 2016. (www.marketingweek.com/2016/04/21/how-ms-transformed-its-schizophrenic-food-marketing/)

The new advertising is a far cry from its seductive past, or is it? In 2005 it was sultry, and not that long ago, it was still fairly sensual with some movement with a bit of 'food wobble' to entice a more emotive connection. However, today, it's safe to say that M&S has become much more dynamic and yes, exciting. Not only is there a lot of movement in the ad, but there is also a definite shift to a younger audience. And price isn't mentioned once. There are no promotional or seasonal offers – yet. What there is a very stylish filmic production with lots of creative advertising content. The music is brisk and moves you along; the colour is primary and bright; there are strong cues in food shapes, textures and types; lots of combinations. And it is very dynamic – there are patterns and there are explosions. It dazzles and it's fun. It makes you smile, it makes you happy. And that of course, is what summer and the holiday season is all about.

It is clear that the brand attributes displayed in the advertising, and across all the different creative treatments of the new campaign, are that its food in its food hall is "different, exciting, fresh and new" confirms Ansall, M&S's global customer director. He now takes on the unenviable task of translating this 'adventurous' positioning across the fashion department. Meanwhile, rewiring our brains away from the infamous, and much parodied food pornography of 2005 where the slow and husky voice told us that "this is not just any chocolate pudding, but a Marks and Spencer chocolate pudding!" is going to be hard. But as Scotland's advertising trade magazine points out, the new advertising finishes on a gorgeous-looking shot of a chocolate orange cake being sliced ready for eating. Meanwhile, Ansall defends M&S saying "we're trying to make new neuro connections"! So, food porn isn't quite dead in the water just yet!

Source: Adapted from www.huffingtonpost.com, 02.04.2014; www.marketingweek.com, 24.03.2010, 12.04.2016 & 09.05.2016; and The Drum, 22.04.2016. All sources accessed on 25/07/2016.

Review questions

To help you develop and gain insight, you can draw on Chapter 7 *Creativity in Advertising and Promotion*.

Identify which type of motivational appeal Marks and Spencer are using to make its creative advertising generate increased attention. Why?

Evaluate the significance of framing creative appeals.

Discuss the tactics M&S uses to get you to sit up and attend to its advertising.

a) Explain what a borrowed-interest device is and evaluate how M&S uses devices in its advertising.

b) Highlight at least three best practice exemplars that use different borrowed-interest devices to attract attention.

11

4: IMC at Standard Life

The investment company, Standard Life plc., based in the UK, is one of the top 500 companies worldwide by revenue, as listed in the 2015 Fortune Global 500. The business has around 4.5 million customers and clients around the world with operations in the UK, North America, Europe, Asia and Australia, while its joint ventures and partnerships in India and China support a further 25 million customers. Around the world the group employs 6,500 people. Listed on the London Stock exchange, Standard Life has around 1.2 million individual shareholders across 50 countries. It is therefore a very large and complex business with an extensive and diverse range of stakeholders to consider. In short Standard Life has multiple communications sources and many other touch-points for a broad range of stakeholders around the world ranging from customers to shareholders. Therefore an integrated approach to communications is critical.

Communications context

Historically, the Standard Life group has comprised a number of distinct business units which each having their own communications functions, focusing on the needs of their own markets and stakeholders. Recognising the need for greater consistency of communications across the group, the Communications Executive was established in 2014, led by the Group Director of Communications and Brand. The Communications Executive, which included members of each business unit, as well as core group-level communications functions, drew up a group communications strategy to support the group's business strategy. This strategy, which sets out the communications objectives and key messages to support the business strategy, is designed to provide overarching guidance for all communications, both internal and external, while giving individual business units the freedom to respond to the needs of their own markets and stakeholder groups. This integrated marketing communications strategy covers the period 2014-2016. Figure 11.1 illustrates the group's communications strategy and its links to corporate goals.

High level communications strategy

Standard Life's corporate goal in 2014 was to "*Drive shareholder value through being a leading customer–centric business focused on long-term savings and investments propositions.*" Figure 11.1 shows how the communications strategy flows from the corporate strategy and is worked all the way through to messaging, and what this should mean for key stakeholder groups. The Communications Purpose, which focuses on enhancing brand and corporate reputation through engagement and advocacy among stakeholders feeds into six communications objectives intended to support the achievement of the business objective. These are then developed into propositions for each of the business's stakeholder groups. Customers for example should be able to look forward to the future with confidence, while the media should see the company as providing thought leadership to the industry, driven by market and customer insight. Key messages are then developed to support the delivery of this strategy and positioning. The group's brand values, shown at the base, support and underpin the whole strategy and framework.

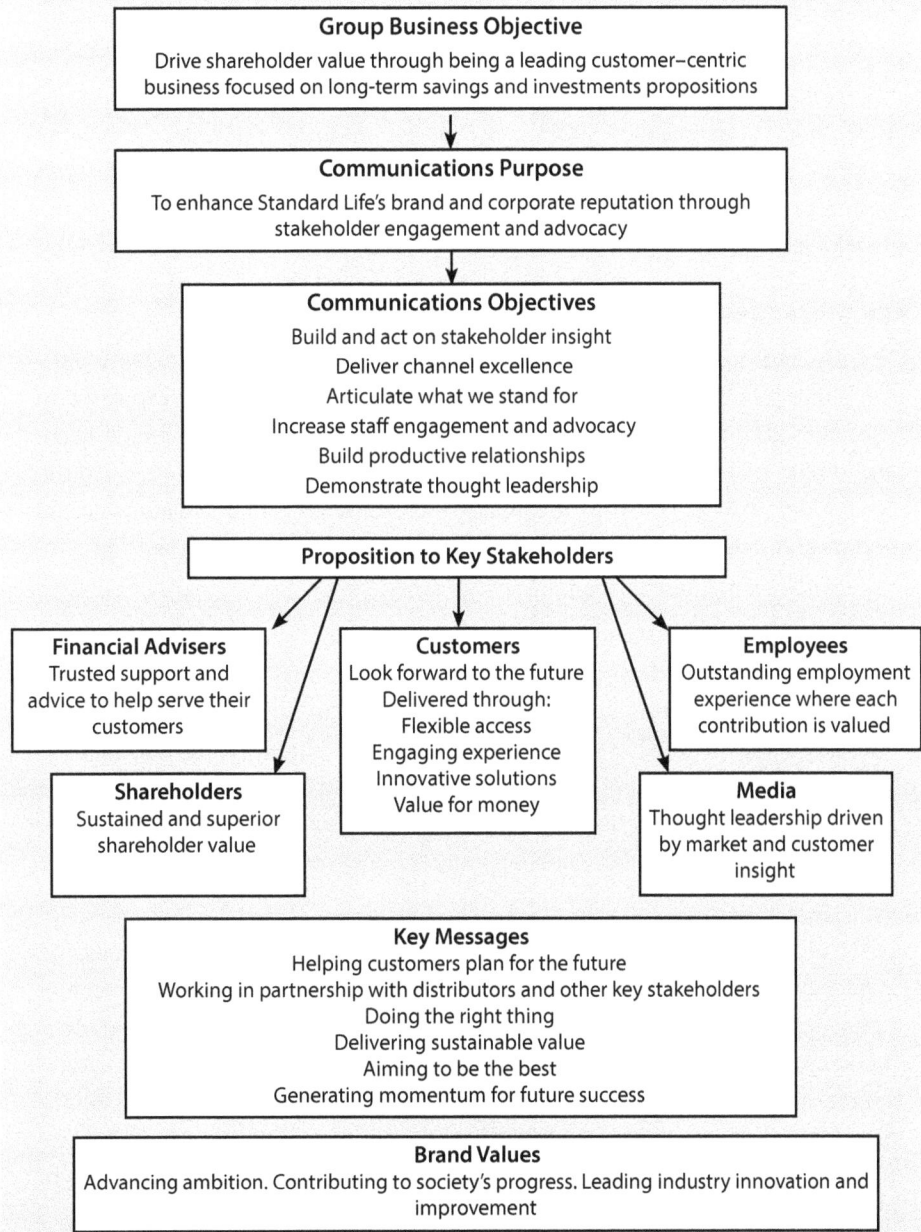

Figure 11.1: Group communications strategy

This is a high-level communications strategy, which is intended to influence and guide all strategic and tactical communications activity across the group whilst still enabling individual business units and geographic operations to have the flexibility to respond to the needs of their particular markets and stakeholders. All individual activities from press releases to social media and sponsorship should have a clear link back to the agreed strategy illustrated in Figure 11.1. As well as ensuring that all communications support this high level framework, it is equally important that there are no communications which contradict the key messages and thus undermine the group's credibility.

This group communication strategy is reviewed annually in line with the wider business planning cycle, to ensure that communications continue to support business strategy. While the high level purpose and brand values remain relevant, individual objectives and key messages may change as business strategy develops.

Key messages

The key messages in the framework underpin all communications activity. They can either be obvious in their expression, or perhaps not explicitly expressed in communications materials. Regardless as to the intensity of expression, they are and should be evident to stakeholders as an expression of the way in which the organisation conducts itself. The messages in the framework articulate what the company and its brand stand for and how the business wants to be seen.

Taking a closer look at how the messaging framework is applied, *'Helping customers plan for their future'* is articulated in a number of ways, including using customer and market insight to drive strategy and thus ensuring that the company's propositions, including its communications, are driven by customer needs, preferences and aspirations. This follows through to shaping the internal culture so that the whole organisation has a customer-centric approach. In this way a core positioning and set of messages is applied across all stakeholder groups and touch-points from media relations to marketing materials and customer servicing communications.

In 2015, at a more tactical level, this resulted in proactive work by UK spokespeople to provide thought leadership pieces on social media, covering pensions and investment related matters. The group has also conducted a number of consumer research projects which have then been released though press releases and social media, and published various research reports which are intended to help customers manage their finances by highlighting important issues, such as the need to plan for retirement, and the possible impacts of changes to legislation for customers, whilst at the same time supporting the group's positioning as a source of thought leadership and influence on issues important to the business.

Evidence of the key messages is one of the ways in which the company measures the success of its communications. Research is conducted on media coverage of the business, which specifically looks for evidence of these messages in how the business is reported in the media. This gives an indication of the success of communications activity in delivering and supporting these key messages.

Stakeholders

There are several different stakeholder groups or audiences to consider in a large and complex business like Standard Life. Table 11.1 below illustrates some of the key audiences to be considered by Standard Life in planning any communications. Individual business units may also have other audiences to consider and any significant Group communication would also need to take account of the London stock exchange and city analysts.

Table 11.1: The multiple stakeholders of Standard Life group.

Customers /clients	Segmented by product and distribution channel
Distributors	Independent financial advisers , Workplace consultants
Prospective customers	Segments targeted for growth
Shareholders	Institutional and Individual
Employees	Segmented by location, function and level
Media	National press, trade press, online news channels (trade and consumer), radio & TV
Other	Joint venture & strategic partners, UK Government & regulators, Overseas Governments & regulators

In planning for any communications, key audiences have to be identified and the needs and preferences of each audience considered. For example a new product launch in the UK may need to consider only UK stakeholders, while changes to the company structure or operating model may also need to be communicated to overseas partners and regulatory bodies. The international nature of the business and the availability of news 24 hours a day mean that it is critical that any major communications are carefully co-ordinated to reach different time-zones around the world in the right order.

Communications planning for individual projects

An integrated approach is also important for any individual communications project. In any initiative, the company must determine which are the key stakeholder audiences and develop messaging relevant to them through channels and media, which are appropriate and effective for reaching that particular group whilst supporting the business objectives. For example, in communicating the recent acquisition of a distributor in the UK where the overall aim of the communications plan was to co-ordinate and facilitate the successful announcement of the acquisition. This was achieved by delivering the right messages to the right audiences via the most appropriate channels for each. The communications team developed a detailed communications plan and identified the following as key audiences and stakeholders, which had to be considered in the communications plan: employees, clients, intermediaries and media and investment analysts. Having developed the key messages for the project, the specific needs and interests of each of these audiences was considered in developing a detailed communications plan. For example while employees would want to understand the rationale for the acquisition and city analysts would want to understand the fit with broader strategy, intermediaries would need to be reassured that this acquisition would not in any way affect the company's relationship with them, or that it would not bring the business into competition with them. Materials were then prepared for each of these audiences, which would deliver the key messages for the project but also address the needs of each audience in terms of the content, communications tools and channels used.

The overarching objective in developing an integrated communications plan here was to ensure that the delivery of messages to a diverse range of stakeholders was coordinated, supported the core business rationale for the acquisition, and addressed the key concerns of the various audience groups. The communications plan for a project like this would contain the elements shown in Figure 11.2.

Communication objectives
For example to communicate the business drivers and rationale for the acquisition
Communication Principles
To position the acquisition in the wider business context
Key stakeholders and their needs
Employees, Clients, and so on.
Key messages
E.g. How the acquisition strengthens Standard Life's business in the affected areas
Sign-off process
The governance process that underpinned the development, approval and delivery of communication outputs.
List of materials to be produced,
Including the responsible person and the target audience for each
Communications Timeline
 Detailing when each audience should receive communications, with which content and through which channel. For example, employees might receive a face-to-face briefing at the same time as the media are to be briefed by emailing a press release.

Figure 11.2 : Outline communications plan

Summary – striking a balance between global and local

The Group Communications strategy developed by Standard Life strikes a balance between ensuring a consistent positioning and messaging framework which supports the business strategy and giving each part of the group a degree of autonomy over their communications, which need to be tailored for their own market conditions. Some examples of how this works in practice can be seen in the screen shots that follow from websites belonging to different parts of the group. The first one is from the corporate website, www.standardlife.com and is about their sponsorship of the tennis player Andy Murray. This is replicated in style and tone on the company's Hong Kong Website, which follows. The next two shown are from the company's operations in the Republic of Ireland and Germany. Sponsorship of Andy Murray is less relevant to customers in these countries and so does not feature, but there is strong similarity in the style and tone of the websites to the Hong Kong one. So content is adapted for local markets but the look and feel are the same.

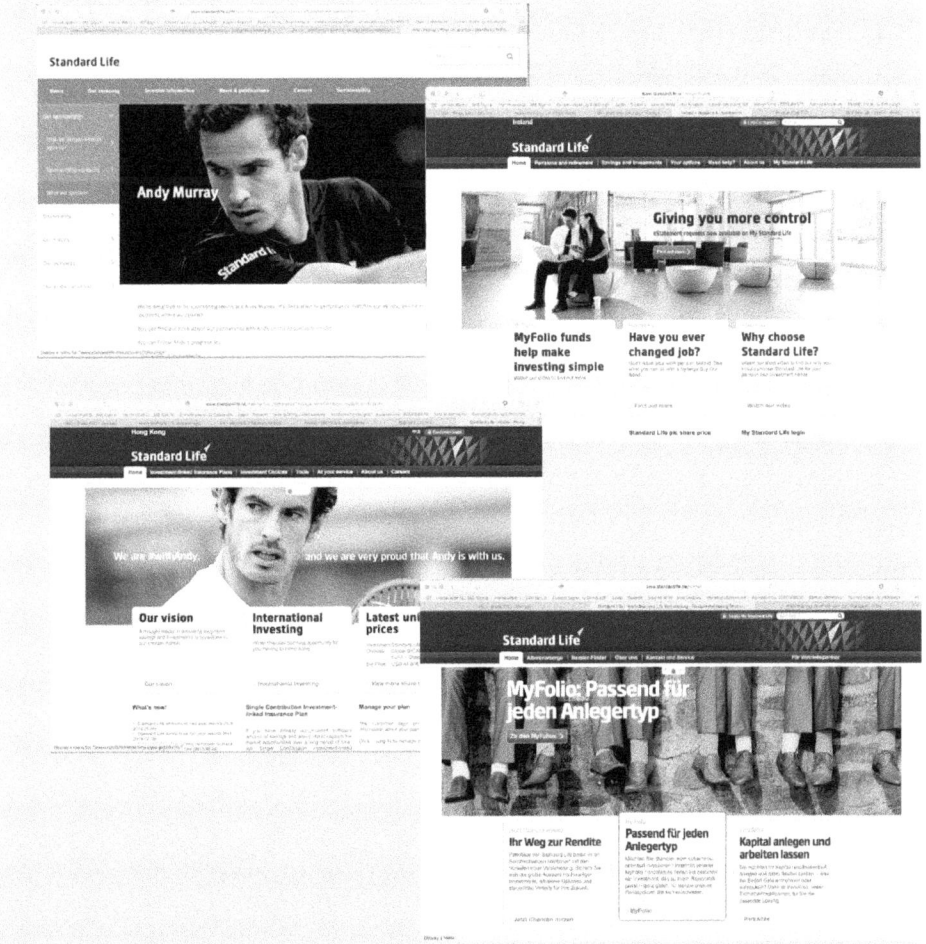

11

Thus the overarching objective is achieved where the messages and appeals that are directed and delivered to a diverse range of stakeholders are fully co-ordinated and integrated thereby addressing the various target audience groups.

Review questions

Why is it important to have a goal-directed communications strategy at Standard Life Plc?

How does this communications strategy provide direction to all Standard Life's stakeholders?

Critically evaluate the role that key messages play in the overall communications strategy.

How important is planning when targeting multiple stakeholders?

In conclusion, what does integration of communications mean to a company like Standard Life?

5: Old Spice Guy: From traditional to new media

This case study and the next draw on material from all marketing knowledge. However, this case specifically draws on Chapter 8, *Digital Marketing*.

Old Spice Guy

Old Spice is a brand of male grooming products which was created in 1938, and was a very popular mass-market brand. The product had distinct smell of orange, vanilla and nutmeg, and its television campaigns promoted the idea of the "Old Spice Man" as an athletic surfer. However by 2010 the Old Spice brand was perceived to be traditional, boring and no longer relevant for the younger consumer. These attitudes resulted in collapsing sales in a growing market-place for male toiletries. In 2010, a video was launched on YouTube and Twitter which featured Isaiah Mustafa, an actor who was formerly an American Football athlete, as the "Old Spice Guy". The video begins with Isaiah Mustafa standing in a shower addressing "Ladies" who might be sitting next to a man who might not look like Isaiah but who might smell like Isaiah. The video is extremely humorous and satirises traditional ideas of machismo. The video was primarily shared on Youtube and Twitter. An advertising agency created "response videos", where the "'Old Spice Guy" replies to comments from online influencers and celebrities. The campaign was immediately successful resulting in significant views, an increase in Twitter followers and an increase in traffic to the company website. In terms of share of voice, Old Spice accounted for 75% of the conversations in the male grooming category during 2010 and half of these conversations came from women. As a result of the campaign there were hundreds of parody videos made and posted online. Sales of the product rose by 55% in the three months during the campaign.

Source: Adapted from Barker, M.S., Barker, D.I., Bormann, N.F. & Neher, K.E. (2013) *Social Media Marketing: A Strategic Approach*. Cengage learning

11

Review questions

Discuss the extent to which the many-to-many marketing communication model can be applied to the 2010 "Old Spice Guy" campaign

Identify how the 2010 Old Spice Guy Campaign matched the brand's marketing objectives.

What might be the risks of this type of viral campaign?

6: Losing control at Qantas : Controlling digital marketing/viral campaigns

Qantas and control over viral campaigns

Qantas Airways Limited is an Australian airline group founded in Queensland in 1920. The company has grown to become Australia's largest domestic and international airline and employs over 30,000 people worldwide (Qantas, 2015). From the marketing and PR perspective, several of the activities organised by the company in the last years are a perfect example of the challenges that organisations are facing when conducting marketing activities in Web 2.0 environments. The airline ran into trouble in October 2011, when more than 68,000 passenger were stranded worldwide due to a labour dispute with three company unions (Rourke, 2011). The Australian government intervened and held emergency court sessions. Qantas aircraft were back in the air after three days, with a ruling from the court to resolve the dispute within 21 days or face a binding arbitration decision (McGuirk, 2011).

With the matter with the unions still unresolved, Qantas launched on November 23rd of the same year another competition to win one of 50 pairs of Qantas first-class pyjamas and a luxury amenity kit (Miller, 2011). The company invited its followers to participate in this contest using the hashtag #QantasLuxury, yet the initiative backfired and the hashtag was used by Qantas' customers to express their frustrations with the airline. The initiative quickly became a mechanism were consumers were complaining for being stranded due to the labour dispute, as well as other unrelated complains such as baggage loss and poor customer service. Within an hour of the hashtag being shared it reached over 500,000 users and resulted in 1.4 million impressions (Social Media News, 2011).

Kennedy (2011), a practitioner in social media monitoring, suggests that Qantas did not pay enough attention to the sentiment of its users prior to launching this initiative. She argues that before launching a social media campaign, companies need to check the temperature of the online channel they are planning to use. Evidence back then suggests that Twitter users had still in their minds the bad experience of the flights that were grounded just a weeks before.

References:

Qantas, (2015). Our Company | Qantas. http://www.qantas.com.au/travel/airlines/company/global/en (accessed 6.14.15).

Rourke, A., (2011). Qantas grounds entire worldwide fleet. *The Guardian*. http://www.theguardian.com/business/2011/oct/29/qantas-grounds-fleet-industrial-action (accessed 6.15.15).

McGuirk, R., (2011). Aussie court ends Qantas strike, fleet grounding. *Yahoo News*. URL http://news.yahoo.com/aussie-court-ends-qantas-strike-fleet-grounding-152252309.html (accessed 6.15.15).

Miller, D., (2011). Qantas Twitter campaign takes nosedive. *ABC News*. http://www.abc.net.au/news/2011-11-22/qantas-twitter-hashtag-backfires/3686940 (accessed 6.15.15).

Social Media News (2011). The #QantasLuxury Fail. http://www.socialmedianews.com.au/the-qantasluxury-fail/ [Accessed on: 22-07-2015].

Kennedy, A., 2011. Qantas makes hash of tweet campaign. *Traveller*. http://www.traveller.com.au/qantas-makes-hash-of-tweet-campaign-1nsa4 (accessed 6.15.15)

Review questions

What motivations can you identify behind the generation of negative eWOM in Qantas' promotional activity?

Once the campaign went live, was there any way in which Qantas could have minimised the impact of the negative eWOM?

According to the steps discussed in this chapter to plan a viral campaign, which ones were overlooked by the Qantas team and resulted in the outcome described in the case study?

11

7: Research and evaluating marketing communications: Aegon and measurement in action

Aegon is an established provider of financial products. Aegon has approximately £542 billion assets under management, with businesses in over 25 countries. In the UK it serves around two million UK customers. The Aegon brand has evolved but stays steadfastly committed to its original purpose - helping people take responsibility for their financial future.

Historically the financial services sector was very fragmented, with products bought through intermediaries with the cost of advice invisible to the customer. In 2012 the regulations changed and this resulted in many "orphaned clients", who typically had a series of individual pensions with previous employers or a self-employed pension, but with limited knowledge of the pension value or how best to invest. The changes led to a seismic shift in the industry requiring the focus on the end customer using direct methods of communication rather than through an agent, broker or advisor.

Aegon used primary research to discover that low numbers were saving towards their retirement and only 32% of working-aged people had a dedicated retirement package. In 2004 they responded to this by launching an innovative on-line product branded as Retiready, which gives all individuals (not just Aegon customers) control of their own financial management via a digital platform. They can use the product to calculate a personal retirement score, work out their readiness for retirement and determine the steps and decisions required to achieve financial security. Retireready proves easy, on-line access to a wide range of products such as savings accounts, pension products and investments from a number of providers, including Aegon. Competing financial service firms usually offer such services to existing customers based around their own products.

Given that this is a digital product the platform was designed to be easy to use and understand and relatively quick to progress through each level. Each stage leads the customer through a series of questions building a picture of their retirement goals, calculating their readiness for retirement, identifying suitable retirement related products and a "shop" facility for additional savings products. Lastly the option of having a financial coach to support the customer is available.

At launch the key objectives of the campaign were to raise visibility, create media awareness and digital chat about the product. Additional support included sponsorship of the 2014 Queens Tennis Tournament, which promoted the Retireready brand alongside the company name. Existing customers were e-mailed to encourage them to transfer their existing products onto Retiready.

Measurement methods included:

- Time taken to transfer existing products
- Unique web visits
- Browsing behaviour
- Uplifts in visits following press campaigns
- Numbers completing Retiready score
- Conversions
- Additional products purchased
- Web fallout point
- Amount of funds under Aegon measurement

In addition to website data, Aegon use Google Analytics with a combination of on-line and manual reports to inform future campaigns. Measures are analysed daily, weekly, monthly and quarterly and refinements made to marketing campaigns where required.

Head of Channel Marketing, Tracy Clifton explains:

"We use the data to refine our targeting, by customer type, those who have upgraded, undertaken score only, or score and email supplied. What all of these refinements have enabled us to do is firstly have much more up to date and comprehensive data on our customers, whilst also integrating our measurement systems……. Our focus now is on retaining a strong customer base, continuing to convert more customers to… Retiready…., whilst up-selling across our products and after sales advice."

The Aegon example shows that measurement is a dynamic process, combining a wide range of measures, both internal and external, but which result in enhanced customer understanding and fine tuning of communications activity. In addition to campaign specific information this business has benefitted from a more integrated approach to customer information management and brand development. For further information, see https://www.aegon.co.uk/index.html.

11

Review questions

Identify the marketing environmental conditions which enabled Aegon to launch this product.

What are the key challenges for a company launching a new product through a new channel?

When measuring how customers were using the product and its success rate, identify the criteria the company used and explain the importance of up to date data.

Answers to review questions

Chapter 1

1 d; 2 a; 3 d; 4 b; 5 b; 6 d; 7 c; 8 d; 9 b; 10 c.

Chapter 2

1 d; 2 a; 3 c; 4 d; 5 a; 6 a; 7 a; 8 c; 9 c; 10 a.

Chapter 3

1 c; 2 d; 3 b; 4 b; 5 c; 6 a; 7 d; 8 c; 9 c; 10 b.

Chapter 4

1 a; 2 d; 3 d; 4 c; 5 b; 6 a; 7 c; 8 a; 9 a; 10 d.

Chapter 5

1 a; 2 d; 3 c; 4 a; 5 b; 6 d; 7 b; 8 a; 9 b; 10 d.

Chapter 6

1 c; 2 d; 3 c; 4 c; 5 b; 6 b; 7 b; 8 c; 9 b; 10 d.

Chapter 7

1 b; 2 c; 3 a; 4 e; 5 a; 6 b; 7 a; 8 d; 9 d; 10 a.

Chapter 8

1 c; 2 b; 3 c; 4 b; 5 b; 6 b; 7 a; 8 d; 9 a; 10 b.

Chapter 9

1 b; 2 a; 3 b; 4 b; 5 c; 6 b; 7 b; 8 c; 9 a; 10 c.

Chapter 10

1 a; 2 c; 3 a; 4 c; 5 c; 6 c; 7 d; 8 b; 9 b; 10 c.

I Index

www.ingramcontent.com/pod-product-compliance
Ingram Content Group UK Ltd.
Pitfield, Milton Keynes, MK11 3LW, UK
UKHW012332151224
452458UK00006B/38

9 781915 097781